ROUTLEDGE LIBRARY EDITIONS: SOCIAL THEORY

Volume 11

CIVIL SOCIETY

CIVIL SOCIETY

KEITH TESTER

Routledge
Taylor & Francis Group

LONDON AND NEW YORK

First published in 1992

This edition first published in 2015
by Routledge
2 Park Square, Milton Park, Abingdon, Oxfordshire OX14 4RN

and by Routledge
711 Third Avenue, New York, NY 10017

First issued in paperback 2016

Routledge is an imprint of the Taylor & Francis Group, an informa business

British Library Cataloguing in Publication Data
A catalogue record for this book is available from the British Library

ISBN: 978-0-415-72731-0 (Set)
ISBN 13: 978-1-138-99134-7 (pbk) (Volume 11)
ISBN 13: 978-1-138-78227-3 (hbk) (Volume 11)

Publisher's Note
The publisher has gone to great lengths to ensure the quality of this reprint but points out that some imperfections in the original copies may be apparent.

Disclaimer
The publisher has made every effort to trace copyright holders and would welcome correspondence from those they have been unable to trace.

Civil society

Keith Tester

London and New York

First published 1992
by Routledge
11 New Fetter Lane, London EC4P 4EE

Simultaneously published in the USA and Canada
by Routledge
a division of Routledge, Chapman and Hall, Inc.
29 West 35th Street, New York, NY 10001

Typeset by Michael Mepham, Frome, Somerset
Printed and bound in Great Britain by
Mackays of Chatham PLC, Chatham, Kent

British Library Cataloguing in Publication Data
A catalogue record for this book is available from the British
Library.

Library of Congress Cataloging in Publication Data
Tester, Keith, 1960–
   Civil society / Keith Tester.
   p.   cm.
   Includes bibliographical references and index.
   1. Civil society. I. Title.
   JC336.T43   1992
   306.2—dc20   92–7782
                                                        CIP

ISBN 0–415–07516–5
       0–415–07517–3(pbk)

Contents

	Introduction	1
1	The imagination	4
2	The symmetry	28
3	The method	52
4	The civilization	76
5	The costs	100
6	The contradictions	124
7	The aesthetics	148
8	Conclusion	172
	Bibliography	177
	Name index	181
	Subject index	183

Introduction

For, on the one hand, men are constantly smashing, replacing and leaving behind them the 'natural', irrational and actually existing bonds, while, on the other hand, they erect around themselves in the reality they have created and 'made', a kind of second nature which evolves with exactly the same inexorable necessity as was the case earlier with irrational forces of nature ...

Georg Lukács

And he watches the flow of life move by, majestic and dazzling. He admires the eternal beauty and the astonishing harmony of life in the capital cities, a harmony so providentially maintained in the tumult of human liberty.

Charles Baudelaire

I think it might be helpful to give a few ideas about how *Civil Society* can be read. However, I am quite aware that the book is in the public domain and so quite separate from whatever I might want for it. It is ultimately impossible for me to stop you doing whatever you want with the book (although I do reserve the right to object if my words are taken to lengths which I hold to be morally indefensible).

The book does not contain copious references to everything which has been said about what Jean Jacques Rousseau, for example, said about civil society. Neither does it refer to everything which has the words 'civil society' in its title. (I am aware that this means that people can respond to my analysis by saying, 'Aha! But what about so-and-so?') My interest is in the hermeneutic stakes of the debates on civil society. I have not been at all interested to ask whether civil society really exists and, if it does, whether it is under attack or is a vibrant milieu of opposition to the state. I am more interested to know why people operate as if the tag 'civil society' can be applied to some reality.

I have not written a 'complete guide' to civil society. Firstly, I have always found diligent pieces of secondary literature to be amazingly boring (to read and, I suspect, often to write); secondly, I do not think that I am especially capable of writing that kind of survey; thirdly, I believe that secondary literature is profoundly dishonest. It is dishonest on the part of the writer, who is implicitly trying to pass off himself as an astonishingly erudite and well read conveyor of bits of objective information. It is dishonest on the part of the reader, who is more often than not trying to find a short cut around books which have a reputation for being tedious and unintelligible. I hope that if this book inspires anyone to do anything, it will be to read the original words of the likes of John Locke, Thomas Hobbes and Karl Marx (the latter in particular stands in very serious need of rescue from the impact of his erstwhile defenders and heirs). They are far more interesting and entertaining than I will ever be.

I suspect that in many ways I might have some sympathy for George Steiner's distaste with 'meta-texts' and with the situation in which, 'Monograph feeds on monograph, vision on revision ... Essay speaks to essay, article chatters to article in an endless gallery of querulous echo' (Steiner 1989: 39).

It might be said that *Civil Society* looks at the immediate problem of the forest rather than at the relatively secondary matter of the foliage of the trees. *Civil Society* is intended to be a commentary on various texts and problems. It is in no way an account of them. I wrote the book as an essay in interpretation which seeks to develop and try out ideas rather than to provide ready-made answers. The book is perhaps best read as a series of sociological and philosophical speculations. Chapter 7 is extremely speculative but, I hope, of some interest. The book is a text to be taken apart and, hopefully, questioned rather than picked up and plundered for the 'right answers'.

If I might be permitted a brief self-advertisement, I should also point out that I wrote this book immediately after completion of my *The Two Sovereigns* (Tester 1992). It is therefore inevitable that *Civil Society* often assumes and alludes to points which were developed at a more leisurely pace in *The Two Sovereigns*. As such, and if anyone can be bothered, I would suggest that the two essays can be usefully read one after the other.

I am deeply grateful to Linda Rutherford, who has continued to give me support and encouragement. I would also like to thank Ian Burkitt and Chris Rojek for their faith in my frequently confused – and confusing – efforts. They are not to be held responsible for anything in *Civil Society*.

Chapter 1

The imagination

Characteristically, Karl Marx saw the question with astonishing clarity. He always had a quite remarkable ability to look through what he took to be mere appearances to grasp a more important basis to the order of things. Marx saw that any analysis of civil society must really do something more than to point fingers ('there it is; that is civil society') or provide descriptions. Rather, and as Marx realized so powerfully, to raise the problem of civil society is to raise frequently very difficult questions, and for that matter cast doubts, about the possibility, meanings and demands of society itself. Marx saw that through an examination of the idea of civil society, it might be possible to explore matters of why we live in the societies we do, and how we understand the delicate relationships between the demands of external sources of authority and our own private interests. Marx saw that an exploration of civil society can help to clarify what might otherwise be seen as the mysterious and difficult mechanisms of society.

The clarity consists in nothing other than the possibility of using the imagination and the idea of civil society as a point of entry into wider questions on the nature of the social world. In many ways, that is why it is interesting and useful to look at civil society. Civil society has important things to say and reveal all the time that we wonder about the societies in which we live. The idea of civil society has had a bad press of late. On the one hand, it has been used simply as an analytic category by authors who cannot be applauded for their literary merits. On the other hand, it has become one of the standard points of reference in political debates which accept civil society in one way or another without really asking what the acceptance actually involves. As such, civil society has tended to be banal or boring.

But it seems to me that if a little time is spent with some of the founding statements of civil society, and Marx gives very fine statements, then it actually becomes rather fascinating, if not plainly exciting. Civil society is not understood too well if it is reduced to questions of this or that democratic politics, or if it becomes an incantation in a circular, self-referential, theoretical debate. Civil society is best understood as a confrontation with the very possibility of society itself – *this* society, *our* society.

To be rather grandiose, if not wildly pompous, that is exactly the kind of challenge that this book hopes to take up. Certainly, in the hands of the young Karl Marx, civil society was moulded into some weird and wonderful shapes. For Marx, civil society was not a point of arcane textual exegesis or definitional nit-picking. Quite the contrary. It was an exciting image which could be examined to explain what it was that made the social world social. Marx also used civil society to try to see what ambitions it was reasonable to place in the hopes and promises of a new kind of society.

The exploration of civil society emphasized the basic experiences of individuals living in societies. It tried to take apart and explain the tensions that we all feel (or say we feel) between what we want to do as individuals but what we are compelled to do, or restrained from doing, as members of society. Civil society is about this fundamental experiential and relational connection between individuals going about their own lives and members of society doing what they are told. The point is, of course, that those individuals and members of society were, and to some extent continue to be, actually one and the same.

As an idea, and as a way of making some sense of the world, civil society looked backwards to provide various kinds of explanation of why private individuals involve themselves in voluntary associations and then accept the legitimacy of authorities external to themselves. It confronted the present to see if the bonds between individuals, associations and authorities were sustainable and acceptable. It looked forwards to ask whether new sources of authority and different associations were at all likely. In so doing, the exploration managed to undermine all the present-day, taken-for-granted meanings of phrases like private and public, freedom, order and responsibility, individual and society. Civil society has the potential of making all our societal relationships rather less than totally obvious; it can demystify or defetishize our present. It can offer new routes of freedom by showing that the world does not have to be like it is. Certainly, Karl Marx managed to turn a discussion of civil society to all those ends. That is why he offers a very good way into the debates.

Now, while I would not even pretend to be a thinker or writer of anything even remotely approaching the stature of Karl Marx, I would like to hope that this book can be read as an extremely modest continuation of the kind of debanalization of the mundane and everyday which is perfectly illustrated in so much of his work.

This book uses an exploration of the meanings and uses of civil society to go some little way towards providing an interpretation of how the possibility of society has been historically imagined and constructed. As such, the book tackles civil society from the point of view of sociology. For my purposes, civil society is perhaps best identified as a specifically, and also a fundamentally, sociological problem. It is discussed as an idea by which seventeenth, eighteenth and early nineteenth-century philosophers tried to explain how society was possible. I argue that those debates, to some extent, provided the basic ground-rules on which the-then new discipline called sociology originally emerged and took its bearings.

Consequently, the variations on the theme of civil society which are to be found in some of the most interesting texts of the sociological discourse can be reflected back on themselves. If that reflexive act of a sociology of sociology is carried out (something which will be similar to the strategy commended by Alvin Gouldner in his evidently forgotten book, *The Coming Crisis of Western Sociology*), at least two very interesting lines of research seem to open up. Firstly, the sociological discourses begin to reveal their own hidden assumptions. Secondly, there arises the possibility that we might be able to offer some kind of interpretation of the stakes in the original discussions of civil society. Those are the paths that this book tries to follow and clarify. That is, this book is something approaching a sociology of the sociology of civil society (or a sociology of civil society as a sociological issue).

That might all seem to be an immensely indulgent set of activities. It might seem to be nothing other than a worthless exercise in sociological navel-gazing and self-congratulation. I hope that the book offers a little more than that. In particular, looking at civil society as a sociological question does indeed seem to have a modicum of contemporary significance.

In the seventeenth and eighteenth centuries, civil society was an idea of quite fundamental importance which was intended to explain how society was possible and why individuals lived in societies which in many ways stopped them (us) doing things that they (we) might have liked to do. Philosophers like John Locke, Adam Ferguson and Jean Jacques Rousseau were, in their different ways, trying to come to terms with those questions at difficult moments when the old and time-honoured answers were collapsing through mixtures of political crisis, intellectual enlightenment, technological development and the increasingly rapid urbanization of social life. Slightly later, in the nineteenth century, sociologists to some extent became aware of themselves as sociologists, working out common concerns through the impact of exactly the same processes. They were all trying to understand how safe society was at a time when it seemed as if individuals were becoming increasingly disdainful and disrespectful of external authority. As such, they did not see themselves as engaging in idle speculation. The men who wrote about civil society were actually very worried. The philosophers and sociologists were offering different ways of avoiding a pit which, to them, promised to be a collapse of civilization into chaos and a complete barbarization of human existence. However, there was also a counter-narrative which placed the blame for everything which seemed to be going wrong firmly in the lap of society itself.

The point is that by the late twentieth century the possibility of society was again being popularly seen as a difficult problem rather than as a self-evident proposition. It might be said that the historical problems have returned to haunt us. To give a couple of exceedingly trite illustrations of that feeling; television and video technology is held to have caused an absolute privatization of pleasure, and a terminal decay of societal relationships and peculiarly human activities (typically, cries are heard that 'the art of conversation is dead', 'nobody reads novels any more'). Sexual activity and sexuality is seen less as an expression of individuality, or of a moment of life, and increasingly as a visit by the Angel of Death. The old social and political allies have turned out to be remarkably prone to become foes, and the old foes have turned out to have rather a lot in common with ourselves ('realpolitik' imitating Orwell). Technology has developed a worrying tendency to explode or behave in a way that the planners had not predicted. The nature which was said to have been tamed has seemingly started to fight back; apparently, the greenhouse effect promises to destabilize all our basic activities. Everything which had been simply assumed for a fairly confident 200 years has been suddenly, or perhaps not quite so suddenly, thrown open to absolutely fundamental doubt.

In the late twentieth century, the possibility of society can no longer be taken for granted. The possibility has to be rendered explicit rather than merely accepted as obvious and basically uninteresting. In Britain in the 1980s, there was a debate about whether society could be said to even exist at all, although it must be said that the debate was not too profound. As such, many of the old seventeenth and eighteenth century worries have begun to express highly topical concerns. Philosophers who had previously been consigned to footnotes or clever references in undergraduate essays have once more become extremely pertinent. Their dusty texts have come to possess something of the quality of the shock of the new. Suddenly, *their* explorations of the possibility of society mirror *our* encounters with exactly the same problem. Whether their answers remain adequate and convincing is a rather different matter.

At least for introductory purposes, the label of 'civil society' can be applied to all those social relationships which involve the voluntary association and participation of individuals acting in their private capacities. In a simple and perhaps even simplistic formula, civil society can be said to equal the milieu of private contractual relationships. It is a coming together of private individuals, an edifice of those who are otherwise strange to one another. In many ways, it is something like the 'architecture for the odd' which Auden mentioned when talking about a rather different set of relationships (the institutionalized Church). As such, civil society is clearly distinct from the state. It involves all those relationships which go beyond the purely familial and yet are not of the state. Civil society is about our basic societal relationships and experiences; it is about what happens to us when we leave our family and go about our own lives. It is about the relationships I have with my colleagues and the person who crashed into my car.

However, a far more interesting grasp on some of the wider implications of civil society can be achieved if the very label of 'civil society' is dismantled and broken into its two constituent parts. That will also give an indication of the relevance of the idea to nearly all interpretations of the meaning of society which sociology has on offer. It will then be possible to see that the idea brings with it a luggage of specific perspectives on the world, a luggage which is predicated on a number of more or less unchallenged and implicit assumptions.

The word 'civil' has a number of very important and interesting social, historical and interpretive loadings. It cannot be divorced from a catalogue of evaluations. The word refers to a condition of education, refinement and sophistication as opposed to a condition of barbarism. To be civil is the opposite of to be brutish or barbaric. As a fairly peculiar example of this identification of the civil with the deliberately and consciously sophisticated, Francis Bacon, in 1626, felt able to make a distinction between the civil and the barbaric on the basis of hairiness, of all things. After all, 'Beasts are more Hairy than Men, and Savage Men more than Civil' (*OED*). So, to talk about *civil* society is certainly to distinguish the milieu of voluntary associations from the institutional arrangements of the state, but rather more interestingly, it is also to suggest a division between a state of civilization and a state of nature.

The civil was not understood to be a condition in which society simply found itself. Rather, society had to be made civil. In the seventeenth and eighteenth centuries, civilization, the condition of becoming or of being civil, was understood to be something in the making and not at all as something in the finding. As such, the end result of civilization was itself taken to be somewhat less significant than the continuing practice and process of civilizing. As Zygmunt Bauman has written of those whom he calls 'the sages and the politicians of the 18th century', that is, the social group which promoted the civil condition: 'Their job was not the contemplation of the world as it was, but making it as it ought to be ... "Civilising" was what they were after: lifting fellow human beings to a new level of existence' (Bauman 1985: 7; see also Bleicher 1990).

'Civil' society was something which had to be made through the deliberate process of civilizing individuals and social relationships. The mark of the success of the process of becoming civil was represented in the extent to which refined, and what the Scottish philosophers called polished, patterns of behaviour and association were taken for granted by individuals and seen as outside of history (Elias 1978a). So, *our* civilization was invariably held to have happened already, whereas *their* civilization was still taking place. In 1641, John Milton was talking about a need, 'To inbreed and

cherish in a great people the seeds of vertu, and publick civility'
(*OED*). It should be noted that these meanings of 'civil' were all
assuming that individuals had to be made to accept the refined
demands of a social existence; there is the implicit assumption that,
left to themselves, individuals will not 'cherish the seeds of vertu'.

The point is that society was held to require such deliberate
activities because the awareness of society itself implies a fairly high
degree of self-consciousness and self-dependence. The patterns of
civility were not only the mark of society; in many ways they were
creating society. To talk in terms of society is to throw into doubt
the meanings and the accepted obviousness of social relationships.
It is to posit something more than the relationships which are
directly experienced and known. It means the drawing of a conceptual distinction between the social and the societal. Arguably,
what Norbert Elias has said of the concept of civilization also holds
true for society: 'this concept expresses the self-consciousness of
the West. One could even say: the national consciousness' (Elias
1978a: 3). The imagination of society immediately and necessarily
divides the things of the world into distinct and distinctive entities
(one society as opposed to another, one nation as opposed to
another), each of which is typified by its own particular and
indigenously reproducible significations of the civil condition.

A society is nothing other than a bounded community which
divides the world into a milieu of those with whom it is acceptable
and safe to associate, and a milieu of those with whom association
is unacceptable and potentially dangerous. And, since the place of
those others within different bounded communities (societies) was
taken as proved and illustrated by their peculiar manners, they
were perhaps inevitably identified as barbarians and in need of
civilization to become 'more like us'. Outside of *this* society lies *that*
society which is invariably defined as inferior and, to one degree
or another, beyond the pale of association. At the very best, *that*
society is accepted only on sufferance (although communication
technology has rather challenged the easiness of that identification
of other societies as more or less inferior). To illustrate, John Locke
was worried about 'those wild savage Beasts, with whom men can
have no Society nor Security' (*OED*).

Importantly, the society was itself interpreted as internally
harmonious. It was the place where individuals could come to
self-awareness and self-consciousness. Society was held to be the
condition of possibility of humans knowing themselves as human

and imposing or simply practising their humanity throughout the world. The *Oxford English Dictionary* refers to a passage written as early as 1580 which talks in fairly epic terms about society as an achieved condition of self-knowledge and harmony: 'Long it was ere that manne knewe hymself ... so that all thynges waxed sauage, the yearth vntilled, societies neglected.'

What all of this means is that civil society is perhaps best understood as the imagination of the possibility and requirements of a distinctively societal and human life. To talk of civil society has conventionally meant to distinguish the milieu of free humanity from the milieu of reification produced either by nature or the state. Both of these sites of external authority were the 'Other' of civil society. In these terms, to be human was to be defining rather than defined. To imagine civil society was to separate the internal from the external, the independent from the dependent, the achieved from the ascribed, the 'Same' from the 'Other', the homogeneous from the heterogeneous, the active from the passive. To separate order and freedom from chaos and compulsion. Civil society meant to never again take the freedom of society and social relationships for granted.

In a word, civil society suggested reflexivity. By reflexivity, I mean the attitude in which the subject of inquiry is seen as an intrinsic part of the object of inquiry. The social world is seen as a product of social relationships and social processes. As such, reflexivity is perhaps exemplified in the great interrogations which are usually imputed to the philosophical enterprise of Immanuel Kant. Invariably, it is said that Kant's work was informed by four questions:

> What can I know?
> What ought I to do?
> What may I hope?
> What is man?

The point is that in all these questions the person asking the question is part of the problem as well as part of the answer. Indeed, it is even possible to go so far as to suggest that reflexivity can be taken as the primary intellectual mark of modernity, and that the first appearance of it is to be found in Kant (Foucault 1986). Reflexivity is also implicit to the early statements on civil society. The philosophers were trying to work out the precise meaning of the society in which they thought they lived; they too

were asking questions which made themselves part of the problem
as well as its solution. The modern sociologists (the sociologists of
modernity) of the nineteenth and twentieth centuries were indulg-
ing in exactly the same activity.

Reflexivity involves a profound and deep undermining of any
assumptions that the order of things should be, indeed could be,
taken for granted. In the useful terms proposed by Agnes Heller,
it might be said that reflexivity involves a deconstruction of 'the
"natural artifice" that for millennia had secured the survival of the
human race' (Heller 1990: 145). Heller continues to stress the
modernity of the deconstruction which 'begins to emerge when
and where the "natural" appears as artificial, a man-made construct'. She writes that the natural artifice was common
throughout pre-modern social relationships, and that it managed
'to integrate men and women into an organized whole, beyond the
pale of a (village) community and the natural ties of blood relationships' (Heller 1990: 145).

The significant point is that in the reflexive deconstruction of
the natural artifice, nature was identified as something to be
pushed outside of the boundaries of societal relationships. That
involved intellectual and increasingly practical projects of the clear
separation of society from nature through, precisely, mannered
and civil practices. Indeed, the emphasis on civil practices not only
made the identification of nature possible, it *actively created* nature.
Nature is not an unchanging and invariant 'out there'. It is a social
construction, a product of the division of the world into societies.
The self-definition of the societal is defining the natural.

But perhaps just as importantly, the modern recognition that
social ties are, and for ever more have to be, confirmed by something other than previously immutable bonds, like very narrow
communities or ties of family, meant that the associations of
individuals had to be explained by something more than a jumble
of assumptions and assertions. These are yet more of the stakes of
civil society.

To the extent that societal relationships and bounded communities could no longer be accepted as completely and utterly
obvious, the understanding of the possibility of society was also
transformed. Concepts like civil society could not be derived from
time-honoured codes (because those codes were based on a decidedly wobbly natural artifice), and neither could they be derived
from mundane social relationships (because with urbanization the

typical social encounters were increasingly with unknown strangers). (For the importance of the stranger see Simmel 1950, and also Wolff 1990.) Consequently, ideals of society, ideals of the separate milieu of social reflexivity, could only be established as imaginations. Essentially, it is for this reason that I repeatedly use rather clumsy phrases like 'the imagination of civil society'. Civil society can only be known to the extent that it is imagined. More than that, outside of the sociological, historical and cultural event of its imagination, the existence or non-existence of civil society is not significant. The map determines the terrain.

It would be rather misplaced, or at best eventually rather uninteresting, to see civil society as an actual state of affairs. It is best interpreted as a social and historical category by which those who have lost, or have been denied, any faith in the natural artifice attempt to explain, confirm and renaturalize (Barthes would say 'mythologize') their social condition. As Benedict Anderson has said, 'all communities larger than primordial villages of face-to-face contact (and perhaps even these) are imagined' (Anderson 1983: 15). What we cannot directly experience or know, we can only imagine. (It is probably true to say that you and I do not know each other, and yet there is a bond linking us; we are involved in some kind of association.)

Cornelius Castoriadis manages to indicate some of the full implications of the concept of imagination. Castoriadis can help to establish the status of civil society, and indeed society itself. Castoriadis writes that 'We cannot understand a society outside of a unifying factor that provides a signified content and weaves it with symbolic structures. This factor is not simple "reality"; and every society has constituted *its* reality' (Castoriadis 1987: 160). He carries on to claim that the unifying factor which makes society a reality is not rationality either. Rather, society can only be understood and made intelligible because of 'the imaginary creation proper to history, that in and through which history constitutes itself to begin with' (Castoriadis 1987: 160).

Society is not a directly known or knowable reality. It is a concept. It is a social and historical intellectual construction which in itself makes sense of the world, and which makes the world sensible. Society is itself a socially constructed reality. A society only exists as an imagination which calls forth those things which are interpreted as proofs and marks of society. For this particular rose, the name is everything. By extension, civil society is to be

understood as an imagination by which philosophers and sociologists have attempted to explain those relationships which we do
not directly experience (as we directly experience the family) but
which are the basis of our safe public existence (society).

Perhaps Georg Simmel put it all more clearly when he suggested that reflexivity (which he narrowed down to the discipline
of sociology) is based on abstraction from the empirical and direct.
Simmel stressed the value of the development of concepts or types
(in my less neo-Kantian vocabulary, imaginations) which establish
certain regularities and consistencies (Simmel 1950: 3–25). To
move beyond the path explicitly indicated by Simmel, and perhaps
to move a little more in the direction indicated by Cornelius
Castoriadis, it might be said that it is the imagination which
establishes the regularities rather than the regularities which
establish the imagination.

To one degree or another, Anderson, Castoriadis and Simmel
are all agreed that society cannot be seen 'out there' in a self-evident, natural or transparent way. Rather, society is only intelligible
through the imaginative (non-natural, epistemologically synthetic) construction of categories which are used *as if* they were
directly derived from something called reality. Civil society is a
prime example of that kind of construction. Consequently, the
fascinating and pressing sociological questions are perhaps best
directed at the conditions of existence of the imaginations rather
than at the realities which are supposedly contained in the
categories.

All these themes can be found in Karl Marx's comments on civil
society. Like so much else in his work, Marx derived the idea of
civil society from a critical engagement with Hegel, in this instance
through a discussion of the *Burgerliche Gesellschaft* mentioned by
Hegel in the *Philosophy of Right* (Hegel 1952). Both Marx and Hegel
saw civil society as a historical phenomenon. They agreed that civil
society had emerged in the-then relatively recent past, with the
post-feudal separation of the realm of the state (public life) from
the realm of the private. According to Hegel and Marx, feudal
society did not conceive of an independent private realm, because
what we define as personal matters (questions of birth, family,
property, occupation and so forth) were all implicated in an
overarching system which determined the place of the monarch's
subject in his kingdom. By this interpretation, to talk about feudal

social relationships in terms of the divide between the private and the public spheres is a fairly serious historical anachronism.

However, Marx was quite explicit that with the rise of capitalist relations of production and the attendant bourgeois social order, there was a definition of property as a free private possession. Similarly, restrictions on occupation because of family origins became unacceptable obstacles to the creation and accumulation of wealth. Consequently, in *The German Ideology*, Marx and Engels felt that it was more than appropriate to declare that 'The word "civil society" ... emerged in the eighteenth century, when property relationships had already extricated themselves from the ancient and medieval communal society' (Marx and Engels 1970: 57).

Now, two points are significant in Marx and Engels's historical location of civil society. On the one hand, civil society is definitely seen as an emergent condition; it has not always existed. Given the reflexive commitments and expertise of Marx and Engels, that recognition of the history of civil society involved nothing other than a profound recognition that since then society and individuality have not always been this way, they do not have to remain this way. Here, Marx and Engels were looking through civil society. They made it historical and consequently demolished any possibility that it might be or become a second nature or a replacement natural artifice. The point was put very clearly when Marx and Engels wrote: 'Civil society as such only develops with the bourgeoisie' (Marx and Engels 1970: 57). However, Marx and Engels were also declaring that civil society is a milieu of relationships which replaces and historically overcomes the face-to-face interactions of relatively stable and small-scale societies. That is, civil society was understood by Marx and Engels to be at least in part an imagination of the possibility of orderly social relationships which can explain a world which is both increasingly complicated and full of strangers.

In the story according to Karl Marx (or perhaps it is better to say, in my interpretation of the story), the strangeness of the multiplicity of individuals is tackled by civil society. The strangers are brought together through a kind of ontological reduction which establishes all individuals as possessed of the same attributes. Indeed, for Marx, the very notion, practice and experience of individuality is a product of the historically emergent civil society. Marx was in little or no doubt that the private individuals of civil society were selfish, possessive and egotistical. This was due to the bourgeois social relationships, and in particular to the state. Marx denied that selfishness is 'human nature'. Instead, he said that it is created in civil society and consolidated by the state. The supposed ability of the state to overcome private individual selfishness (that is, the universality of the state as opposed to the particularity of individuals) was identified by Marx in nothing other than the ability of the state to depoliticize very important questions. (In this book, the notions of universality and particularity will more usually be discussed in terms of the problem of social order and society. Consequently, I usually prefer to use the words 'homogeneity' and 'heterogeneity'. I use those words interchangeably with the words 'universality' and 'particularity'.)

For example, Marx stresses that in bourgeois civil society questions of birth, education and profession are defined as issues of no public or political consequence. They are issues which have been emancipated from the realm of public political life. Yet Marx sees a paradox because 'the state still allows private property, education and profession to have an effect [on 'participation in popular sovereignty'] in their own manner, that is as private property, as education, as profession, and make their particular natures felt' (Marx 1971: 93). So, Marx is saying that certain matters are seen as having a purely private relevance; they are understood to have nothing to do with the state. They have, as such, been emancipated from the political sphere.

But in a typical move of turning the insight back against itself, Marx argues that the depoliticization of the private sphere is actually a political act. That is, particularity (heterogeneity) is created by the state in order to confirm its own claims to universality (homogeneity). For Marx, it is the political state which establishes questions such as birth, class, education and profession as purely private. As such, the claim of the state to a homogeneity which can oversee and look after all these heterogeneous private concerns of all the particular private individuals is thoroughly self-serving. The bourgeois political order is parasitic on a bourgeois private order, and both confirm and justify each other. Moreover, since these private concerns are taken out of the realm of politics, and instead interpreted as an intrinsic clothing of the bourgeois individual (who is thus made inevitable), they are naturalized and removed from the agenda of reflexivity. Marx says of the state that 'Far from abolishing these factual differences, its

existence rests on them as a presupposition, it only feels itself to
be a political state and asserts its universality by opposition to these
elements' (Marx 1971: 93).

As such, the state according to Marx establishes itself as precisely
Auden's 'architecture for the odd'. The odd-ness (strangeness) of
the private individuals of the bourgeois order resides in their lack
of knowledge of each other, and in their ontological and existential
duality. Marx illustrates the nature of the duality when he says of
the private individual: 'He has a life both in the political community, where he is valued as a communal being, and in civil
society where he is active as a private individual' (Marx 1971: 94).
The point is that the political establishment of communal being
(that is, of homogeneity through the state, of the state's homogeneity) is drastically undermined yet made all the more necessary by
the requirements of the practice of private individuality. In civil
society, each individual 'treats other men as means, degrades
himself to a means and becomes the plaything of alien powers ...
Man in the reality that is nearest to him, civil society, is a profane
being' (Marx 1971: 94).

In Marx's scheme, the result of this schizophrenia at the heart
of bourgeois ontology, the irreconcilability of the demands of the
public/private dichotomy, is nothing other than a series of turns
to the natural artifice. On the one hand, the ability of the state to
promote its own universality over private particularity means that
it is made inevitable and put beyond doubt. The state is able to
rebuke any challenges to it on the grounds that they are fundamentally selfish. On the other hand, the private realm where,
in explicit defiance of Kant's categorical imperative, each individual treats the other as a means and not as an end is embodied in
reified structures of representation which seek to exempt themselves from the challenge of reflexivity (although, of course, Marx
had little affection for Kant).

For Marx, one of the most significant of those representations
is religion. Religion is understood to be nothing other than the
natural artifice which establishes itself as a timeless and time-honoured since time-immemorial architecture for the odd. According
to Marx, even the state, in its own way, can be interpreted as
religious. Individuals look to the apparent universality of the state
and trust it to do what is in the best interests of all. In respect of
the individuals, Marx talks of 'their belief that life in the state is the

true life even though it leaves untouched their individuality' (Marx 1971: 99).

Marx stresses that to the extent that religion is depoliticized and identified as a question of private conscience, it is also able to operate as the legitimation, the cement, the artifice, which renders intelligible and even inevitable the fundamental selfishness and egoism of civil society. In his early essay 'On the Jewish Question', Marx argues that 'religion has become the spirit of civil society, the sphere of egoism, the *bellum omnium contra omnes*. Its essence is no longer in community but in difference' (Marx 1971: 95). Religion is seen to be nothing other than a gloss on depoliticized privatism – ironically, nothing other than a myth which says, against the attitude and the condition of reflexivity, that all is as it must be. 'It has become the expression of separation of man from his common essence, from himself and from other men, as it was originally. It is still only the abstract recognition of a particular perversion, private whim and arbitrariness' (Marx 1971: 95). In other words, religion is existential heterogeneity in opposition to essential homogeneity.

So, in Marx's astonishingly powerful assault on natural artifice, an assault which uses civil society precisely to see through civil society, there is a recognition of nothing other than the separation of man from man. As such, bourgeois civil society occasions Marx's most withering contempt. Marx is basically saying against the strongest myths of bourgeois order that, in the private sphere, man most emphatically does not find himself and his freedom. On the contrary, in the private sphere, man is thrown back on to himself against others, and on to the assumed certainties of reification rather than the difficult freedom of reflexion. According to Marx, civil society is basically a terrible lie.

It is not too surprising, then, that Marx should refuse to identify any traces of humanity (or even humanity itself) in civil society. Rather the opposite. Civil society is seen to be the milieu of the animalization and dehumanization of man. Certainly, in his early works, Marx upholds a notion of Man as a species-being; Man as a community of all men which is truly universal without mediation or external compulsion. In the *Paris Manuscripts*, the alienation of man from his species-being is seen as one of the most awful results of capitalist production. According to Marx, the point should be that 'It is just in his work upon the objective world ... that man really proves himself to be a *species-being*' (Marx 1959: 69). But capitalist production makes sure that this proof is impossible.

Species-being consists of that which makes the life of the human species distinct from the life of any other species. For humans, the species-being is the ability consciously to make something out of the given world of objects and objectivity. Man's species-being is represented in a deliberate act of the division of the human and the social from the animal and the natural. 'In creating a *world of objects* by his practical activity, in his *work upon* inorganic nature, man proves himself a conscious species-being, i.e., as a being that treats the species as its own essential being ...' (Marx 1959: 68). Essentially, Marx is proposing, and indeed predicating his system on the assumption, that nature is the pliant stuff of the realization of species-being. Nature is something to be escaped and rendered distant. Indeed, the success of the attainment of species-being is recognized as involving nothing other than the continuous production of the objects which make man distinct. Man is defining of himself. Nature is defined. As such, any institution or arrangement which hinders that division, or which even diverts it, becomes a historical and an ontological offence. Civil society was charged just so.

Marx argues that in capitalist production, the things which man makes, and which should therefore be the mark and the measure of species-being, are themselves objectified and constructed as something alien to the worker. Capitalist relationships create a zone of mediation between the man and the products of his labour. As such, the objects of labour are taken away from the activity of labour. The work is estranged. This has serious implications. Estranged labour is simply a means for the achievement of the physical needs of individual existence rather than an expression of all that it is to be human. The universality of the human species-being thus collapses into the particularity of capitalist production and, by extension, the bourgeois civil society. After all, 'the proposition that man's species-nature is estranged from him means that one man is estranged from the other, as each of them is from man's essential nature' (Marx 1959: 69).

Furthermore, and to make the connection between estranged labour in capitalist production and the individuality of civil society quite explicit: 'The estrangement of man, and in fact every relationship in which man [stands] to himself, is realised and expressed only in the relationship in which a man stands to other men' (Marx

1959: 69). And, since each man stands to the other as a private individual guided by egotistical concerns and interests, each man is estranged from himself and from his fellow human beings. By this account of Marx, the individual does not find himself in the private sphere; rather, he finds only estrangement and alienation. The private sphere is hardly civil; for Marx, it presages something quite beastly.

The private concerns of civil society mean that the species-being remains an 'ought' rather than an 'is'. In civil society, man appears 'uncultivated and unsocial, man in his accidental existence, man as he comes and goes, man as he is corrupted by the whole organization of our society, lost to himself, sold, given over to the domination of inhuman conditions and elements' (Marx 1971: 99). In other words, civil society is only a society because it is compelled to be so (and it is therefore an offence to the true society of species-being), and it certainly has only the most marginal connection with anything truly civil.

Marx examines civil society and sees it as a valley of tears and shadows, and the tossing of man into a cauldron of selfishness where each individual struggles against others to meet material needs. He uses man as man is to look forward to man as man should be. From the false and uncivil society of the individual of the bourgeois order, Marx can reflexively imagine the possibility of the truth of humanity. As he put it in the tenth thesis on Feuerbach, 'The standpoint of the old materialism is *"civil"* society; the standpoint of the new is *human* society, or socialised humanity' (Marx 1946: 68). The achievement of the truly human society will thus involve the obsolescence and redundancy of civil society. We will have direct, unmediated relationships with all. Man will be himself universal; Man will he homogeneous as a self-conscious species and being. As such, the mediating architecture for the odd, which bourgeois order needs so much, will simply crumble into dust.

Marx's analysis of civil society, and his profound unravelling of the order of things, can be seen to have achieved three ends. Firstly, Marx shows that society, and even more so civility, should not be taken for granted. Secondly, he reveals the historicity and the particularity of the foundations of the natural artifice of bourgeois universality. Marx shows that this freedom is no freedom at all. Thirdly, Marx shows that the meanings of terms like public and private are not at all self-evident but are themselves highly problematic.

This third achievement is quite significant. In much of the literature on civil society, there is a tendency to use the words 'public' and 'private', or to refer to a public sphere as opposed to a private sphere, as if it was entirely obvious what was being referred to and what was meant. But Marx shows that these dichotomies are themselves part and product of the problem of civil society. The imagination of civil society does not simply embody the public and the private; it constitutes them as distinct and yet linked milieux. The imagination of a public sphere only makes sense to the extent that there is a simultaneous and continuous imagination of a private sphere, just as the imagination of a private sphere only makes sense to the extent that there is a simultaneous and continuous imagination of a public sphere. Once again, it is the cartographer who creates the landscape. (A number of feminist philosophers and theorists have also sought to make the point that the meanings of the public and the private warrant investigation rather than assumption. For a survey of this work, see Moller Okin, 1991. Moller Okin seems to ignore Marx's achievement of exactly the kind of qualification of obviousness which she wishes to promote.)

Marx worked from the claims of universality to the attributes of particularity and revealed both to be rather less obvious than they at first appeared. The strategy is in many ways a fine mark of the extent to which Marx moved in a radical direction away from Hegel. In Marx, there is a critical interrogation of the claims to universality which are made by the state, and the claims to particularity which are invested in the individuals of civil society. Marx looks through the claims and discovers that they are neither self-evident nor natural. As such, Marx is able to imagine the possibility of the deliberate construction of a better society in the future. For Marx, society can be rendered truly self-sufficient and truly human through an imaginative leap from a revelation of the reification which makes the existing societal relationships possible. As the tenth of the *Theses on Feuerbach* made plain, Marx used the present to construct a narrative of the past and a teleology of the future.

Hegel's critical project did not go quite so far. Hegel accepted the claims which were made by the state and, indeed, in many ways confirmed them. Hegel thought that civil society was indeed a sphere of private egoism riddled by conflicts between individuals. But, for him, the state was what it claimed to be. It was indeed the overarching architecture which could control and reconcile those conflicts. Hegel makes his essentially descriptive and uncritical use of civil society quite plain when he calls it 'an association of members as self-sufficient individuals in a universality which, because of their self-subsistence, is only abstract' (Hegel 1952: 110). Hegel stresses the status of civil society as the sphere of individuals operating in their private capacities. But he also emphasizes that the particularities are subsumed within a wider universality; that universality is unsurprisingly identified as the state, which is thus interpreted as a generalized institution of homogeneity in which individuals can practise their selfish interests but without unduly threatening each other. For Hegel, the state is 'an external organization for attaining ... [individuals'] particular and common interests' (Hegel 1952: 110).

The extent to which Marx built on the Hegelian analysis of civil society, but in the process turned it upside-down, is quite evident when Hegel begins to talk about the selfishness of civil society. According to Marx, that selfishness is a product of the bourgeois order, and it is destructive of man's species-being. But Hegel saw a great deal of benefit coming out of the conflict. He said that: 'In the course of the actual attainment of selfish ends ... there is formed a system of complete interdependence, wherein the livelihood, happiness, and legal status of one man is interwoven with the livelihood, happiness, and rights of all' (Hegel 1952: 123). Here, Hegel seems to be anticipating the sociological recognition of the division of labour and its implications for social solidarity. Hegel continues to announce that the interdependency is confirmed by the state standing above the selfish interweaving of private interests. 'On this system, individual happiness, &c., depend, and only in this connected system are they actualized and secured. This system may be prima facie regarded as the external state, the state based on need ...' (Hegel 1952: 123).

Ultimately, then, Hegel's disruption of the natural artifice stops at precisely the point where it might have become extremely interesting – something more than a description of the arrangements of the age in terms of the ideals of the age. Marx started at the point where Hegel finished. (A very different, and a far more sustained, interpretation of Hegel and Marx can be found in Rundell 1987.)

But this does not mean that Marx picked up the baton from others and pushed and pushed until he could push no further. Marx did not take reflexivity so far that he ran over the edge of an abyss where everything became reflexive and nothing at all was left self-evident. Quite the contrary. Despite his very deep and profound undermining of reification, and indeed despite his ability to identify social and historical reification in places where others had seen nothing of any interest at all, there were certain assumptions that Marx never questioned. The point is, of course, that had Marx questioned absolutely everything everywhere, he would scarcely have been able to imagine and write about a better society of the future.

Perhaps the most important assumption which informed Marx's project was that of universality (the homogeneity of the species, and the homogeneous future). For Marx, universality was many things. It was a desirable social and historical condition, a reflection of the species-being of humanity, a category by which the existing social relationships and arrangements could be known and condemned. Universality was ontological and political. It was the condition which ought to be. Indeed, it was precisely the deep and unquestioned commitment to the ideal of universality, and the struggle for homogeneity in a world which was otherwise heterogeneous, which enabled Marx to propose that there was some fundamental reality lurking behind the appearance of things and, moreover, which caused him to be able to identify the existing arrangements as particular. It was only the assumption of universality which rendered the existing order of things particular in the first place; it was the ideal of universality which enabled Marx to express some dissatisfaction with things as they appeared. The need for reconstruction which runs like a thread through all Marx's work was, then, pulled by a needle which was aiming for the future.

The further point, of course, was that since particularity could be seen, since it was part of the world of appearances, it could not possibly be at all approximate to the demands of universality, whatever the likes of Hegel might have said. The universal was an ideal, therefore the particular was real, therefore the real was particular, therefore the universal remained to be attained. Civil society was real, therefore it was particular, therefore it could not possibly be universal. The same was true of the state as well.

But the commitment to universality had another side. Marx

assumed the universality of the species-being of man. And, when he said man, he meant man (see also Sayer 1991: 5). In the modern tales of universality, and indeed in the modern imaginations of civil society, women were seen to have an entirely secondary significance. The imagination of civil society was conventionally an entirely patriarchal imagination. Carole Pateman has rightly noted that in its historically most important expressions, 'civil society is patriarchal' (Pateman 1988: 3). The tendency to universalize experiences or interests under the sign of 'man' is something to be confronted and shown as significant in itself.

It is for that reason that this book talks about 'man' and 'men'. I do not use the now orthodox gender-neutral language of social science, because to do so would be to render invisible and inconsequential absolutely fundamental issues. The imaginations of civil society which are found in writers like Marx, Hegel, Locke and, most obviously, Rousseau were not meant for women and, as such, it would be a mistake to imply that the use of the word 'man' was a simple oversight of habit. Here, to talk in gender-neutral terms would be to invoke or at least imply a false homogeneity of human beings. Women were not part of the traditional stories of civil society, and it would be inappropriate to imply that they were, however well meaning the implication might be.

When the imagination of civil society emerged in the seventeenth, eighteenth and early nineteenth centuries, it was more or less implicitly assumed that the experiences of women were either fully accommodated under the sign of man or, if they were not, could be dismissed as of no great importance. But to imagine civil society today, in the late twentieth century, involves a confrontation with that patriarchal gender bias (which presented itself as gender neutrality, human homogeneity). Perhaps the different significance of gender then and now can be taken as an illustration of quite how important the question of civil society remains. Perhaps it is also one reason why the texts of the likes of John Locke and Karl Marx can leap across the centuries and say things which are important and meaningful to us. The point is that when they developed the imagination of civil society, the philosophers were trying to tackle the question of how society is possible and how it might be created as a self-sufficient milieu of human self-consciousness free from the dictates of reification and the natural artifice. Women were given a very modest walk-on part (at most) in that story precisely because men held them to be incapable of a complete freedom from reification.

But now, in the very late twentieth century, the question of the possibility and demands of civil society has evidently been reinvigorated. Perhaps the reason is that while the founding statements of civil society were attempting to understand the possibility of society at the dawn of modernity, we are trying to confront the possibility of society in the twilight of modernity. Locke and the others speak to us so directly because they confronted the same questions as us. They knew that society, civility and freedom were things which could not be taken for granted. Similarly, we know that the imaginations of society and civilization which underpinned the remarkable confidences of modernity are not really adequate to the challenge of explaining immense events like Auschwitz or Hiroshima. They cannot even explain mundane events like the nature of the relationship which I should, and could, have with my daughter. More than that, the very late twentieth century is plagued by the imagination that the Earth may no longer be able to support any society, even less a civil society.

The imagination of civil society emerged in conditions where nature was interpreted as a threat to the self-sufficient freedom of humanity. The imagination of civil society has re-emerged in conditions where humanity is interpreted as a threat to the self-sufficient freedom of nature.

At the threshold of modernity, the debates on civil society constructed nature as a threatening and awful 'out there'. As such, the historical construction by men of women as closer to nature than men meant that women were to some extent pushed outside of the taken-for-granted boundaries of civil society. They were silenced and left to bear children (pregnancy was a natural act precisely because it was something outside of societal – men's – control.) But the feminist-inspired debate on gender, the free debate self-sufficiently practised by women, proves precisely that the historical interpretation by men of women as natural is, to say the least, slightly shaky. The old boundaries between self-sufficient society and reified nature have been challenged, if not completely dismantled. Those whom modernity and the men of modernity identified as silent and virtually incapable of societal participation have demonstrated an ability to behave in precisely the ways that civilized society demands. The appearance and brilliant success (in some respects) of feminist discourse can be taken as a prime example of the post-modern ability of that which modernity defined as passive and natural to become defining, active and social. The boundaries of society have thus been reinserted into history.

The imagination of civil society can be confronted once again. The confrontation suggests a turn to the founding fathers of civil society, be that turn in admiration or outrage. Note here, not a return, just a turn. While I would indeed want to argue that, in many ways, the founders of the imagination of civil society were explicitly confronting problems which are implicitly being raised today, that does not mean that I think their answers can be taken up as policy documents for the end of the millenium. Certainly, a similar problem is being wrestled with, but the answers which are given and the answers which are actually useful are different. We are thinking at the end of modernity, with the experience of modernity. They were thinking at the beginning of modernity, with the optimism of modernity.

Essentially, this book seeks to discuss the imagination of civil society in precisely this way. It seeks to explore why civil society, an old idea from seventeenth and eighteenth century social and political philosophy, has been revived in the closing years of the twentieth century. To see why, the most useful strategy will be to interpret the stakes of the founding imaginations of civil society. Hence, this book says a lot about Locke, Ferguson and Rousseau, and about versions of civil society in sociological discourse. It has even spent a little time looking at civil society in the early work of Karl Marx. But this book does not really say anything at all about the discussions of civil society which were developed in twentieth century political discourse by Marxists and neo-Marxists in particular. In those debates, the main question of civil society is 'how do we change this society?' Of course, the importance of that question cannot be underestimated, but a possibly more significant issue is to ask 'why and how is the transformation of society held to be a possibility in the first place?' That is far more fundamental inquiry.

Indeed, it is a sociological inquiry. By following civil society from social and political philosophy to the founding assumptions of sociological narratives, it might be possible to see if the old imaginations of society, and the disciplines which flourished on them, are likely to continue to be important after modernity. As such, dusty books are discussed very much with contemporary questions in mind. This book is not a history for the sake of the past. It is rather a history for the sake of the present.

Hopefully, the book can, in some little way, live up to Samuel Taylor Coleridge's belief: 'There is one sure way of giving freshness and importance to the most commonplace maxims – that of reflecting on them in direct reference to our own state and conduct, to our own past and future being' (Coleridge 1985: 667).

Chapter 2

The symmetry

Perhaps it will be useful to recall very quickly Agnes Heller's idea of the natural artifice. It should be stressed that this is an interpretation of Heller's argument rather than a direct and undistorted summary of it. She says that the natural artifice characterizes all the great pre-modern civilizations. All these civilizations tried to come to terms with a multiplicity of individuals, and they all tried to do so by implicitly or explicitly stating that the prevailing social relationships or institutional arrangements were in fact the only possible relationships or arrangements. As such, they were defined as natural because they were interpreted as an arrangement by nature. There was nothing that could be done about it; this was simply the way it had to be (Heller 1990: 145).

The use of the word 'artifice', however, indicates that for the moderns, looking back on pre-modern arrangements, what was previously taken as existing according to nature is interpreted rather as existing by man. As Agnes Heller says: 'What is natural to the pre-modern conception is no longer natural to the modern one. Modern imagination begins to emerge when and where the "natural" appears as artificial; a man-made construct that can be deconstructed' (Heller 1990: 145). A sense of that imagination of artificiality can be found in the work of the Scottish Enlightenment historian William Robertson. He was in no doubt that 'When we survey the face of the habitable globe, no small part of that fertility which we ascribe to the hand of nature, is the work of man' (Robertson quoted in Swingewood 1970: 174). Robertson was clearly implying that at least in some respects, the natural is in fact artificial.

Where pre-modern forms stressed the inevitability of reification and natural ordination, modern interpretations saw only attempts to legitimize and render incontestable essentially social and societal relationships. For Heller, the modern imagination would seem to consist in nothing other than a declaration that the natural world and the social world are two distinct milieux which have to be forced apart and thereafter kept apart.

Heller continues to point out rightly that the dominant arrangement of the natural artifice (whenever and wherever it was identified from the perspective of modernity) was patriarchy; the rule of a single male. 'In society, that is, within the family, in the *oikos*, this was the case even during the very short periods of republican or democratic constitutions when a few males, instead of one, ruled in the political arena' (Heller 1990: 147–148). The most obvious instance of patriarchy as the natural artifice was, undoubtedly, the pre-modern principle of the divine right of the monarch.

In essence, the concept of divine right proposed that the authority and rights of the monarch were attributable to the direct commission of God. As such, whatever the monarch did, he did on the basis of sacred authority. The theory had a number of implications. Firstly, and most obviously, it reified the existence of monarchy and the notion of a royal genealogy; they were rendered natural and consequently put far beyond the orbit of mundane men. Secondly, divine right made patriarchy natural. To the extent that the monarch ruled over his subjects as if the head of a family, so the individual man became the head and sole authority in the individual family. Thirdly, the ascribed status of the monarch as the head of the realm, and the corollary of the status of the father at the head of the family, suggested a very rigid structure of social relationships in which each individual had a definite, determinate and invariant place.

The father was in charge of his family, but he looked up to the monarch who was the father to his realm, who in his turn looked up to God the Holy Father. Going in the other direction, the word of God was communicated to subjects through the monarch, who in his turn communicated to all other individuals through their fathers. This was a highly rigid system which denied the possibility of different social arrangements. It was a system which staked its continuation, its legitimacy and its hold on the extent to which it could make itself seem to exist as if by nature.

Within the natural artifice, and as Agnes Heller points out very clearly, social relationships were, then, arranged in terms of asymmetric reciprocity. The participants in social relationships were ordered hierarchically and did not conceive of themselves as equals – he is superior to me, I am superior to you. As Heller explains: 'The members of each cluster are equals among themselves, and they are all unequal in relation to the members of other clusters, higher or lower' (Heller 1990: 148). The point is that this hierarchical ordering of what Heller calls 'clusters' was accepted as if it existed by nature and therefore was legitimated on the grounds of unchallengeable inevitability. The individual could do absolutely nothing about this state of affairs. Quite the contrary. After all, 'One belongs to a social cluster even in the mother's womb; the destiny of the newborn is written upon the cradle' (Heller 1990: 148).

Arguably, it is necessary to add to Heller's account of the natural artifice the point that its geographical spread tended to be fairly restricted. The natural artifice was an ordering of social relationships which could only accommodate essentially face-to-face interaction. It could cope with wider interaction only by making it fit a hierarchy of clusters which was said to be the same in all places at all times. Perhaps one very minor illustration of the restricted horizons assumed and created by the natural artifice is provided by the character of the midwife in Laurence Sterne's wonderful novel *The Life and Opinions of Tristram Shandy, Gentleman*.

The interesting point is that while the midwife had achieved that status after she had been widowed with three or four children to look after, it had been decided by others that she would assume the role. In other words, the midwife's achievement was in fact an ascription within a hierarchically ordered system of social relationships. It was the parson's wife who determined that the widow would become the midwife: 'it came into her head, that it would be doing as seasonable a kindness to the whole parish, as to the poor creature herself, to get her a little instructed in some of the plain principles of the business' (Sterne 1983: 11).

Just as significantly, the geographical sweep of this very hierarchic and more or less inescapable system of ascription and definition was extremely limited. The midwife was famous throughout the world. But that world of the natural artifice was not as wide as the world of specifically modern imagination. For the midwife, the world spread as far as 'a small circle described upon the circle of the great world, of four *English* miles diameter, or thereabouts, of which the cottage where the good old woman lived, is supposed to be the centre' (Sterne 1983: 11). The natural artifice suggested a universe of restricted horizons; restricted both spatially and imaginatively.

But in the modern condition, asymmetric reciprocity is forced to give way to symmetric reciprocity. In pre-modern arrangements, the individual is, basically, born unequal and dies unequal. But in the arrangements of modernity, the situation was very different indeed. Heller explains that 'men and women are not thrown into its network by birth; they enter into such a division later, potentially (although not really) by their own choice ... One is born equal and becomes unequal' (Heller 1990: 148). Of course, Tristram Shandy's midwife had been born unequal and lived as someone with little or nothing of that which modernity defined as private life; every aspect of her existence was defined for her, by others, from the top down, as if by nature. But in modern arrangements, asymmetry gave way to symmetry. Definition was in principle replaced by self-defining.

It is important to notice the different terms that Heller uses. When she is discussing the asymmetric reciprocity of the natural artifice, she talks about social clusters. But with the symmetric reciprocity of modernity, clusters are given an entirely secondary importance (at best) to the sovereign individual. Arguably, Heller is trying to make the point that in the conditions and imagination of the natural artifice, the individual is not free, if indeed it is at all viable to talk in terms of individuals. But with the deconstruction of the natural artifice, individuals indeed became free; they were imagined as possessing the potential to choose to do some things and not others. They were understood in terms of the possibility of practising alternative relationships, or of subjection to alternative arrangements, in the here and now. Whereas Marx looked at the existing individual with a mixture of sadness and loathing, Heller refuses to give up so easily on individuals and individuality. She tries to understand rather than repudiate (however grand the intentions of that repudiation might have been).

So, asymmetric reciprocity created a human and social milieu which was seen as indivisibly tied in with nature. It emphasized ascription, acceptance and reification. But symmetric reciprocity emphasized achievement, freedom and construction. As such, the natural artifice did not see societal relationships as a terribly pressing problem, because the imagination of a distinctive sphere called society did not exist. All that existed was the place dominated by the monarch or the father in a wider and all-encompassing, timeless (natural) order of things. God was the chief superintendent and the only active agent. However, symmetric reciprocity involved nothing other than the imagination of society as a separate and separable milieu of freedom and action. Whereas asymmetric reciprocity was given, symmetric reciprocity had to be made. The modern imagination of society was consequently totally unnatural and synthetic. Modern imaginations were aware of nothing so much that modern societies did not continue by nature, but that instead they continued by the efforts of society on itself.

The question is, of course, why the natural artifice collapsed. It must be said that Agnes Heller's solutions to that problem are just a little vague. She talks fairly simply of a process of deconstruction which systematically revealed the strands of the natural artifice to be not at all necessary: 'deconstruction of one element was followed by the deconstruction of several others with increasing speed, until the aim of an *alternative* socio-political arrangement appeared on the horizon' (Heller 1990: 146). To solve Heller's problem for her, it can be proposed that the deconstruction was a direct consequence of the appearance of the stranger.

The point is that the stranger could not be accommodated by the hierarchic arrangements of the natural artifice. Instead, the sheer freedom of the stranger to come and go (if he pleased) presaged the irrelevance and eventually the obsolescence of all imaginations which sought to allocate each person to a once-and-for-all status. Any attempt to come to terms with the stranger had to allow for the fact that he had not been present from time-immemorial, that his presence was a historical event and that, therefore, it could not possibly be treated as an event by nature. While the natural artifice might struggle to accommodate the stranger, that accommodation was necessarily extremely rickety.

Georg Simmel makes this point extremely clear at the beginning of his immensely important essay 'The Stranger'. As Simmel says of the stranger: 'He is fixed within a particular spatial group, or within a group whose boundaries are similar to spatial boundaries' (Simmel 1950: 402). So far, the situation is not much different to that which applied to the midwife in *Tristram Shandy*, but Simmel continues to draw out the challenge which the stranger posed to the natural artifice: 'But his position in this group is determined, essentially, by the fact that he has not belonged to it from the beginning, that he imports qualities into it, which do not and cannot stem from the group itself (Simmel 1950: 402). Whereas the midwife served a group from which no escape was imaginable, a group which ascribed even her modest accomplishments, the stranger is an embodiment of achievement. Any attempt to ascribe his qualities is more or less temporary. The attempt to pull the stranger within the narrow horizons of the natural artifice was itself historical (because the attempt had not always been needed) and therefore a deconstruction of the natural artifice.

The presence of the stranger did indeed become an increasingly pressing problem in Europe, especially the north-western tip of Europe, through the course of the seventeenth, eighteenth and nineteenth centuries. Geographically, the problem was due to the rapid development and process of urbanization. Urbanization pulled people away from worlds which stretched no further than four miles from a cottage and inserted them into metropolises where every social encounter was with an individual who was to a greater or a lesser extent a stranger. In the metropolis, the possibility of society could not be assumed because there could be no natural artifice which said that things were simply as they had to be. Quite the contrary, the fleeting appearances and relationships of the urban milieu indicated nothing other than the ceaseless possibility of different kinds of social relationships (for more on this, see Simmel 1950: 409–24).

The awareness of the possibility of different arrangements was exacerbated by the development of cosmopolitan communication networks which meant that even if an individual was not a physical stranger, he might quite possibly be an intellectual stranger. With these figures, the possibility of difference was not demonstrated by their coming, going and staying. Instead, it was represented in their ability to write blueprints of alternatives on the basis of their ability to read reports of social relationships from elsewhere. In principle, it was the case that an individual could become a stranger without ever leaving his study. The prime example of this kind of stranger is Immanuel Kant and, to a slightly lesser extent, Jean Jacques Rousseau. (This aspect of the stranger is discussed in some detail in Tester 1992.)

Within this urban and cosmopolitan context, social relationships were not stable enough to be interpreted or practised through the rigid restrictions of asymmetric reciprocity. They could be predicated only on the imagination and practice of symmetric reciprocity. This point can also be illustrated with an example from literature. The social relationships and society of the urban individuals who are strangers to one another is quite frequently illustrated with Baudelaire's discussion of the *flâneur*, but an equally fine illustration can be found in Jean-Paul Sartre's *Nausea*.

The fundamentally pre-modern world recalled in *Tristram Shandy* was predicated on a hierarchy in which those 'at the top' knew everything, and defined everything for those 'lower down'. But the urban and cosmopolitan world of Sartre's book is very different indeed. One of the important episodes in *Nausea* concerns a Sunday walk by the central character, Antoine Roquentin, around the small town of Bouville. Roquentin perceives the town and its inhabitants from the objective and subjectively detached point of view of the stranger. He knows that despite his keen sense of self, his is simply one face in a crowd of many faces. But, although each individual is more or less unknown to each other individual, there are still powerful ties of social reciprocity. The crucial point is that the reciprocity consists in rituals of civil society and is structured by the ability of individuals to signify inclusion within the bounded community of society.

In Sartre's presentation, urban life involves the individual as a subjective agent looking at the world of other subjective agents. The urban sphere is one of free individuals, coming, going and staying more or less as they please, rather than clusters which define everything for all time. Moreover, from his own experience, Roquentin is very aware that even familiar faces might hide intellectual strangers. Sartre has Roquentin record in his dairy this sense of strangeness mediated through ritual: 'I have arrived: this is the rue Tournebride, all I have to do is take my place among my fellows and I shall see the gentlemen of substance raising their hats to one another' (Sartre 1965: 64). The attitude of these individuals towards one another is not deep involvement, as it was for the parson's wife and the widow in *Tristram Shandy*; rather, it is one of a symmetric reciprocity (raising hats to each other) and it is generally blasé. The endless requirement to treat strangers as if they were friends leads to the exhaustion of the meaning of reciprocity, leading instead to its solely habitual performance.

Simmel recognized the point very clearly indeed when he said that the demands of urban life have great effects on individuals. The metropolis tears 'the nerves so brutally hither and thither that their last reserves of strength are spent; and if one remains in the same milieu they have no time to gather new strength' (Simmel 1950: 414). Symmetric reciprocity led to a formalization of social relationships and to the ritual construction of civil society. The differences between individuals which were so fundamental to the natural artifice were reduced to a purely private concern. Consequently, civil society was conceived as constituted by a multiplicity of formally equal citizens. (Marx came to this conclusion by a rather different route.)

Hence, and to put it all extremely schematically, the imagination of civil society is best interpreted as a modern social and historical attempt to understand the possibility of the reproducibility of society in situations where the natural artifice had been drastically deconstructed. Civil society explained society when no explanation was possible as if by nature.

So, the emergence of symmetric reciprocity as the formal signification and the basis of the relationships of civil society, and the disruption (if not the destruction) of the asymmetric relationships of the natural artifice, had at least two very important implications. Firstly, any assumptions that social relationships and arrangements were immutable began to decay extremely rapidly, so that they became either anachronistic or the stuff of nostalgic returns to a time when all was as it should be. Secondly, the possibility of society had to be explicated on the basis of the reciprocity of strangers rather than on the basis of taken-for-granted authority structures. That is, symmetric reciprocity involved and implied the search for imaginations of society which could respond to the challenge of freedom without falling into the trap of offering revisions of reification. The imagination of civil society was in principle able to do just that.

These themes and concerns can be found in John Locke's development of civil society in the *Two Treatises of Civil Government* (Locke 1924). Essentially, it is possible to identify two dimensions of the reflexive imagination in Locke's treatises. They consist of an observation and a subsequent question. Firstly, the observation. Locke was in no doubt that society has to be deliberately and actively constructed as a free realm. This is a fundamental act of the deconstruction of the natural artifice. Secondly, the question. Locke asked how the construction of society could be maintained while at the same time avoiding reification into something which was simply taken for granted. The observation involved a withering and a frequently witty attack on the patriarchal hierarchy of the divine right of the monarch. The question involved an answer which emphasized civil society as the milieu of the symmetric reciprocity of strangers.

The observation (or, at least, that which was treated as an observation) that social relationships and society do not exist as if by nature was Locke's main concern in the first treatise. Significantly, the treatise is entitled 'An Essay concerning Certain False Principles'. The title itself is a fine indication of the attitude of John Locke towards the notion of divine right. It was false; he was, in knowing that falsehood, therefore right. This is of more than intellectual or rhetorical importance. Locke's ability to condemn divine right because of its falsity can also be taken as a significant moment in the history of social reflexivity.

The point is that divine right involves an extraordinarily high level of passivity. If the monarch is believed when he says that he rules by and with the grace of God, then any possibility of change becomes more or less completely impossible. A century or so after Locke, David Hume made this implication very plain. Hume said that the attempt to trace a direct causal line between the authority of God and the authority of the monarch served to, 'render it [i.e. the latter] so sacred and inviolate, that it must be little less than sacrilege, however tyrannical it may become, to touch or invade it in the smallest article' (Hume 1947: 209). Social change is quite unimaginable.

The concept of divine right was so offensive to any reflexive imagination because it implied that social relationships and society are not defining of what it means to be human. Rather, they are defined and are, to the extent that they continue in the shadow of the unimpeachable monarch, tantamount to slavery. The practices of divine right, when challenged from the point of view of reflexivity, made it quite impossible to distinguish between the slavish and the free (even the monarch was God's slave). As such, ethics, the problem of living virtuously as a free individual, the problem of responsibility in reciprocity, collapsed into simple coercion. The defined subjects of divine right were invested with neither the ability to govern themselves nor, for that matter, the ability to imagine alternative social relationships. (Recall the illustration of the widow in *Tristram Shandy*: she unquestioningly accepted the definition of herself from outside as a midwife.) The problematic of ethics as modernity understood it was impossible in the asymmetric system of divine right because only God was absolutely free and absolutely responsible. More than that, God was the precondition for any notion of the virtuous life. As such, he was placed beyond ethics. God was the figure which halted reflexivity.

Locke was quite aware that divine right meant that men were slaves (because they were defined rather than defining). He expressed this awareness through a critique of Sir Robert Filmer's book *Patriarcha*. Filmer's book was one of the more significant and sustained attempts to reinforce the practice and the principle of absolute monarchy in the seventeenth century. According to Locke's summary, Filmer argued that all men 'except only one, are all born slaves, and by divine right are subjects to Adam's right heir' (Locke 1924: 4). That 'right heir' was, of course, represented in the figures of the monarch and the father. Filmer was obviously imagining a world of inescapable ascription and definition. The logic of the case was quite simple. For Filmer, man cannot possibly be free because 'Men are born in subjection to their parents' (Locke 1924: 6). (For 'parents' read 'father'.) Therefore, all men in general are born in subjection to their parent in general (the monarch), who in turn is born in subjection to his parent (God).

It might well be that John Locke thought that Sir Robert Filmer's defence of arrangements which seemed to exist as if by nature was abhorrent. He definitely thought that it was so much nonsense. Not the least, Locke thought that Filmer was attempting to make asymmetric reciprocity seem inevitable purely because he had a considerable personal stake in that kind of interpretation of the world. According to Locke, then, Filmer's frequent citations of biblical authority were rather offensive: 'The prejudices of our own ill-grounded opinions, however by us called probable, cannot authorise us to understand Scripture contrary to the direct and plain meaning of the words' (Locke 1924: 25). Locke was using the Bible precisely to reveal all previously taken-for-granted interpretations of scriptural authority as simply socially and historically dependent constructions. Locke was trying, and to a very large extent succeeding, to lay bare the artificiality of the self-evidence of a biblically sanctioned patriarchy.

The identification of the artificiality of all that was accepted as if by nature is perhaps the central theme of Locke's attack on 'false principles'. Principles were false precisely to the extent that they ascribed and defined. By extension, and in a simple logical reversal, principles were therefore true in Locke's scheme to the extent that they were achieved and defining. Locke seemed to think that one of the best ways of proving the close dependency of divine right and false principles was to link expressions of absolute monarchy to the interests of ascribed social groups which were at or near the top of the hierarchy of asymmetric reciprocity. The charge of the connection between divine right and the interests of privileged social groups runs through at least the first of the *Two Treatises of Civil Government*.

Locke was in no doubt that the arguments and understanding of the world of Sir Robert Filmer could be reduced to social relationships and, more specifically, social hierarchies. As such, for Locke, to reveal the social basis of divine right was to deconstruct it fundamentally as an unchallengeable order, as a realm 'sacred and inviolate' (to recall David Hume's prose). Locke looks at the arguments for absolute monarchy and repudiates them as completely lacking in credibility. Locke says that the men who support divine right should therefore look towards themselves 'to consider whether they do not give the world cause to suspect that it is not the force of reason and argument that makes them for absolute monarchy, but some other by-interest' (Locke 1924: 11).

John Locke's strategy of reducing the natural principle of divine right to purely social and historical conditions of existence had a number of significant implications. Firstly, he showed the principle to be not at all natural, and therefore he turned absolute monarchy into something to be subjected to reflexive interrogation. He did not let it remain as the social site where reflexivity stopped (or rather the site which made reflexivity actually impossible). Secondly, Locke was fleshing out the details of the false principles that he wanted to demolish. If a principle could be tarred with the brush of self-interest then, for John Locke, it lost all credibility. Indeed, in many ways the inability of Sir Robert Filmer to establish divine right as anything other than an assertion was taken as clear proof of the falsity of the idea.

The point is that assertion relies on hierarchy to become legitimate. An assertion can only secure widespread acceptance because it is made from prestigious and powerful social locations. As such, divine right was a dominant assertion precisely because it was made by the monarch and his supporters (people like Knights of the Realm), and because it claimed the sanction of God. In an order where expressions were accorded credibility on the basis of the social location from which they were uttered, that was indeed a pretty hard act to follow. But Locke was not persuaded. For him, as indeed for the modernity at which Locke was at the threshold, principles derived their truth and their acceptability from the degree of achievement which was associated with them. Given that modernity fundamentally involved the deconstruction of the natural artifice, its criteria of truth similarly reflected the free achievement of individual human action and inquiry in the world. For Locke, a principle was only true to the extent that it appeared to be quite independent of any social, historical and, even more so, natural conditions of existence.

Crucially, this thesis led Locke to identify two different kinds of man. On the one hand, there were all those who accepted the legitimacy of the time-immemorial and who saw no need to look any further than the self-evident. These men, typified of course by Sir Robert Filmer, thought that asymmetric reciprocity was the way that things had to be, and that therefore the pressing social problem was simply one of making sure that the order of evidently inescapable inequality was secured. But John Locke was writing for, and as, a different kind of man – a man for whom nothing could be taken for granted and for whom the truth of a principle could only be established at the end of difficult intellectual endeavour.

Essentially, Locke was writing as a modern about the arrangements and order of a pre-modern universe which was falling apart. As such, he refused to accept the natural inevitability of the pre-modern arrangements. More interestingly, perhaps, his comments on the work of Sir Robert Filmer reveal a deep intellectual and interpretive incommensurability. Locke's point was that the men of modernity simply could not understand and engage in a dialogue with the inheritors of the pre-modern. As Locke said, the protagonists of divine right should try to rely on something more than assertion from near the top of social hierarchy: 'I hope they do not expect that rational and indifferent men should be brought over to their opinion' (Locke 1924: 11). The modern imagination was deliberately making itself immune from trespass by the tattered remnants of pre-modern systems.

According to their own self-images, the rational and indifferent men could only be persuaded by rational and indifferent principles. But Sir Robert and all the other defenders of absolute monarchy had, according to Locke, quite failed to provide any means of persuasion. After all, the *Patriarcha*, the great statement of divine right, 'has said so little to prove it, from whence it is rather naturally to be concluded that there is little to be said' (Locke 1924: 11). The pre-modern orders were simply unconvincing in conditions of modernity and therefore modernity simply reconstructed those once self-evident systems as either horrible or ridiculous.

It is at this point that attention turns from the observation, which can be identified in the *Two Treatises of Civil Government*, to the question. Basically, with the assault on divine right and the creation of the incommensurability of pre-modern interpretations of asymmetric reciprocity to the conditions of modernity, Locke was abandoning all the taken-for-granted explanations of society. Locke could not admit that society was a natural and intrinsically hierarchic situation. Rather, the deconstruction of such a natural artifice meant that the basis of society, the basis of its possibility and its future, had to be located in society itself. Hence, the centrality of civil society to John Locke. At the very threshold of modernity, Locke used the imagination of civil society to explain how society was possible and, moreover, to explain how reification could be avoided. For Locke, civil society was the guarantee of modernity.

Locke understands civil society to be the associations of individuals which are beyond the family and which are, in my (quite heavily borrowed) terminology, based on the symmetric reciprocity of strangers. Civil society involves the practices and confirmation of a free milieu as distinct from any trace of reification. It involves the reciprocity of strangers who equally and individually give up the state of nature in order to enter into a society. Locke did not doubt the proposition that 'Men being ... by nature all free, equal, and independent, no one can be put out of this estate and subjected to the political power of another without his own consent' (Locke 1924: 164). Furthermore, 'Wherever ... any number of men so unite into one society as to quit every one his executive power of the law of Nature, there and there only is a political or civil society' (Locke 1924: 160). Natural law has given the individual 'a power not only to preserve his property – that is, his life, liberty, and estate, against the injuries and attempts of other men, but to judge of and punish the breaches of that law in others' (Locke 1924: 159).

The state of nature for Locke was not at all one of complete brutishness, but it was certainly a condition of unease and more or less isolated individuals. Locke argues that each individual is pre-formed and already capable of exercising deliberation in the state of nature. Each individual possesses property which he is able, and has a right, to defend against others. That defence was seen by Locke to require developed senses of proportion. The breaches of the natural law were punished by the individual 'as he is persuaded the offence deserves, even with death itself, in crimes where the heinousness of the fact, in his opinion, requires it' (Locke 1924: 159). So, it is right to talk about individuals when discussing Locke's image of the state of nature. He is quite clearly saying that the inhabitants of the state of nature have peculiar and specific possessions which they already know how to defend according to some, however rudimentary, standards of justice.

The point is that this state of nature is one in which individual challenges and threatens individual. It is a state in which there is no symmetric reciprocity. More specifically, it is a state in which the stranger is seen as a definite threat. But Locke was trying to understand a world in which strangers were simply too many to be threatening all the time, a world in which the strangers had to be friends if life was to be possible at all. Hence, the imagination of civil society.

It is perhaps worth quoting Locke at some length on this point. He is making it quite plain that civil society involves reciprocity, the overcoming of strangeness and the confirmation of reflexivity. Civil society also means the social construction of clarity and homogeneity. In the second treatise, Locke wrote about civil society occurring 'wherever any number of men, in a state of Nature, enter into society to make one people one body politic under one supreme government' (Locke 1924: 160). Locke continued:

> For hereby he authorises the society, or which is all one, the legislative thereof, to make laws for him as the public good of the society shall require, to the execution whereof his own assistance (as to his own decrees) is due. And this puts men out of a state of Nature into that of a commonwealth, by setting up a judge on earth with authority to determine all the controversies and redress the injuries that may happen to any member of the commonwealth, which judge is the legislative or magistrates appointed by it. And wherever there are any number of men,

however associated, that have no such decisive power to appeal to, there they are still in the state of Nature.

(Locke 1924:160)

So, the commonwealth is the signification of the bounded community of the strangers who have entered into reciprocity by moving out of the state of nature. That commonwealth is expressed in, perhaps even is the same as, a legislative authority which is able to make decisions in the public interest. As such, the legislative authority operates on the basis of a legal universality (homogeneity) which transcends particularity (heterogeneity). The universality is enforced without regard to persons (as Max Weber might have put it). The authority, which is in turn expressed by and through legal codes, is the guarantee of the symmetric reciprocity of civil society. Nature is thus identified as the condition in which individuals see others as actual or potential threats and in which, therefore, individuals are unable to overcome their heterogeneity. Obviously, Locke is imagining a foundation of society which has no place whatsoever for any criteria of asymmetric reciprocity.

In John Locke's system, then, civil society is the mark of the entrance of humanity into universality and self-determination. Moreover, it is the practice of reflexivity, both in terms of individuality (I am able and willing to subordinate some of my possessions in natural law to the *common*wealth, to the common*wealth*) and in terms of the ability of individuals, through symmetric reciprocity, to see a mirror of themselves in others. Locke was quite clear that civil society represented something beyond the isolated and particular individual: 'wherever any two men are, who have no standing rule and common judge to appeal to on earth, for the determination of controversies of right between them, there they are still in the state of Nature' (Locke 1924: 161). In the *Two Treatises of Civil Government*, Locke was making a profound statement of social independence and freedom; he was moving away from the simple deconstruction of the natural artifice and perhaps even into its destruction.

However, the strategy employed by Locke contained an extremely unfortunate possibility. If civil society was synonymous to legal authority and the executive apparatus of the law, and if it was only through those institutions of homogeneity that society and humanity could be established as defining of themselves, then there was the distinct possibility that the expressions of homo-geneity could themselves become reified. That is, Locke's interpretation of the basis of free society in many ways implied the emergence of a new network of definition from outside. It could be that modernity had emerged in the moment of the deconstruc-tion of one natural artifice, only to lead to the reification of society through another artifice – from the state of nature to the state; from reification to reflexivity to, well, another reification.

Locke was subtle enough a thinker to see this implication, and so he went to great lengths to tackle it head on. He stressed the point that individuals only enter into civil society, and only subject themselves to its authority, on the basis of freely given consent (the social contract). Individuals are prepared to enter into society with each other because, although they have the right to enjoy their property in the state of nature, 'yet the enjoyment of it is very uncertain and constantly exposed to the invasion of others; for all being kings as much as he ... the enjoyment of the property he has in this state is very unsafe, very insecure' (Locke 1924: 179). As such, civil society is derived from and is an expression of individ-uals' 'mind to unite for the mutual preservation of their lives, liberties and estates' (Locke 1924: 180). Men will withdraw their consent to subject themselves to the institutions of symmetric reciprocity if it fails to guarantee life, liberty and property.

By this tactic, John Locke managed, to his own satisfaction at least, to work around the possibility that the homogeneity of civil society might become a new reification. Locke invested all individ-uals with the natural right to withdraw from society and, consequently, he made society a reciprocity of sufferance rather than a reciprocity of necessity. Individuals always retained the right to interrogate reflexively the existing societal arrangements and either withdraw from them or reconstitute them if they were found to be wanting.

Locke argued that the institutional arrangements of civil society are founded on the trust that individuals place in them. Where the trust is found to be misplaced, the existing civil society can be rightly dissolved and a new one constituted:

> Wheresoever, therefore, the legislative shall transgress this fun-damental rule of society, and either by ambition, fear, folly, or corruption, endeavour to grasp themselves, or put into the hands of any other, an absolute power over the lives, liberties,

and estates of the people, by this breach of trust they forfeit the power the people had put into their hands for quite contrary ends, and it devolves to the people, who have a right to resume their original liberty, and by the establishment of a new legislative (such as they shall think fit), provide for their own safety and security, which is the end for which they are in society.

(Locke 1924: 229)

The right of the people to withdraw their trust means that the arrangements of society can never be taken as existing as if by nature. It also means that individuals and institutions have to practise and subject themselves to a ceaseless reflexivity. In the civil society imagined by John Locke, nothing, absolutely nothing, could be taken for granted because there was not, and rightly neither could there be, any absolute source of authority other than the creative, self-defining, individual. For Locke to suppose otherwise, to argue that some authority was indeed invariant and beyond questioning, was to fall into the archaic trap of false principles.

But it is quite noticeable that while John Locke was perfectly happy and able to identify civil society as an independent realm which had achieved freedom from reification, there were certain things that he actually did assume in a quite unquestioning way. Most obviously, Locke simply assumed that in the state of nature there is something called natural law, which is concerned with the life, liberty and property of the individual. In many ways, Locke took the bourgeois property holder entirely for granted and simply universalized and mythologized the experiences and social conditions of existence of a group of strangers who had nothing in common except their private accumulation of wealth. (That is by no means to imply any crass economic reduction of Locke's work. I hope it is clear that I think Locke's work goes far beyond that.) Locke's exercise in reflexivity and the deconstruction of the natural artifice was predicated upon the assumption of certain qualities of being human, qualities which were themselves never questioned.

However, while the virtual reification of property ownership might have been unfortunate, it was not so serious as the story that Locke told about the origins of civil society. Locke had said that civil society was founded in a moment of consent by individuals who had voluntarily entered into symmetric reciprocity with each other. This is the social contract which turns men in the state of nature into citizens of civil society. 'Nothing can make any man so but his actually entering into it by positive engagement and express promise or compact' (Locke 1924: 170). So, Locke assumes a moment of free social activity which is prior to the moment of the emergence of, or individual entry into, civil society.

Arguably, Locke did not actually mean to imply that there really was a historical moment when everyone signed something called a social contract, or indeed that such a contract existed on paper in a library. Undoubtedly, Locke was offering nothing other than an interpretation, arguably even a mythological account, of the possibility of society which was in line with the self-images of the threshold of modernity. But it was fairly easy to criticize Locke on the grounds that his assumption of the contract itself represented a reification which required deconstruction. Precisely that kind of a critique was offered, unsurprisingly, by David Hume.

According to Hume, contract theorists like Locke see the contract as the foundation of civil society. Hume simply pointed out that if this was indeed the case, if all society everywhere was indeed represented in some contract, then the awareness of a contract should be more or less historically constant. But it was not. Hume took reflexivity at least one stage further than even Locke was prepared to go. Hume deconstructed even the imagination of a contract and showed it to be historically contingent. Hume put the matter with quite remorseless logic: 'If scarce any man, till very lately, ever imagined that government was founded on compact, it is certain that it cannot, in general, have any such foundation' (Hume 1947: 236). Hume is saying that the very act of talking about the contractual and associational basis of civil society, the very historical act of that imagination, proved nothing so much that civil society was not at all predicated on such a contract. In Hume's analysis, then, any principle which asserts that society rests on freely given consent is not prior to civil society at all. Rather, it is a product of civil society.

Hume offered a radically different, and a far more cynical, story. As a modern, and perhaps the leading, exponent of reflexivity, David Hume refused to find the possibility of civil society in any thing at all which might be construed as a reification. To Hume, there was originally nothing more to civil society than brute force: 'Almost all the governments which exist at present, or of which there remains any record ... have been founded originally, either on usurpation or conquest, or both, without any pretence of a fair consent or voluntary subjection of the people' (Hume 1947: 216). Hume found the justification of that bitter comment in contemporary history. Here, he is also revealing the extent to which his imaginations have been freed from any notion of invariance: 'The face of the earth is continually changing, by the increase of small kingdoms into great empires, by the dissolution of great empires into smaller kingdoms ... Is there anything discoverable in all these events but force and violence?' (Hume 1947: 216).

Where John Locke saw consent and contract, David Hume saw coercion and compulsion. Now, it can be easily objected that David Hume was simply offering an ironic counter-point to the rather nicer tale told by John Locke. Perhaps Hume was doing precisely that, but he was also doing something of far greater importance when he raised the possibility that civil society might be explained without a turn to more or less mythical stories. Hume managed to provide an explanation of the possibility of civil society which was fully sociological.

Hume's explanation contained two fairly sophisticated sociological components. Firstly, he assumed absolutely nothing except the effects of social relationships. Secondly, he tried to use a (fairly rudimentary if not ultimately crass) cross-cultural methodology to unravel general trends in the formation of societies. With these sociological orientations, Hume was reflecting one of the dominant strands of the eighteenth century Scottish Enlightenment. (For a brief sketch of the Scottish Enlightenment, see Phillipson 1981. For the sociological aspects of the Scottish Enlightenment, see Swingewood 1970.)

The theme explored by David Hume, that civil society has its roots in conflict, was also important in the work of Adam Ferguson. Indeed, it is fascinating to look at the virtually forgotten books of Ferguson. It is quite remarkable how contemporary they seem to be. For example, in the *Principles of Moral and Political Science*, which was published in 1792, Ferguson was hinting at the notion that society is best understood as an imagination which orders and creates regularities and which, moreover, represents a moment in human freedom. Rather like David Hume, Ferguson argued that while laws and institutions contain some contractual elements, it is more significantly the case that 'such agreements are all of them posterior to the existence of society, and not the foundations upon which society was erected' (Ferguson 1975: 220).

In other words, Ferguson was implying that the imagination of civil society involves also the construction of essentially mythological stories about the foundation of society. The myths serve to give the imagination some degree of credibility. An example of such a mythology would undoubtedly be nothing other than Locke's emphasis on the contractual moment of civil society and the free consent given to government. Ferguson's point was quite simply that any concept of a contract necessarily implies a social act prior to the contract, else it could not be drawn up, and even less could be drawn up as able to *already* secure universal consent.

Ferguson agreed that civil society emerges from the requirements of a reciprocity which bonds individual with individual. He wrote: 'from a regard to the welfare of our fellow-creatures, we endeavour to pacify their animosities, and unite them by ties of affection' (Ferguson 1980: 25). This involves a struggle to make individuals move beyond the limits of their heterogeneity: 'we may hope to instil into the breasts of private men sentiments of candour toward their fellow-creatures, and a disposition to humanity and justice' (Ferguson 1980: 25). So far, so enervating. But Ferguson started to move on to very original ground when he suggested that while civil society might be understood as the creation of a bounded community of reciprocity, each community does not exist in a vacuum. Ferguson dealt with the problem of treating some strangers as friends, but he was brilliantly aware that any classification of 'us' also means a classification of 'them'.

In Locke's system, there is a sense that it is enough to provide a single interpretation of civil society, and that the interpretation will be universally valid. Perhaps that trend was due to Locke's assumption of a certain ontological and anthropological baggage brought by the individual to society. But Ferguson made the crucial point that different civil societies exist in difficult relation to other civil societies. This meant two things. Firstly, Ferguson did not pretend that civil society represented complete harmony: 'But it is vain to expect that we can give to the multitude of a people a sense of union among themselves, without admitting hostility to those who oppose them' (Ferguson 1980: 25). Secondly, without that hostility towards outsiders, or even strange insiders/strangers inside, the community of civil society would simply collapse.

It is precisely the identification of an abhorrent 'them' which makes 'us' possible. On the one hand, Ferguson knew well that 'The names of *alien*, or *foreigner*, are seldom pronounced without some degree of intended reproach. That of *barbarian* ... and that of *gentil* ... only served to distinguish the stranger, whose language and pedigree differed from theirs' (Ferguson 1980: 205). On the other hand, however, 'Could we at once, in the case of any nation, extinguish the emulation which is excited from abroad, we should probably break or weaken the bands of society at home, and close the busiest scenes of national occupations and virtues' (Ferguson 1980: 25).

Like Hume, Ferguson looks at civil society and sees something which is rather less than glorious, and which yet represents civilization. Ferguson made his position quite clear: 'Without the rivalship of nations, and the practice of war, civil society itself could scarcely have found an object, or a form' (Ferguson 1980: 24).

For Ferguson, then, civil society emerged out of the problem of dealing with others who could not be known already. But the definition of those others who were relevant to the given private individual necessarily involved clear and vigorous projects of boundary drawing. The boundary drawing in turn meant a rivalry between nations, and this yet further exacerbated the problem of internal homogeneity in the face of external heterogeneity. Indeed, it is only through the threat of the stranger that symmetric reciprocity can be formalized. It is only through the creation of clear boundaries between us and them, between the same and the other, that it is possible to 'decide every contest without tumult, and to secure, by the authority of law, every citizen in the possession of his personal rights' (Ferguson 1980: 188).

The establishment of institutions and relationships of homogeneity was held by Ferguson to be the precondition of a subsequent trend towards internal division. But the division was unproblematic precisely because it occurred within pre-ordered boundaries. Ferguson saw the diversification as a sign of progress, but his work contains hints that the division might involve future reification: 'Mankind, when in their rude state, have a great uniformity of manners; but when civilized, they are engaged in a variety of pursuits; they tread on a larger field, and separate to a greater distance' (Ferguson 1980: 188).

So, civil society makes possible a division of labour, and this in turn signals a movement away from the reification of uniformity. But the problem of the division of labour is that it too can become a reification: 'It enables the statesman and the soldier to settle the forms of their different procedures; it enables the practitioner in every profession to pursue his separate advantage' (Ferguson 1980: 188–9). (This point almost seems to anticipate Durkheim and Weber on the implications of rational or professional special-ization.) In other words, the marks and the guarantees of freedom might become too easy. They might begin to seem natural and thus presage a new kind of evidently inevitable artifice – a second nature.

Similar worries run through the work of Adam Smith. He believed that men in feudal societies had been corrupted by dependency, but the emergent commercial culture promised to change all of that because it freed humanity from any traces of the natural. Smith wrote: 'Nothing tends so much to corrupt and enervate and debase the mind as dependency and nothing gives such noble and generous notions of probity as freedom and independency' (Smith 1977: 333).

But that freedom and independence does not mean that the individual is to be conceived as a hermit. Quite the contrary. Smith argued that individuals can only know such fine sentiments as freedom to the extent that they associate with other individuals in society. For Smith, society is the achievement of man, because it is a mirror which enables the individual to go beyond the particular and experience the pulls of morality. Smith did not doubt that man becomes free in relationships with other men. After all, if 'a human creature could grow up to manhood in some solitary place, without any communication with his own species, he could no more think of his own character ... than of the beauty or deformity of his own face' (Smith 1976: 110).

Smith continues to draw out the idea that society is a milieu in which the individual can know himself by knowing others: 'Bring him into society, and he is immediately provided with the mirror which he wanted before ... it is here that he first views the propriety and impropriety of his own passions, the beauty and deformity of his own mind' (Smith 1976: 110). The point that Smith did not emphasize, however, is that a mirror is a technology of symmetric reciprocity. It reflects that which is put in front of it and is made by strangers for us. For Smith, the moral principles which make individuals free are derived purely from the reciprocity of equals. He states that 'our first moral criticisms are exercised upon the characters and conduct of other people ... But we soon learn, that other people are equally frank with our own' (Smith 1976: 112).

The situation signalled by Smith is, to say the least, highly reflexive. He is not simply saying that we worry about what others think of us. He is also saying that through the criticism of others, we are able to criticize ourselves and treat ourselves as if we were a stranger to ourself. That is, we become precisely the kind of self-conscious individual, walking in a world of other self-conscious individuals, which was illustrated by Sartre in *Nausea* and in Georg Simmel's discussion of the blasé attitude of the metropolis.

So, thanks to the sociological narrative of Adam Smith, civil society can be understood as the sphere in which individuals are confronted with the mirror of their actions and sentiments. It is through that mirror that the individual man can transcend himself and enter into relationships with others. The relationships are based on mutual reflexivity. But the mirror effect helps the cause of social order in quite another way. According to Smith, when we enter into society and reflect upon the practices of ourselves and others, we quickly realize that some individuals are more wealthy or more virtuous than ourselves. We envy and try to imitate them: 'Upon this disposition of mankind, to go along with all the passions of the rich and the powerful, is founded the distinction of ranks, and the order of society' (Smith 1976: 52). This is yet another kind of cement between strangers, yet another cause for symmetry between those who would in different times and in different imaginations have been understood as thoroughly asymmetric.

Moreover, Smith implicitly states that none of this should be taken as existing as if by nature. The entire architecture of morality, reciprocity and society is identified as the result of social and historical processes. But Smith had a keen sense that the commercialism that he applauded had potentially disastrous implications for continued reflexivity and for the perpetuation of freedom. In the *Wealth of Nations* he proposed that tendencies towards mass production would result in the creation of dehumanized labourers. In common with the other Scottish philosophers, especially Adam Ferguson, Smith expressed serious misgivings at the reifying implications of the division of labour. They anticipated Marx, and perhaps even in a fairly accidental way, the thesis of the Dialectic of Enlightenment, when they suggested that the processes of human freedom were also the technologies of human oppression.

Like John Locke, although in a very different way, David Hume, Adam Ferguson and Adam Smith were all attempting to make a compelling case for symmetric reciprocity, and for the freedom of society and humanity from reification. They were quite vividly aware that at the time that they were writing, the seventeenth and eighteenth centuries, society could not be taken for granted. They also knew that authority structures had to be examined and interrogated rather than taken purely at their own word as inevitable by the grace of God. In various ways, they all located the hope of freedom and the proof of social symmetry in the imagination of civil society.

As such, it might be said that these expressions of the imagination of civil society reveal two key features of modernity. Firstly, the texts show that, in the seventeenth and eighteenth centuries, the possibility of society was becoming increasingly worrying. The worry was due to the intellectual, spatial and political transformations which were all represented in the figure of the stranger. Secondly, the texts show that the collapse of the divine right of the monarch represented a most profound liberation.

With the enthusiastic deconstruction of the natural artifice, which turned the likes of Sir Robert Filmer into mere footnotes of history, the bounded community of civil society became imaginable; civil society as the free and independent realm of free and independent humanity; as the universal compass of the particularity of the individual; as the achieved milieu of the civil. Quite simply, civil society was the creative and homogeneous world as distinct from the passive and heterogeneous state of nature. Civil society was the self-image of modernity.

Chapter 3

The method

The Scottish philosophers like David Hume, Adam Ferguson and Adam Smith were extremely aware that the processes associated with the production of wealth, refined manners and societal diversification, were themselves to some extent harbingers of terrible forms of reification. Those future arrangements promised to turn societal freedom against itself, and to denude human life of the symmetric reciprocity which should have been its modern defining trait. The philosophers seem to have hoped that by calling attention to the worrying tendencies of the division of labour and industrialization, they could also sound a caution which would always be kept in mind by following generations. Either that, or the philosophers simply issued cautionary declarations in densely packed texts because they could offer nothing else against the forward march of manufacture.

In either case, Hume and the others were working only a relatively short while after the wide spread of the practice of reflexivity. They knew that reflexivity could not at all be assumed to happen all of its own accord. Quite the contrary, the Scottish philosophers were aware that the conditions for existence of reflexivity had to be revealed and reproduced if the great chance of freedom was to be seized. For them, the movement out of the state of nature and the creation, or at least the posterior imagination, of civil society meant nothing other than the self-sufficiency of the social and its release from any arrangements which were evidently simply as they had to be. The deconstruction of the natural artifice meant that any possibility of reification in the future had to be located, removed and for ever carefully watched.

Something similar was also implied by John Locke. He too, and of course before the Scottish philosophers, was careful to avoid the trap that the deconstruction of one natural artifice might create the space for the construction of another. That is why Locke put the social contract at the very centre of his imagination of civil society, and why he deliberately made the point that the maintenance of any existing contractual arrangement ought not to be taken for granted. When he reserved for individuals the right to withdraw from any contract, and from any existing civil society if it was not protecting life, liberty and property, Locke was also making sure that no social constructions could ever be removed from the perpetual questioning of reflexivity. For Locke, any government, any milieu of association, had to prove itself continually to be adequate to the demands of the individuals who voluntarily participated within it.

Moreover, Locke's emphasis on the contract itself indicates an imagination of social relationships and arrangements as things which need to be negotiated and renegotiated rather than simply imposed or assumed. 'In the prudent discussion of "the social contract" or a "new covenant", the early moderns found an apposite metaphor for this renegotiation' (Heller 1990: 148).

In other words, Locke gave an interpretation of civil society and its requirements which was actually quite optimistic. Of course, Locke was not a Panglossian who was prepared to brush aside any terrible occurrences on the grounds that everything would be for the best eventually. But it is nevertheless the case that the *Two Treatises of Civil Government* can be read as statements of the freedom, opportunity and improvement, which reflexivity was assumed to bring to social relationships. Locke provided an image of modernity as, according to many of its leading protagonists, modernity ought to have been and could have been. (For more on the enthusiasts of modernity, their social position as well as their social interests, see Bauman 1987.)

Locke was apparently fairly sure that once individuals had entered into civil society, they would not wish to return to the state of nature. All the individuals would want by way of an alternative to *this* civil society would be *another* civil society. But for some of the early modern philosophers, the picture was not at all so clear and, more importantly, neither could individuals be assumed to do anything so sensible as choose between societies rather than between society and nature. For some, there were few, if any, reasons for optimism in the study of man. Certainly, these less optimistic thinkers did not at all wish to exempt the natural artifice from deconstruction, but neither did they wish to allow an unceasing reflexivity which could possibly cast doubt on everything and leave absolutely nothing certain.

Thomas Hobbes is perhaps the most important among these philosophers. (Most important, that is, in so far as he was fully pulled into the heritage of European modernity.) The problem embodied in the work of Hobbes, and most obviously in the *Leviathan*, is rather different to that which can be found in Locke. Basically, Locke's problem was one of making sure that civil society could defend the natural rights and possessions of individuals. As such, he was careful to emphasize the point that, in theory at least, no social arrangements should emerge which could deprive individuals of their natural rights of property and liberty. But for Hobbes, the problem was a lot more awkward.

The sense of the *Two Treatises of Civil Government* is that, for Locke, the state of nature is experienced by individuals as uncertain and potentially highly dangerous, but as little more than a possible difficulty. Yet Hobbes saw the state of nature as completely and utterly terrible and terrifying. For Hobbes, the main question was one of making sure that civil society could be maintained in the face of the overwhelming threat presented to it by the state of nature. Hobbes was not too worried if social reflexivity was halted by a reification of society's own making, just so long as the state of nature could be avoided. If it can be said that Locke's work is characterized by a perpetual dialogue between the societal and the natural (a dialogue which, however, involves the ever firmer separation of the two), then Hobbes's work is rather more concerned with a single, total, irrefutable moment of absolute rupture.

There are a small number of passages in the library of European thought which are, perhaps, rather too well known for their own good. It is impossible to read them without either complacency or disdain. Their challenge and, often, rhetorical brilliance have been quite lost through over-familiarity. A number of passages from Karl Marx immediately spring to mind, possibly a couple from Jean Jacques Rousseau and, most notably, the famous description of the state of nature that Thomas Hobbes gives in the *Leviathan*.

Hobbes argues that in the state of nature, all men should be treated as equal individuals. He does not mean equal in any moral sense, but equal simply in terms of what they can do to each other: 'the weakest has strength enough to kill the strongest, either by secret machination, or by confederacy with others, that are in the same danger with himselfe' (Hobbes 1991: 87). But this is not the only problem in the state of nature. Hobbes also thought that individuals are quite astonishingly vain and arrogant, since each believes himself to be the wisest person alive. Each individual believes that he has the mental and physical resources to secure whatever are his ends, and yet in the state of nature, there simply are not enough resources for the securing of all individual ends. In Hobbes's interpretation, the state of nature is one in which egoistic individuals create a condition of scarcity. (Marx saw much of this as the product of bourgeois and capitalist arrangements.) The result is, perhaps, inevitable. Individuals equally hope to secure their ends; 'And therefore if any two men desire the same thing, which neverthelesse they cannot both enjoy, they become enemies; and in the way to their End ... endeavour to destroy, or subdue one an other' (Hobbes 1991: 87).

Clearly, this state of nature is immensely more threatening and horrible than anything that Locke imagined. Certainly, the Hobbesian themes are not incompatible with Locke, but Locke never declared that 'men have no pleasure, (but on the contrary a great deale of griefe) in keeping company, where there is no power able to over-awe them all' (Hobbes 1991: 88). Hobbes put it a little differently in one of his wonderfully pithy statements: 'during the time men live without a common Power to keep them all in awe, they are in that condition which is called Warre; and such a warre, as is of every man, against every man' (Hobbes 1991: 88). Hobbes was not saying that the state of nature is consequently a condition of perpetual fighting, but simply that it is a condition in which there could be no guarantee that there would not be perpetual fighting.

After sketching these outlines of the state of nature, Hobbes comes to fill in some of the detail. He does so through a quite magnificent rhetorical stroke in which the emptiness, the want, the reification of the state of nature is appreciated by a remorseless catalogue of everything that it lacks. Hobbes imagines the state of nature in terms of its failings. It is only through the rhetoric of the absent that Hobbes feels able to say what the state of nature actually means. But what the state of nature means would have been better left unsaid:

> there is no place for Industry; because the fruit thereof is uncertain: and consequently no Culture of the Earth; no

Navigation, nor use of the commodities that may be imported by Sea; no commodious Building; no Instruments of moving, and removing such things as require much force; no Knowledge of the face of the Earth; no account of Time; no Arts; no Letters; no Society; and which is worst of all, continuall feare, and danger of violent death; And the life of man, solitary, poore, nasty, brutish, and short.

(Hobbes 1991: 89)

After this devastating passage, which would be famous for its prose regardless of the charge of the message, Hobbes asks any one who disagrees with him to consider why, if the natural relationships between men are not so awful, they lock away all their valuables, carry weapons and secure their houses against burglars. He suggests that when we lock our doors, we are actually signalling our acceptance of the terrible picture of the state of nature. As such, to disagree with Hobbes while sitting in a house with a burglar alarm is to give evidence of nothing more than our own dishonesty.

It is extremely interesting, however, that when Hobbes makes this point, when he refers to all those traces of the state of nature which lurk behind the deeds of civilization, he refers to milieux or conditions which are outside of the boundaries of everyday civil society. Hobbes talks about the dangers of taking a journey. He asks why an individual, 'when going to sleep, he locks his dores; when even in his house he locks his chests; and this when he knowes there bee Lawes, and publike Officers, armed, to revenge all injuries shall bee done him' (Hobbes 1991: 89). The vestiges of the state of nature are to be found in those places and in those moments where the bonds of reciprocity are stretched to breaking point. The fear of the possibility of the war of all against all arises either when the individual moves outside the boundaries of the known and into the spaces of the stranger, or when the individual closes his eyes to the societal world and relapses into the nightmares of reason. (It would be very interesting to spend some time exploring the history and sociology of the fear of sleep in European discourse, a fear which was vividly portrayed for modernity by Goya and later, albeit with a little more ambivalence, the Surrealists.)

Despite the stark impact of his prose, and the vulgarization to which it was consequently susceptible, Hobbes's point was actually extremely subtle. He argued, that in themselves, the actions of men in the state of nature could not be called wrong, sinful, bad or immoral. The actions cannot be labelled with those evaluations precisely because in the state of nature the actions are not forbidden by any law. As Hobbes says: 'The notions of Right and Wrong, Justice and Injustice have there no place. Where there is no common Power, there is no Law: where no Law, no Injustice' (Hobbes 1991: 90). The implication is, then, that it is only through, and because of, the imagination of civil society that it is possible to imagine the state of nature as something horrible.

But while Hobbes himself provides a reason to see the state of nature as nothing more than an 'Other' created in the interest of defining the 'Same', he rather seems to have missed the full implications of what he was hinting at. Hobbes hesitantly opened the possibility of a deconstruction of civil society. But perhaps the opportunity came too early in the history of modernity, when society was still in the founding rather than established as the accepted and overly familiar milieu of social relationships. Instead of moving from the social construction of the nasty, brutish and short life of nature to the meaning of civil society, he failed to see beyond the concern to deconstruct the natural artifice. As such, Hobbes seems to have been deceived by the nightmare of his own waking hours. He constructed a powerful and compelling theory of escape from natural reification and into civil society and freedom, when he might have offered an exploration of the social construction of the imaginations which create the intelligible order of things.

Hobbes saw the escape route from nature as being opened in the first instance by a contract or covenant. Essentially, Hobbes understood that contract to be the basis of the 'common Power' which could guarantee the symmetric reciprocity of individuals and overcome the egoism, reification and scarcity of the state of nature. For Hobbes, the contract was operating on the terrain of symmetric reciprocity in two ways: firstly, because all the subjects of the contract came to it as equals in the state of nature; secondly, because all the subjects were established as more or less identical from the point of view of the 'common Power'.

Hobbes builds on his point that in the state of nature, there is nothing to stop anyone from doing whatever he might please other than the actual or potential threat of violence by others. In the state of nature, 'every man has a Right to every thing; even to one anothers body' (Hobbes 1991: 91). However, the paradox is that men cannot possibly secure this natural right in the state of nature. If it is a natural right that every individual has a right to everything, then my right undermines your right. As such, we either collapse yet further into war, as our conflicting natural rights create scarcity, or we each give up some of our natural rights. We avoid war by each renouncing our natural rights or by transferring them to some external authority (Hobbes 1991: 92–3). 'The mutuall transferring of Right, is that which men call CONTRACT' (Hobbes 1991: 94).

However, for Hobbes, it was not enough to say simply that men can overcome the possibility of the war of all against all through the contractual transference of natural right into a system of reciprocal costs (I cannot have that) and reciprocal benefits (you cannot have that either and so we shall not fight over it). For Hobbes, it was also very important that the continuation of the contract had to be institutionalized and put beyond doubt. This is the basis of Hobbes's concern to identify a single moment of division between the societal and the natural. The contract overcomes fear to the extent that it represents external compulsion. All the time the contract is externalized, it can compel individuals and it can never become obsolete. The requirements of the contract make sure that the individuals who would otherwise be strangers are pulled together. For example, if the relationships between just two men are considered: 'if there be a common Power set over them both, with right and force sufficient to compell performance; it is not void' (Hobbes 1991: 96).

Consequently, the contract is understood to be something like the basis of civil society because it confirms the associations of individuals. It is the reciprocity of the contract which overcomes the problem of the stranger by uniting all individuals into a societal system. The contract can achieve that if it is externalized; if it can become an artifice which works on a broader horizon than the dull immediacy typical of the state of nature. It is consolidated because it manages to do two things. Firstly, it makes sure that individuals fear the state of nature and have something to lose by any return to it. Individuals lose the benefits of reciprocity (Hobbes 1991: 96). Secondly, the contract can secure itself through coercion. After all, 'Covenants, without the Sword, are but Words, and of no strength to secure a man at all' (Hobbes 1991: 117).

In the work of Hobbes, the fear of the state of nature is so great, and so much an ever-present whisper from behind the rigorous prose, that no cost is too great if it means a final and irreversible escape from that most awful of reifications. As such, Hobbes pushed the project of reflexivity only so far. Certainly, he went a long way in the deconstruction of the natural artifice. After all, the main challenge of Hobbes's argument is precisely that the lives of men do not have to be experienced as nasty, brutish and short. Hobbes was indubitably a modern thinker because he went to great lengths to show that other kinds of social arrangement were possible. Indeed, the realization of that possibility of alternatives was closely linked with 'The finall Cause, End, or Designe of men'. Hobbes was quite certain that the human mission consists of, 'the introduction of that restraint upon themselves, (in which wee see them live in Commonwealths), [which] is the foresight of their own preservation, and of a more contented life thereby' (Hobbes 1991: 117).

But the central charge of Hobbes's work is that despite the assumption of some kind of *telos* to societal arrangements, there could be no certainty that men would be up to the demands of achieving their ends. As such, the final cause of man was quite unattainable 'when there is no visible Power to keep them in awe, and tye them by feare of punishment to the performance of their Covenants' (Hobbes 1991: 117). Consequently, given that to be secure the move out of the state of nature required a potent mixture of obligation and force, Hobbes was prepared to exempt the 'visible Power' itself from too much questioning. Indeed, the drift of Hobbes's argument seems to be that the societally con-structed external authority should become a new reification. But that price would be a small one to pay since, while it might have involved a limitation to quite how far deconstruction could go (everything can be deconstructed except the institution of the contract), it did mean that the reification of nature could be avoided once and for all.

Hobbes turns the commonwealth, as the societal representation of the contract, into nothing other than an immense force working in the direction of complete and utter homogeneity. In Hobbes's commonwealth, nothing can be left to be strange because strange-ness means difference, and difference implies vestiges of the natural.

It is quite clear from *Leviathan* that anything which smacked of heterogeneity was, for Hobbes, absolutely abhorrent and in need of extirpation. He offers a list of the 'Infirmities' of a commonwealth and shows why they have to be refuted (Hobbes 1991: 221–30). The list reads like a series of extracts from Machiavelli. I will only outline the infirmities which are relevant for this discussion.

Firstly, Hobbes says that any sovereign power must be absolute and must never weaken its authority, because 'when the exercise of the Power layd by, is for the publique safety to be resumed, it hath the resemblance of an unjust act; which disposeth great numbers of men ... to rebell' (Hobbes 1991: 222). Authority must be absolute otherwise difference will flourish.

Secondly, Hobbes attacks moral relativism and subjectivism. He says that it is quite erroneous to assume that every individual is a self-sufficient judge of good or evil. He says that relativism and subjectivism are part of the natural state, but that civil society requires external and universal criteria of the good. Without the imposition from outside of moral values, homogeneity is quite impossible because 'men are disposed to debate with themselves, and dispute the commands of the Common-wealth; and afterwards to obey, or disobey them, as in their private judgements they shall think fit' (Hobbes 1991: 223). That would mean the weakening of the community.

Hobbes's third infirmity is in many ways an extension of the second. Hobbes refuses to agree with the postulate that it is wrong for a man to do something against the dictates of his conscience. In a discussion which rather anticipates Rousseau on the 'general will', Hobbes says that in the commonwealth, the public conscience is embodied in the law that the individual has, through the contract, undertaken to obey. As such, if the law demands something, then it has to be done, totally regardless of individual conscience (Hobbes 1991: 223).

Hobbes continues to show quite clearly that he was prepared to reify the authority of the commonwealth and put it beyond reflexivity. In many ways, he laid the ground for another natural artifice (for a second nature). Hobbes says that the sovereign simply cannot be subjected to civil law, because to be subject to law is to be subject to the commonwealth. But, logically, that would make the commonwealth (as the sovereign) subject to itself. Hobbes was in no doubt that such an argument is both absurd and very dangerous. He expresses his fears in a manner which clearly illustrates the disastrous consequences of an unbridled reflexivity: 'because it setteth the Lawes above the Soveraign, setteth also a

Judge above him, and a Power to punish him; which is to make a new Soveraign; and again for the same reason a third, to punish the second'. Once in motion, the train would not stop: 'and so continually without end, to the Confusion, and Dissolution of the Common-wealth' (Hobbes 1991: 224). Dissolution would result because the safe and definite heart of the commonwealth would always be receding into the distance, and confusion because there would be no single meaning of homogeneity against which an order of things could be constructed.

However, Hobbes did not see, despite the vague opportunity that he gave himself, that the entire perspective of *Leviathan* was little more than a kind of optical illusion. Hobbes was not looking from the state of nature to civil society; rather, he was constructing the state of nature in terms of a prior imagination of civil society. What Hobbes took to be nature was nothing more than the fears generated from within the bounded community of society. In these terms, Hobbes provides an excellent philosophical example of what Kenneth Clark, after a usage which has been known since the time of John Ruskin, has called the pathetic fallacy (Clark 1956: 152). Clark mentions the idea of the pathetic fallacy in his analysis of the European tradition of landscape painting, and he uses it to refer to 'the use of landscape as a focus for our own emotions' (Clark 1956: 152). Hobbes was indeed engaging in the pathetic fallacy. He was using nature, and its non-societal landscape of the possible war of all against all, as an extension of the interpretation of his own world and his own security within it. Hobbes was writing at the dawn of modernity, at a time when the natural artifice was apprehended as utterly unable to explain social relationships and the basis of reciprocity between individuals. (Whereas Locke did not want the natural artifice to have any explanatory use, Hobbes was convinced that the natural artifice must not have any such use.)

The intellectual fear which runs through *Leviathan* was due to the possibility that any replacement for the natural artifice might not be able to develop in time. Hobbes was expressing a fear of the *interregnum* between one foundation of reciprocity and another. That *interregnum* was understood to be something without order rather than something between order. Hence, it was conflated with the nature which ostensibly existed outside of civil society. As such, the state of nature became the condition of man without order and without any certainty of reciprocity. Since Hobbes was concerned with the society of individuals (that is, with their reciprocity), any state in which that reciprocity could not be taken for granted could not possibly be civil society.

So, while Hobbes thought that he was providing an empirical description of the foundations of civil society, he was in fact merely asserting it. Hobbes turned nature into myth when, in the name of reporting the reality outside of society, he actually provided only an imaginative reference to it. If Hayden White is right, then it might be proposed that Hobbes's turn to the state of nature is a typical imaginative move in times of social and cultural tension, when the old orders are being systematically reduced by deconstruction, and new orders have not yet emerged which can fully come to terms with problems like rapid change, increasing cosmopolitanism or the multiplicity of urban strangers. The point is that Hobbes wanted to assert his humanity and, moreover, to establish the need for a civil society which demanded the restraint and constraint of individuals. The natural artifice could not be the basis of that assertion, but nature could be.

Hayden White says that in times of stress, and Thomas Hobbes was writing at a time of massive social and cultural tension, the problem of asserting humanity and society when there is no basis for humanity and society can be resolved because 'it is always possible to say something like: "I may not know the precise content of my own felt humanity, but I am most certainly *not* like that", and simply point to something in the landscape that is manifestly different from oneself' (White 1978: 151). Basically, Hobbes was expressing the fears of men who 'were uncertain as to the precise quality of their sensed humanity' and he 'appealed to the concept of wildness to designate an area of subhumanity that was characterized by everything they hoped they were not' (White 1978: 152). The tenuous basis of the approach, which White calls the technique of ostensive self-definition by negation (White 1978: 151–52), is confirmed by the serious doubts that Hobbes entertained as to whether it was actually reasonable to suggest that he was not like that.

In other words, it is the imagination of civil society which creates and determines the imagination of nature. Where civil society is imaginatively constructed as something which is sensed but not known, nature is a massive threat which must be pushed away. The act of pushing will create the boundaries of civil society and, moreover, create the principle of homogeneity which will make society knowable. Where civil society is imaginatively constructed as something which is known but not sensed, then nature becomes less threatening. It becomes the resource by which individuals can sense their humanity and know the existing arrangements of civil society as bad or in some way unpleasant. Nature, rather than society, becomes the basis on which the boundaries of civil society can be drawn.

Where Thomas Hobbes perfectly illustrates the former strategy, Jean Jacques Rousseau perfectly illustrates the latter. Where Hobbes's interpretation moved from the wild man of the state of nature to the fully homogeneous commonwealth, Rousseau moved in a different direction, from the heterogeneity of existing society to the homogeneity of the civil society constituted on the basis of the social contract. Despite their very substantial disagreements, Hobbes and Rousseau are rather like two miners digging the same tunnel from different ends and who finally meet underground (a metaphor I have borrowed from Mahler, who had in turn borrowed it from Schopenhauer). Just like Hobbes, Rousseau ended up making great pleas for the universality of some social arrangements and their exemption from reflexive deconstruction.

It must be said that it can be quite difficult to derive a coherent story from the body of Rousseau's writing. As Jacob Talmon put it, 'The *Social Contract* was the sublimation of the *Discourse on the Origins of Inequality*' (Talmon 1952: 39). Now, it seems quite likely that Talmon has rather too easily reduced the complexities of Rousseau's work to questions of personality (although it cannot be denied that Rousseau was certainly an extremely idiosyncratic character). While it can be said with some validity that Rousseau's work does tend to reveal some inconsistency of implication, it is nevertheless the case that *A Discourse on Inequality* and *The Social Contract* do indeed talk about the same problems in a morally consistent fashion. The two books are part of the same project. In both, Rousseau was trying to explain the basis and institutions of the kind of society which would be most appropriate, 'taking men as they are and laws as they might be' (Rousseau 1968: 49).

When Rousseau says that he wishes to take 'men as they are', he does not mean that it is enough to abstract out to the figure of universal man on the basis of observation or knowledge of individual men (and perhaps even women, although with Rousseau probably not) who live in any given society. Much like Karl Marx some years later, Rousseau wanted to grasp the universal truths which, according to him, lurked somewhere behind the particular appearances. As such, the reference to 'men as they are' is arguably intended to be understood in an ontological sense. Rousseau was trying to take man in his essential being and basic relationships, man before and without civil society.

That was Rousseau's point of departure, and from it he attempted to construct a blueprint of the minimum institutions which could, firstly, be reconciled with man in his essential being and, secondly, nevertheless express and ensure the modern imagination of the conscious human definition of humanity and society. Whereas the method of Hobbes was relatively simple, involving little more than the interpretation of the reified state of nature as simply the 'Other' of civil society (that is, Hobbes basically looked out *from* civil society *to* nature and back again), Rousseau's method was a lot more complex. He looked at laws as they were and men as they might be made by those laws, and dialectically negated that investigation in terms of men as they were and laws as they might be. As such, Rousseau managed to ground his critique of existing social arrangements through the provision of a bench-mark beyond which the exercise of reflexivity could not go (the universal ontology of men) and simultaneously deconstruct the natural artifice.

Rousseau was proposing that the existing relationships and arrangements of civil society (laws as they are, polished manners as practised in the salons of Paris) create asymmetric reciprocity. He knew this, and could define it as a terrible problem, because the ontology and anthropology behind appearances (men as they are) implied and required symmetric reciprocity. (Clearly, Rousseau was going some way towards a mythologization of the categories of modernity; he saw the notion of symmetric reciprocity as a report of reality.) Rousseau demonstrated all of this through an emphasis on the state of nature and, specifically, the natural status of man as the 'noble savage'. Rousseau deconstructed the existing social relationships of nobility (again, as typified in the salons of Paris) in terms of the ontological being of nobility: 'As thus envisaged, the Noble Savage idea represents not so much an elevation of the idea of the native as a demotion of the idea of nobility' (White 1978: 191).

Rousseau spelt out the meanings of his version of the state of nature in *A Discourse on Inequality*. The difference with Hobbes, a difference due to Hobbes's belief that civil society is our only chance and Rousseau's belief that it might be only one chance, is stark indeed. For Hobbes, the state of nature was completely and utterly terrible. It was a pit of strangers, strangeness and the strange which needed to be kept at bay at all costs. But the state of nature imagined by Rousseau as the 'Other' of civil society is basically something of an idyll. For Rousseau, it was the existing social arrangements, the demands of laws as they are, which became the great problem.

Throughout *A Discourse on Inequality*, Rousseau engages in a running battle with Thomas Hobbes. Whether Hobbes was represented entirely fairly in the battle is another matter. For example, Rousseau says that if Hobbes had endeavoured to construct an argument which was internally consistent, then he 'ought to have said that the state of nature, being the state where man's care for his own preservation is at least prejudicial to that of others, is the one most conducive to peace and the most suited to mankind' (Rousseau 1984: 98). According to Rousseau, the point is that Hobbes had constructed an image of man in the state of nature which was actually nothing more than an expression of some of the worst consequences of existing civil society. Hobbes was accused of having merely naturalized the egoistic result of existing social arrangements (precisely the charge that Marx levelled against most of his contemporaries). As Rousseau saw it, Hobbes had performed a sleight of hand and slipped 'into the savage man's care for his own preservation the need to satisfy a multitude of passions which are the product of society and which have made laws necessary' (Rousseau 1984: 98).

Hobbes understood the state of nature in terms of the coercive reciprocity of thoroughly egoistic individuals. But Rousseau pushed the implications of egoism rather further. Rousseau's 'noble savage' is noble precisely because he lives in himself; he is honest and self-sufficient. This is an imagination of man without society, and of man all the better for it. But the cost of the peace, tranquillity and truth of the state of nature was such that the life of men could barely be called human. With a kind of ambivalent amazement, Rousseau wrote in *A Discourse on Inequality*:

> that savage man, wandering in the forests, without work, without speech, without a home, without war, and without relationships, was equally without any need of his fellow men and without any desire to hurt them, perhaps not even recognizing any one of them individually. Being subject to so few

passions, and sufficient unto himself, he had only such feelings and such knowledge as suited his condition; he felt only his true needs, saw only what he believed it was necessary to see, and his intelligence made no more progress than his vanity.

(Rousseau 1984: 104)

The passage can be read as an eulogy to a perfect symmetry of individuality in which there is no divergence between the homogeneous and the heterogeneous, between the universal and the particular.

According to Rousseau, the emergence of civil society (that is, the institution of laws as they are), signalled a once-and-for-ever movement out of the state of nature. Civil society means that the state of nature is quite beyond any return which is not simply speculative (Rousseau 1984: 68). This is because civil society is taken as meaning two things. Firstly, it involves the appearance of man as a distinctively human being separate from nature. Secondly, it is the institution of men in relationships so as to overcome scarcity.

In *The Social Contract*, Rousseau was in no doubt that the state of nature collapses with the onset of scarcity. As such, the association of individuals and civil society itself is equated with want rather than abundance. He commented that 'men reach a point where the obstacles to their preservation in a state of nature prove greater than the strength that each man has to preserve himself in that state. Beyond this point, the primitive condition cannot endure' (Rousseau 1968: 59). The scarcity of resources can only be overcome if individuals recognize that their personal interests in warmth, sustenance and so forth are shared by all other individuals. Rousseau sees the emergence of civil society in a two-fold process. On the one hand, men see homogeneity in their heterogeneous concerns: 'It is what is common to those different interests which yields the social bond; if there were no point on which separate interests coincided, then society could not conceivably exist' (Rousseau 1968: 64). To this extent, then, civil society is necessary but beneficial. It assists each individual in the attainment of his interests. But, on the other hand, Rousseau thought that the need for civil society to resolve the problem of reciprocity in conditions of scarcity was quite terrible. In *A Discourse on Inequality*, he was in no doubt at all: 'The first man who, having enclosed a piece of land, thought of saying "This is mine" and found people

simple enough to believe him, was the true founder of civil society'
(Rousseau 1984: 109). Interestingly, then, for Rousseau, to be
human is at one and the same time to transcend heterogeneity
through necessary involvement in institutions of homogeneity,
and to want.

In Rousseau's modern hands, civil society is the milieu of the
specifically human. And it is therefore both an artificial realm and
a realm of artificiality. Consequently, to be human is to be alienated. 'Being and appearance became two entirely different
things, and from this distinction arose insolent ostentation, deceit-
ful cunning and all the vices that follow in their train' (Rousseau
1984: 119). In civil society, 'behold man, who was formerly free
and independent, diminished as a consequence of a multitude of
new wants into subjection' (Rousseau 1984: 119).

For Rousseau, then, civil society as it is has rather disastrous
implications. It has turned free men into masters and slaves. Civil
society has replaced symmetry with asymmetry. Consequently, the
relationships and the arrangements of civil society as they are
become offences against that order of things which should obtain.
A new kind of society is needed which can overcome the problem
of the stranger which has been generated (rather than solved) by
civil society. It is the blueprint of that new society which is provided
in *The Social Contract*. In other words, Rousseau does indeed end
up sounding a little like Hobbes. Both are trying to confront the
problem of how to create a peaceful society consisting of individuals who have few or no personal reasons to be peaceful towards
one another. The difference is that Hobbes saw civil society as part
of the solution, and Rousseau saw it as a big part of the problem.

Rousseau responds with the proposition of a civil society as it
might be, which can deal with the difficulty created by all previous
civil societies and yet also express the interests of men as they are.
His point is that whereas civil society had previously been based
on the scarcity which is the other side of private property, the new
society can be fully based on an entirely symmetric reciprocity
through the moment of contract. After all, 'Since no man has any
natural authority over his fellows, and since force alone bestows
no right, all legitimate authority among men must be based on
covenant' (Rousseau 1968: 53).

According to Rousseau, the contract could overcome the problems of all previous civil societies because it made the same
demands of each individual and gave to each the same promises.

That is, the contract was primarily an ontological act of symmetry which had no connection at all with the artificial practices and beliefs which the societies of scarcity required of men. The contract involves 'the total alienation by each associate of himself and all his rights to the whole community. Thus, in the first place, as every individual gives himself absolutely, the conditions are the same for all' (Rousseau 1968: 60). Symmetry is indivisible from Rousseau's interpretation of the contract since, because its terms are the same for each individual, 'it is in no one's interest to make the conditions onerous for others' (Rousseau 1968: 60). For Rousseau, the social contract could ultimately be reduced to just one clause: ' "Each one of us puts into the community his person and all his powers under the supreme direction of the general will; and as a body, we incorporate every member as an indivisible part of the whole" ' (Rousseau 1968: 61).

The new society would be based on a 'general will' which would subsume within a bounded community the particular interests of all. The general will is at one and the same time the expression and the act of the social construction of civil society. It is the quality of homogeneity. As Rousseau puts it: 'the general will derives its generality less from the number of voices than from the common interest which unites them'. He continues: 'for the general will is an institution in which each necessarily submits himself to the same conditions which he imposes on others' (Rousseau 1968: 76). It is created in the contract since, 'in place of the individual person of each contracting party, this act of association creates an artificial and collective body ... and by this same act that body acquires its unity, its common *ego*, its life and its will' (Rousseau 1968: 61). The point is that this artificial body is not a problem because it is truly universal and capable of subsuming within itself, on the basis of complete equality, the heterogeneous interests of each.

The demands which this true civil society can make of the individual are immense indeed. Rousseau was in no doubt that, firstly, any individual who threatens the continuation of the 'general will' as expressed in law should be executed and that, secondly, the 'general will' can demand total allegiance and acquiescence. The first point, concerning the execution of the law-breaker, is expressed in very interesting language. Since Rousseau understands the 'general will' to be the bounded community of symmetric reciprocity in which there are no strangers because all are the same, any law-breaker is a stranger to that community and, therefore, a problem to be solved. As Rousseau puts it, 'since every wrongdoer attacks the society's law, he becomes by his deed a rebel and a traitor to the country; by violating its law, he ceases to be a member of it; indeed he makes war against it' (Rousseau 1968: 79). There can be only one solution: 'the preservation of the state is incompatible with *his* preservation; one or the other must perish; and when the guilty man is put to death, it is less as a citizen than as an enemy' (Rousseau 1968: 79).

The law-breaker is an enemy; a stranger and a personal expression of illicit heterogeneity who has to be pushed away if homogeneity is to survive. Consequently, any individual who opts to live within the bounded community is required to obey all laws absolutely. Anyone who lives within the orbit of a 'general will' is under its universal surveillance and must therefore either obey or move out (Rousseau 1968: 79). Rousseau also made the point that 'After the state is instituted, residence implies consent: to inhabit the territory is to submit to the sovereign' (Rousseau 1968: 153). In many ways, this was not an original point. According to Plato, Socrates had made a broadly similar argument in his dialogue with Crito. Socrates had accepted the claim that anyone who lived in Athens was obliged to obey each and every law of Athens. Socrates agreed with the law in the proposition that 'those of you who remain here, with full knowledge of how we administer justice and generally manage the State, have thereby entered into an agreement with us to do what we ordain' (Plato 1963: 80). The implication of this argument is that the 'general will' is always right, and only the individual person can be wrong (Rousseau 1968: 72).

Now, this situation might seem to involve absolute domination over the individual. It might seem to imply a complete entrapment. But, for Rousseau, it was a condition of freedom. Rousseau argued that the civil society which was expressed in law – 'Laws are really nothing other than the conditions on which civil society exists' (Rousseau 1968: 83) – meant that men could escape from the dull compunction and the reification of the state of nature. Instead, men would become moral subjects. Rousseau said that 'man acquires with civil society, moral freedom, which alone makes man the master of himself; for to be governed by appetite alone is slavery, while obedience to a law one prescribes to oneself is freedom' (Rousseau 1968: 65).

By this analysis, Rousseau was able to make a number of points. Firstly, he was able to make a compelling case for the distinction of society and humanity from any form of reification. Secondly, he was able to imagine society as internally homogeneous and possessed of the moral right to defend that homogeneity so that hard-won humanity does not backslide into either artificiality or the pre-human state of nature. Indeed, *The Social Contract* is haunted by a fear of heterogeneity, by the fear of an inability to understand the meaning and significance of the stranger. Symmetric reciprocity has to be defended at all costs, because 'when the social bond is broken in every heart, when the meanest interest impudently flaunts the sacred name of the public good, then the general will is silenced' (Rousseau 1968: 150). As such, the sovereign power of the society must make sure that a situation never arises in which 'particular interests make themselves felt and sectional societies begin to exert an influence over the greater society' (Rousseau 1968: 150).

The possibility of a slippage out of the civil society appropriate for men as they are requires an active policy of the moulding of men to the demands of society. Here, Rousseau has quite clearly abandoned any traces of the natural artifice. He explicitly declares that reciprocity demands a reconstruction of human nature 'to transform each individual, who by himself is entirely complete and solitary, into part of a much greater whole, from which that same individual will then receive, in a sense, his life and his being' (Rousseau 1968: 84). The argument continues to emphasize the need 'to replace the physical and independent existence we have all received from nature with a moral and communal existence' (Rousseau 1968: 85). It is only through this societal moulding of the raw stuff provided by nature that each individual can be constructed as adequate for reciprocity.

Rousseau placed such importance on the possibility of creating a universal and homogeneous civil society which would be suitable for men as they are that he ultimately ended up reifying that society. His concept of the 'general will', which was intended to guarantee the contract and confirm the boundaries between society and nature, was, in the final analysis, nothing more than a massive barrier beyond which reflexivity could not go. Rousseau simply assumed the existence and universality of the 'general will', because to do otherwise would, in terms of the logic of his own analysis, mean that he would have had to give up on either the possibility of freedom or the possibility of civil society itself. In other words, without the assumption of the homogeneous and homogenizing 'general will', Rousseau would have virtually had to give up the challenge of modernity.

It is instructive to compare the work of Thomas Hobbes and Jean Jacques Rousseau. Firstly, they provide very clear and, certainly with Rousseau, concise examples of the method which made the imagination of civil society possible. Both were crucially concerned to create a very clear distinction between a state of nature, which was understood as reified in one way or another, and a civil society, which was interpreted as a milieu of human self-sufficiency and freedom. Their work demonstrates the possibilities, the insights and the interpretation of the world which could be generated with the pathetic fallacy. Both Hobbes and Rousseau constructed a realm called nature, projected all their hopes and fears on to it, and concluded with the assumption that, in one way or another, civil society was desirable or at least necessary.

Secondly, Hobbes and Rousseau were worried by the question of how that division of the order of things might be maintained given that it could not be assumed as existing by nature. Albeit in different ways, they argued that the division had to be defended at all costs and so they were prepared to reify some societal constructions because they were in principle the guarantee that there need never be a return to the natural artifice. Ironically, then, the great fear of an order of things which seemed to be immutable resulted in nothing other than the assumption of the immutability of the institutions and arrangements of social homogeneity. More or less by default, then, Hobbes and Rousseau illustrate the subtlety of John Locke's argument. Locke was able to avoid placing any barriers on reflexivity and deconstruction.

But there is another explanation as to why Thomas Hobbes and Jean Jacques Rousseau are so crucially important in the story of the imagination of civil society. With them, it is possible to see two of the originating statements of the idea that society is a force which can make men moral. This was indeed one of the main assumptions, if not the main assumption of the modern sociological discourse. Zygmunt Bauman has pointed out that 'The etiological myth deeply entrenched in the self-consciousness of our Western society is the morally elevating story of humanity emerging from pre-social barbarity ... By and large, lay opinion resents all challenge to the myth' (Bauman 1990: 12). Perhaps the myth has proved so powerful for a number of reasons. Most obviously, the kind of stories told by Locke, Rousseau and even that old pessimist

Hobbes are actually quite flattering. They all say that humans can indeed make the world on their own terms. Perhaps the making simply involves an escape from absolute horror, but it remains a sovereign act of making nevertheless. Moreover, what humans make is understood to be an improvement of what went before. The myth was so popular because it told the subjects of modernity what they wanted to hear, and it continues because of its habitual and common sense acceptance.

The story of emergence from a savage state and into the clear milieu of homogeneity actually made sense of the world. The basically speculative commentaries of the likes of Hobbes and Rousseau became so deeply entrenched in the self-understanding of modernity precisely because they could be taken to be reports of reality. The myth could make a compelling case for the need for firm laws and possibly even the coercion of individuals. It could do more besides. Firstly, it could explain why some individuals seemed to be so loathe to accept legal compulsion. Secondly, it could explain why some individuals evidently threatened everything which was held so dear. Thirdly, it could account for the presence of those who should be distant but were experienced as near. And it could do all of that while confirming the status of humanity as the defining subject of its own being.

The contract interpretations of civil society are based on the assumption that men are born natural (either individually, as a species, or historically) and are made social. As such, the civil society which is held to be the context of the subjective achievement of humanity as a moral condition is itself an achievement. To this extent, it is civil society which makes man what he is, and which makes it possible for man to imagine becoming something else. The regulations of a specifically societal existence are understood in contract theory to be identical with freedom. But there is another side to this analysis, the side that the myth of modernity rendered as the hidden face of civilization (but the hidden face had to be spoken of, in order to make the known face of civilization that much more compelling). Without civil society, man is nothing. In different ways, and for different reasons, philosophers as otherwise different as Locke, Hobbes and Rousseau were all in agreement that without civil society man is simply one beast among many.

In other words, the narratives embodied, and were largely impossible without, a fundamentally ambivalent conception of man. On the one hand, man is the malleable, potentially free and moral, subject of his own history. On the other hand, man wallows in reification and is unable to see beyond his savage interests. Man is both the foundation of understanding and simply one thing among many to be understood.

This difficulty at the heart of the discursive figure of man has been emphasized by Michel Foucault. In his book, *The Order of Things*, Foucault makes the point that the figure of man is a historical artifact which can only emerge in certain epistemological configurations. Foucault explicitly ties the emergence of the problem of man as a simultaneously natural and social being to the modern epoch. As Foucault puts it: 'Man ... is a strange empirico-transcendental doublet, since he is a being such that knowledge will be attained in him of what renders all knowledge possible' (Foucault 1970: 318). Foucault expresses himself a little more clearly when he proposes that man as he is understood in the conditions of modernity is 'at the same time at the foundation of all positivities and present, in a way that cannot even be termed privileged, in the element of empirical things' (Foucault 1970: 344). Man is that which explains, and that which has to be explained.

The figure of man which runs through the contract imaginations of civil society is, then, both the condition and the cause of reflexivity. It is the unstable and more or less indeterminate status of man which makes it possible for civil society to be imagined as, essentially, the 'other' of nature, and, through the pathetic fallacy, for the state of nature to be understood as the 'other' to the condition of being societal. Foucault puts all of this down to epistemological events, but perhaps the ambivalent status of man reflects the historical and social appearance of the ambivalent urban and intellectual character of the stranger.

The stranger is a person who should be distant from orderly social relationships. But the stranger is, by definition, present within those relationships. The status of the stranger cannot be known in advance, and his involvement within any civil society cannot be taken for granted. In other words, the figure of the stranger represents a personalization of the possibility of wildness. In the natural artifice, wildness is 'out there'. The world structured by the patriarchal order of things was understood as itself orderly, and any threats to it, any outbursts of disorder, were explained as attributable to the encroachment of the outside. The natural artifice responded to these threats by attempting to restate the unchanging relationships of authority.

But in the modern imaginations, the possibility of disorder was all around (since strangers were all around), and therefore the threat of the wild itself became something which was ever present. Consequently, with the consolidation of the modern imaginations there was also a reinterpretation of the wild. The threat and fear of the wild was reinterpreted as less of a geographical problem and more by way of a psychological problem. Hayden White makes the implication of this transformation quite clear. In so doing, he helps to indicate the extent to which the contract interpretations of civil society are founded on a set of assumptions which structure the answers of civilization as much as the problems of society.

White says that with the despatialization of the wild (which I have attributed to the phenomenon of the stranger), 'instead of the relatively comforting thought that the Wild Man may exist *out there* and can be contained by some kind of physical action, it is now thought ... that the Wild Man is lurking within every man' (White 1978: 153–54). In other words, the problem of the state of nature, the threat of an attack on the moral integrity of civil society, comes not from outside but from inside. Those who are moral are themselves the biggest problem for morality. Hence, the need for unceasing projects of homogenization and relentless pursuits of the last traces of the wild and the savage within the boundaries of society. The modern demands of, and the demands for, civil society were unceasing because each of us harbours the 'wild man' who 'is clamoring for release within us all, and will be denied only at the cost of life itself' (White 1978: 154).

Hobbes and Rousseau show that, within this line of thought, the beast within had to be firmly shut out, and by extremely different routes, they imply that a new reification is a small cost to pay for that exclusion. But, perhaps more interestingly, the modern sociological narratives shared the assumption of the psychic interiorization of the wild. Indeed, many of the founding figures of sociology, most obviously Emile Durkheim and Sigmund Freud, assumed that society was a moral force which made symmetric reciprocity reproducible. Even the rather more Romantic critiques of modernity, which are to be found in the work of Karl Marx and Max Weber, are predicated on the assumption that there is something about being human which is repressed by societal regulation and by the practices of civil society. The difference is that whereas

Durkheim accepted the necessity of that repression, the likes of Marx and Weber saw it with the deepest pessimism (although Marx identified reasons for optimism in the longer run). Freud straddled the opposite positions: he recognized necessity and expressed profound pessimism.

The deconstruction of the natural artifice meant that man could be understood as the free sovereign of his own history, and of his own existence. But the conditions of reflexivity also meant that man became identified as the biggest threat to that self-sufficient self-production of the human milieu. That is, in the imaginations of civil society as they appeared in the work of social philosophers and fed into the problems, assumptions and interpretations of sociology, it is possible to see 'a transition from myth to fiction to myth again, with the modern form of the myth assuming a pseudo-scientific aspect in the various theories of the psyche currently clamoring for our attention' (White 1978: 154). The remythication of man and civil society can also be seen in modern sociology. Perhaps, even, modern sociology was the remythication.

Chapter 4

The civilization

With ever-increasing urbanization and the improvement of cosmopolitan communications, the existence of the stranger could no longer be explained in terms of the temporary presence of a visitor from the wild places. Rather, and as Georg Simmel realized so well, the stranger became the basic unit of presence in the self-sufficient metropolis. As such, the wild traces of the state of nature, whether that state be imagined as an idyll (Rousseau) or as completely awful (Hobbes), were interpreted as interior to civil society as well as external to it. That interiorization took two forms. Firstly, it was internal to the urban spaces which consequently had to be carefully watched in order to stop any expressions of the relationships of the state of nature. Secondly, the wild was rendered psychological and removed from the places 'out there' to the recesses of the heart of darkness lurking in every man. It is possible to see the emergence of the imagination of civil society as, simultaneously, a moral condition of human being and a moral regulation of the reciprocity between strangers.

By the eighteenth century, this rounding of the meaning of societal relationships also meant that the meaning of civil society as a moral regulation was supplemented with an additional dimension. Certainly, civil society continued to be what it had been since the threshold of modernity. It continued rather monolithically to suggest the subsumption by a homogeneous universal of the heterogeneous particularity of the state of nature. But the interiorization of the wild meant that moral regulation was additionally understood as something which was necessary within civil society itself. The monolith was slightly cracked.

For people like Locke, it was more or less enough to ensure the moral regulation of an external state of nature. But by the late eighteenth century, the state of nature had been pulled within the spaces normally occupied by the bounded community of civil society and therefore civil society itself had to be characterized by practices which vigorously kept the wild at bay. Hence, the mid to late eighteenth century obsessions with civilized manners. Perhaps this worry can also be identified as the basis of the charge and sociological-historical significance of the work of Jane Austen. It seems reasonable to suggest that Austen's novels can be read as accounts of what happened to the behaviour of the upper classes at a time when they could not be certain that they were not slightly beastly. With the interiorization of the wild, moral regulation continued to be a problem for the relationship between civil society and nature, but it also became a problem which was held to be internal to that civil society.

Anthony Pagden has tried to draw out some of the features and implications of the additional meaning of civil society. He points out that by the mid-eighteenth century, the words 'civil', 'civility' and 'to civilize' 'had become, largely if not exclusively, attached to a set of formal behavioural characteristics, to what were broadly called "manners" ' (Pagden 1988: 33). The words continued to refer to the qualities and processes which were meant to signify uniquely human and societal activities as opposed to the activities associated with nature. But they came to mean something else as well, something internal. 'They still described those qualities which separated social man from the savage; but they were now far more heavily freighted with the sense of what criteria might be used to distinguish between individuals *within* civil society' (Pagden 1988: 33).

In other words, by the end of the eighteenth century, the imagination of society involved both a division of the things of the world into the societal and human, on the one hand, and the natural, on the other hand, and a division of the societal into the more and the less human. Any assumption of an ontological or anthropological unity of man was thus placed in a social context which seemed to prove nothing other than that some men were more human (because they were more civil, more mannered, more closely approximating a true Jane Austen *beau*) than others. Indeed, some social groups possessed the cultural and social resources which enabled them to define their own manners as approaching the ideal of civility, whilst repudiating the practices of others as wild and, therefore, in need of civilization. (For a very specific episode in this story, see Tester 1991). Anthony Pagden has recognized in these debates 'the implicit claim that only the civilized can know what it is to be "civilized" ' (Pagden 1988: 33).

These transformations of meaning and interpretation (which clearly did not occur in a realm of pure ideas, but were attempts to come to terms with rapid and radical social and historical processes) tended to mean that man as an individual and as a species became a problem which had to be civilized (made civil). Civilization was established as the process of the regulation by civil society of the wild within man. It is possible to understand the establishment of the wild as an internal question as a remythication of the meanings of man and society, because it designates 'the existence of things or entities whose attributes bear just those qualities that the imagination, for whatever reason, insists they must bear' (White 1978: 154). The deconstruction of the natural artifice meant that modernity created replacement myths of its own to explain what things are really and truly like.

Arguably, one of the high points in this particular narrative can be found in the work of Sigmund Freud. In his very late work, *Civilization and its Discontents*, Freud succinctly defined civilization as 'the whole sum of the achievements and the regulations which distinguish our lives from those of our animal ancestors and which serve two purposes – namely to protect men against nature and to adjust their mutual relations' (Freud 1985: 278). So, according to Freud, civilization refers to all those practices and norms by which man is defining rather than defined. Civilization essentially means the ability of men, living a communal life, to separate themselves off from the natural and then consciously construct their own networks of interaction. Furthermore, the ability to separate also means that man is able to reinterpret the order of things. It ceases to be an immutable and dull compulsion; instead, through technology (which Freud understands as a product of civilization), the world is turned into something which is 'serviceable' (Freud 1985: 278). That is, the products of civilization are indivisible from, and indeed clearly signal, an act of human and social self-sufficiency.

According to Freud, civilization was necessary for man. Two pressures forced man to move into a regulated communal existence. Firstly, Freud makes the point that since civilization is synonymous with the ability of man to turn nature into a resource, 'it cannot have been a matter of indifference to him [i.e., the individual] whether another man worked with him or against him.

The other man acquired the value for him of a fellow-worker, with whom it was useful to live together' (Freud 1985: 288). To this extent, then, civilization has its roots in a compulsion to work in order for man to overcome the scarcity of resources and thus ensure protection against natural forces. According to Freud, it was quickly realized by 'primal man' that such an aim could be best secured through co-operation.

The second pressure towards a communal existence relates to sexual relationships. In many ways, Freud seems simply to assume some neo-Rousseauian points, because he says that there was a time when genital satisfaction 'made its appearance like a guest who drops in suddenly, and, after his departure, is heard of no more for a long time' (Freud 1985: 288). But this transient satisfaction of genital pleasure which required no continuous societal reciprocity collapsed when genital pleasure 'instead took up its quarters as a permanent lodger' (Freud 1985: 288). The transition of genital pleasure from the status of one who comes today and goes tomorrow to one who comes today and stays tomorrow (another variation on the theme of the problem of the stranger) had a profound impact. It heralded the appearance of the family as a form of reciprocity in interdependence since 'the male acquired a motive for keeping the female, or, speaking more generally, his sexual objects, near him' (Freud 1985: 288). Here, then, civilization is understood from the point of view of men as an appropriate solution to the problem of securing a readily available source of genital pleasure. Freud continued to spell out the advantages which, he thought, the emergence of the family had for women: 'the female, who did not want to be separated from her helpless young, was obliged, in their interests, to remain with the stronger male' (Freud 1985: 288).

Perhaps Freud's discussion of the basis of civilization provides one of the clearest possible illustrations of the argument that modernity was essentially about the defining ability and subjectivity of men. In Freud's modern and entirely conjectural imagination of civilization and society (Freud 1985: 288), women are defined and objectified. It is important that this dimension of Freud's work is recognized because in many ways it goes to the heart of the imaginations of European modernity. But I am not saying something as trite as 'Freud was a sexist' and proposing that his work be thrown out of court accordingly. Freud's thought is far more profound and important than that kind of intellectual stone-throwing can possibly allow.

Indeed, the connection of women with civilization, over and above the claims that they make to love, is seen by Freud as more than a little tense. Freud argues that the achievement of civilization is the business of men, who therefore employ a great deal of their energy in solving difficult puzzles and carrying out hard tasks. But this has serious implications for men since 'What he employs for cultural aims he to a great extent withdraws from women and sexual life' (Freud 1985: 293). Women consequently resent civilization. Furthermore, they retard its development because they make men devote energy to genital pleasure which therefore cannot be used in cultural achievement. But even if women are not making men use valuable energy, they are simply being ignored by men (who for Freud have better things to do) and so 'the woman finds herself forced into the background by the claims of civilization and she adopts a hostile attitude towards it' (Freud 1985: 293). At least Freud could, in his own terms, provide a coherent explanation of the defined status of women.

Freud was, then, prepared to understand civilization as 'a process in the service of Eros' (Freud 1985: 313). Civilization consequently means the overcoming of the state of nature and, perhaps more significantly, the establishment of an external authority over the wildness which remains within each individual. Freud was in no doubt that the state of nature, whether as a social or an individual matter, was completely hellish. Indeed, in Freud's hands, the state of nature is turned into something far more awful than it was even for Thomas Hobbes. According to Freud, civilization is under permanent threat because 'man's natural aggressive instinct, the hostility of each against all and of all against each, opposes this programme of civilization' (Freud 1985: 313–14). There is a subtle and yet significant difference between the state of nature as conceived by Freud and Hobbes. For Hobbes, the state of nature was not actually one of the war of all against all; rather, it was a state in which any individual could not be sure that there would not be such a war. Freud removed the doubt. For him, the war of all against all did indeed rage.

As such, Freud had a far from optimistic notion of what man was like without the work of the process of civilization. Freud was not contemptuous of his fellow men; he simply felt that it was misplaced to have very great expectations of them. Despite the drift of Freud's comments about a primal age in which genital pleasure occurred without conscious deliberation, he otherwise had an opinion of the state of nature which could not be further away from that held by Rousseau. Freud rejected the claim that men are 'gentle creatures who want to be loved, and who at the most can defend themselves if they are attacked'. On the contrary, Freud said that men are 'creatures among whose instinctual endowments is to be reckoned a powerful share of aggressiveness' (Freud 1985: 302). More forcefully even than that attack on Romantic assumptions: man without civilization is 'a savage beast to whom consideration towards his own kind is something alien' (Freud 1985: 302; see also Freud 1985: 351).

This state of nature is overcome to the extent that individuals practically realize that through co-operation they can secure a somewhat safer life. But the movement into civilization has serious costs. Freud expresses the costs more or less in terms of a utilitarian calculation: 'Civilized man has exchanged a portion of his possibilities of happiness for a portion of security' (Freud 1985: 306). In order to reap the secure benefits of civilization, the individual has to renounce the possibility of achieving a full gratification of instincts.

For example, the communal life, which is at the same time the basis and the product of civilization, means that the sexual instincts of the individual have to be restrained and subjected to the most rigorous surveillance. For Freud, there is, in fact, a most deep and serious antithesis between the demands of civilization and the demands of sexuality. The point is quite simple. According to Freud, sexual love is a relationship between two people which normally treats any third person, at best, as superfluous and, at worst, as an irritation. So, in these terms, the individual achieves a high degree of satisfaction of instincts in relationships with a single other person. But civilization is fundamentally predicated on relationships with more than one other person. Civilization requires 'relationships between a considerable number of individuals' (Freud 1985: 298). Consequently, civilization stands in a relationship of antagonism to sexual instincts, and so if civilization is to be possible 'a restriction upon sexual life is unavoidable' (Freud 1985: 299). Civilization means security for the objects of sexual love, but it also means that the instinct of sexual love cannot be freely expressed. Hence, civilization is a cause of unhappiness.

In Freud's system, then, the individual is simultaneously

looking in two directions. On the one hand, the individual is permanently seeking to satisfy entirely egoistic instinctual urges which are in opposition to stable life with others. This egoism is an expression of the death instinct which is oriented towards 'presenting the ego with a fulfilment of the latter's old wishes for omnipotence' (Freud 1985: 313). It is a death instinct because it takes the form of a will to destruct civilization, its relationships and its artifacts. The act of destruction confirms to the individual his instinctual omnipotent power. On the other hand, the individual is seeking to live a communal existence in order to secure access to scarce resources (of various kinds). This is an expression of the love instinct. Freud reveals the nature and the implications of the instinctual tension inside the individual when he explores the meanings of the ethical precept, which is so important to Christianity that we should love our neighbour as we love ourselves.

Freud makes the point that the precept rather seems to fly in the face of reason. According to Freud, love is something which is important to the giver, and which is only given to other individuals who are in some way deserving of it. Moreover, the love I feel for someone 'imposes duties on me for whose fulfilment I must be ready to make sacrifices' (Freud 1985: 299). In other words, love is an attitude which can only be meaningful in already bounded communities of one sort or another. Love, and the ability to love, imply an already known relationship with the other. But the neighbour is a stranger, towards whom I feel nothing other than an instinctual aggression. The precept to love my neighbour is antithetical to my instinctual relationships towards him.

For Freud, that antithesis makes the precept, and its imposition, all the more necessary. The precept represents a significant attempt to ensure some stable reciprocity between individuals who are otherwise linked by nothing more than a mutual hostility. Without injunctions of this kind, civilization would be impossible, and even with them the civil existence cannot be taken for granted. As Freud said:

> Civilization has to use its utmost efforts in order to set limits to man's aggressive instincts and to hold the manifestations of them in check by psychical reaction-formations. Hence, therefore, the use of methods intended to incite people into identifications and aim-inhibited relationships of love, hence the restriction upon sexual life, and hence too the ideal's

commandment to love one's neighbour as oneself – a commandment which is really justified by the fact that nothing else runs
so strongly counter to the original nature of man.

(Freud 1985: 302–3)

As such, it is the aim of civilization to tie each individual into social
relationships which are directly opposite to those which would be
dictated by human nature.

In many ways, the point is not too dissimilar from that made by
Thomas Hobbes, but there is a crucial difference. For Hobbes,
individuals could be tied to reciprocity through external authority.
Freud agrees that external authority is indeed very significant, but
he breaks new ground when he suggests that individuals are
involved in the process of civilization through the operation of an
internal authority. Just as Freud played an important part in the
mythical interiorization of wildness, so his solution to the problem
also concentrated on the operations of something within.

This is an important dimension of the meaning of Freud's
reference to 'psychical reaction-formations'. However, while
Freud was making an important contribution to modern imagination, the point about internal authority was, perhaps, not itself
wholly original. In a section for the Chorus in *The Eumenides*, the
Greek poet Aeschylus had written that the life of moral regulation
requires that fear 'Must somewhere reign enthroned'. Aeschylus
continued to have the Chorus declare that men learn that sin (in
modern vocabulary, immoral behaviour) cannot be condoned
through the operation of emotional reactions of 'self-inflicted
sorrow' (Aeschylus 1956: 165). Aeschylus identified the agents and
place of the fear and sorrow with the 'Furies' who drew the
boundaries between the moral community and the wild 'out there'.
But for Freud, the agent and place were located in the psychical
formation of individuals in civilization.

For Freud, civilization can be understood as the moral regulation of individuals, and as the community of morality, in so far as
it is able to inculcate in individuals a due measure of fear (of
external authority) and of self-inflicted sorrow (occasioned by
internal authority). The demands of civilization are represented
to the individual, and interiorized as moral authority, through the
formation in each of a superego. The superego refers to the means
which civilization employs to deal with the instinctual aggressive
impulses. It turns aggression back to the place from which it came.

The superego, 'in the form of "conscience", is ready to put into action against the ego the same harsh aggressiveness that the ego would have liked to satisfy upon other, extraneous individuals' (Freud 1985: 315).

To put the matter a little more succinctly: 'Civilization ... obtains mastery over the individual's dangerous desire for aggression by weakening and disarming it and by setting up an agency within him to watch over it, like a garrison in a conquered city' (Freud 1985: 316). The result is that the individual becomes a policeman of himself. He becomes his own regulatory authority and is guilty if any hints of aggressive impulses are felt. The external authority of civilization can only punish manifest aggression, but the superego, according to Freud, punishes the latent aggression within each of us. In other words, the superego requires of each individual that he practises a high level of relentless reflexion on the basis and implications of his own actions. The wild is domesticated.

Freud's diagnosis of civilization quickly became an essay on the human condition. Freud was saying that civilization means unhappiness and guilt for all individuals, at all times, and in all places. He was thoroughly denying that the experience of civilization could be heterogeneous in any meaningful sense. A more explicitly sociological discourse in principle offered a way out of this tendency of Freud's theory towards a remythication. Sociology promised the possibility of an awareness of the heterogeneity of the human experience of civilization, and it could in principle show precisely what that civilization meant in the past and what it meant for the modern present. Sociological interpretations of civilization could, in their own terms, work without any category of the inevitable human condition. A most suggestive encounter with these promises can be found in the work of Norbert Elias. The parallels between the process of civilization, which Freud unravelled, and the civilizing process, which is, perhaps, the main contribution of Norbert Elias to modern sociology, is quite remarkable. Indeed, Elias explicitly acknowledged a debt to Freud (see Goudsblom 1987: 330).

Like Freud, Elias was concerned to draw out the networks of societal restraint and self-constraint which are involved in the formation of the individual as a social being. Both Freud and Elias were concerned to explore the roots of the feeling of guilt in social relationships, although where Freud with his universalistic story saw guilt as an ahistorical component of personalities in society,

Elias brilliantly realized that feelings of guilt have radically changed over time. Similarly, the story of what civilization has to do to transform the individual's instinctual urges was dismantled and reconstructed by Elias in a manner which meant that it was quite impossible to see the individual as an always the same anthropological and ontological fact who simply (or, perhaps it is better to say, not so simply) enters into civilization. Despite the many similarities between the interpretations of civilization pro-vived by Freud and Elias, the latter's account of the civilizing process is, on the fact of it, quite incompatible with any remythi-cation of the catergories of the modern imagination.

It is possible to get a good idea of Elias's originality by consid-ering his ideas on human nature. Of course, the conventional interpretation, which was implicit to Locke, Hobbes and Rousseau even before Freud, was that human nature was something intrinsic to the human being which individuals brought with them to civil society. As such, the problem for these thinkers was one of explain-ing how and why society could moralize that human nature and reconstruct it as something which was amenable to the demands of symmetric reciprocity. The likes of Rousseau and Freud also tried to understand the moral and psychological costs of that work on nature. Elias's point is that human nature is not at all something which comes to society from outside. Rather, Elias argues that human nature is thoroughly social. That is, Elias refused to draw a distinction between human nature and social being; his argument was that social being is actually human nature.

Elias implied that an explanation like that developed by Freud might well be right to place a very great emphasis on the instinctual urges of human nature. To this extent, Elias would not disagree with Freud that humans are influenced by unlearned patterns of behaviour and compulsions. But Elias does not agree that identi-fication of these innate capacities can be used as the foundation of an analysis of some essential human condition in civilization. Elias's point is that there is much about human nature and human being which cannot be explained in terms of unlearned drives. Indeed, the unlearned aspects of human being 'have become softened and weakened to such an extent that human beings can neither orien-tate themselves in their world nor communicate with each other without acquiring a great deal of knowledge through learning' (Elias 1987: 345).

In other words, it is human nature that humans' innate and

natural capacities become less significant to all that is done than those capacities which are learnt through participation in social relationships. It might be said that 'people are *naturally* adapted to change and constitutionally equipped with organs which enable them to learn constantly ... and to change the pattern of their social life together' (Elias 1978b: 115). For Elias, human nature is fundamentally and radically malleable. It should not at all be understood as an all-inclusive immutable state which always remains the same. As such, there is no bench-mark of some universal human condition.

Elias does not deny that there is some core of being human which is part of biological, natural, constitution. But his point is that the process of social relationships means that natural capacities become decreasingly significant. Human nature as it is realized in social relationships consequently involves a separation between that which is immutable within the individual and that which is open to change and education: 'By nature – by the hereditary constitution of the human organism – human behaviour is directed less by inborn drives and more by impulses shaped by individual experience and learning than is the behaviour of any other living creature' (Elias 1978b: 109).

Elias's position has a number of implications. Firstly, he sees the subordination of unlearned to learned patterns of behaviour in terms of social and historical processes; he refers to the subordination with words like 'more' or 'have become'. Secondly, Elias is arguing that it is impossible to understand individuals without an understanding of the relationships between them. Thirdly, he is saying that the natural (that is, unlearned) patterns of human behaviour have been so overlaid with learned patterns that 'nowhere, except perhaps in the case of madmen, do men in their encounters with each other find themselves face to face with psychological functions in their pristine state, in a state of nature that is not patterned by social learning' (Elias 1982: 285). So, much like Rousseau and Marx, Elias supposes that men as they are, living in societies in the here and now, are not driven by immutable instinct, but, on the contrary are driven by the consequences of a societal and historical existence.

Elias understands these conditions of existence which make individuals what they are as figurations. Elias tries to explain his concept of figuration with the example of a game of cards and says that the concept refers to 'the changing pattern created by the players as a whole – not only by their intellects but by their whole selves, the totality of their dealings in their relationships with each other' (Elias 1978b: 130). As such, figuration is advanced by Elias as a conceptual means to overcome the conventional divides (which are invariably implicit to the debates on civil society) between the individual and the society. Elias is arguing that social relationships are to be understood in terms of figurations in which individuals create society (in this example, the society of the card game), and in which the society creates the individuals (there is no card game without card-players). The example of the card game makes another important point for Elias: figurations are not internally homogeneous, and all the individuals do not have the same interests. Quite the contrary, a figuration is at its core 'a fluctuating, tensile equilibrium, a balance of power moving to and fro, inclining first to one side and then to the other' (Elias 1978b: 131). The figuration itself, then, is not to be reified, but is instead to be understood in terms of the density of the interaction between individuals and the chains of interdependency which tie individuals to one another.

To the extent that each individual becomes more dependent on each other individual, the personality becomes divided. While each individual comprehends himself as the hub of a figuration, the individual is also aware that continued participation within that chain of interdependency can only be maintained to the extent that his patterns of behaviour are moulded in such a way that he does not prejudice interaction through a misplaced deed or word. As the relationships of the figuration become both more dense and more complex, the threshold of the prejudicial is raised and, as such, each individual feels guilt and embarrassment over, to give the richest example, bodily functions which are considered too much like unlearned behaviour. In many ways, Elias is simply recalling Freud's discussion of superego formation, but Elias's departure consists in his recognition that 'the superego, like the personality structure of the individual as a whole, necessarily changes constantly with the social code of behaviour and the structure of society' (Elias 1978a: 190). The process of change is the civilizing process (Elias 1978a: 191).

If Elias's interpretation of civilization is applied to the specific problem of civil society, a very rich picture seems to emerge. Elias would refuse to accept that civil society emerges out of some foundational act like a moment of contract. He would also disagree with the other dimension of the conventional imaginations which proposes that it is possible to find the unchanging face of human nature somewhere behind the world of appearances. Instead, Elias's work would lead to the conclusion that the symmetric reciprocity of civil society is a moment in a continuing process, called civilization, of the separation of the human from the natural.

Now, with that kind of explicitly sociological and historical perspective, Elias is indeed offering something quite new. But perhaps that originality is deceptive. Elias ends up saying little more than it is in and through society that humanity is achieved, and that individuals learn to become defining rather than defined. Elias also equates exclusion from the chains of interdependency with some kind of non-moral condition. When he speculates that only the madman reveals a pristine state of nature, Elias is also implying that those of us who are not considered mad have managed to learn to be social, and at the same time learnt what it means to be human. Elias's actually rather orthodoxly modern conclusion is, then, that when humans learn (through society to be human), there is simultaneously a division of the order of things into categories of the non-moral and the moral, the strange and the known, the dangerous and the domesticated.

Elias writes:

> As human society develops, people experience themselves increasingly strongly as separate beings, distinct both from other people and from natural objects. Reflection and conscience increasingly interpose themselves through the process of social training as controlling and taming influences between people's own spontaneous impulses to action and other people, other natural objects.'
>
> (Elias 1978b: 122)

So, Elias is saying that an action or a pattern of behaviour is denigrated as natural (and therefore as something to be worked on by and through the mannered practices of civilization) if it occurs spontaneously. The natural is that which takes places habitually and without thinking. There is no invariant standard of the natural or of natural behaviour which civilization pushes further and further away (although the reference to the madman does suggest some kind of bench-mark condition). Rather, Elias is arguing that the civilizing process brings its own natural baggage with it.

As Elias demonstrated brilliantly in his book *The History of Manners*, the actual patterns of behaviour which individuals carry out habitually are themselves the product of a processual lengthening of the figurational chains of interdependency and of the density of interaction. As such, with the civilizing process, certain actions which have not always been performed become spontaneous (such as blowing our noses after sneezing) and therefore they are carried out as if they have never been learned. For us, nose-blowing is part of our armoury of seemingly unlearned patterns of behaviour. It is apprehended as natural, when previously it was a virtually unknown activity. Consequently, the civilizing process is propelled once more, as a new site of the natural is identified and constructed, as standing in need of separation from the bounded community of society.

In other words, civilization is a process which crucially involves a forgetting of itself as a process. Civilization itself is elevated to the status of a myth which seems to occur of its own momentum. Its social and historical conditions of existence involve precisely an amnesia and an embarrassed attempt to forget social and historical conditions of existence. Elias takes up a point from Freud and suggests that the changes associated with civilization are rendered inevitable and processually put outside of reflexion through a legitimating rhetoric of hygiene (Elias 1978a: 116; Freud 1985: 289). The point is that as soon as an activity is commended because it is hygienic, it is more or less pushed off the agenda of those things which can be discussed.

In its own terms, Elias's sociological enterprise consequently becomes a most devastating exercise in the demystification of society, social relationships and patterns of behaviour. In his own terms, Elias is looking at the history of civilization, showing that the order of things did not at all have to be the way it is, and demonstrating that it is human nature to change societal arrangements and social practices. In many ways, Elias is calling on individuals to make their world anew continually. He is also saying that if the making is carried out under the guidance of an object-adequate knowledge which is aware of the requirements of the chains of interdependency, then the world might actually become a less destructive and more meaningful place (Elias 1978b: 32).

Certainly, Elias gives the narrative of civilization a number of highly original twists, and he carries deconstruction of the natural artifice a very long way. But his account of civilization is clearly within the tradition of the relationship between society and the wild. Elias sees the wild in the individual as mutable and as a social construction in itself, but when he talks about the wild at any given moment of the civilizing process, he does indeed deal with it as if it was an immutable condition 'out there'. Despite its emphasis on processes, and social and historical transformations, Elias's sociology actually does not move outside fairly conventional narrative conventions. (Elias can be seen as one of the leading protagonists of what Bauman sees as the 'etiological myth' of modernity.) To some degree, Elias simply told the subjects of modernity what they wanted to hear: the world can be changed, the world is changing.

Since Hobbes, Rousseau and Freud in particular, there had been a very powerful awareness of the costs which had to be paid in the name of civilization. But, for Elias, those costs are seemingly of little or no significance. This failure to talk about the costs of civilization is perhaps due to Elias's refusal to see human nature as an ahistorical constant. But it is likely that it can, in large measure, be put down to Elias's modern trust in the potential abilities of knowledge (a faith expressed in Elias 1956), and to the developmentalism of his thought. Throughout his enterprise, Elias is always trying to make some connections linking entities at lower levels of interdependence to entities at higher levels. (Goudsblom says that the concept of interdependence is the core of Elias's perspective (Goudsblom 1987: 330).)

This does not at all mean that Elias was an evolutionist thinker, he emphatically was not, but it is to say that he sees continuities between the less complex and the more complex. These continuities are identified by him whether he is talking about biological organisms, learning processes in human individuals and complex social networks, or the succession of figurations. (For some examples of the assumption of developmentalism, see Elias 1987.) Elias simply assumes that all chains of interdependency (whatever their ontological or epistemological status) are in some way equivalent from one sphere of inquiry to another, and that they can be understood in terms of lengthening and increasing density (and hence increasing complexity). For Elias, the logic of developmentalism means that civilization and society will become increasingly complex, and he seems to see that logic as to some extent a precondition for a knowledge of the reality of the world which will actually improve things for men and women.

Civilization is elevated to the status of a developmental fact. To complement that position, Elias also assumes that it is only through the interdependencies and implications of civilization that humanity can practise its nature. In a typical figurational move, Elias is saying that civilization might well make us what we are, but we make civilization. As such, Elias's work might offer a very deep deconstruction of the natural artifice; Elias is evidently able to put the previously assumed categories under a very bright light of reflexivity. But Elias harnesses these possibilities to a narrative which virtually gives the answers even before the questions are asked. Consequently, it is difficult not to come to the admittedly quite harsh conclusion that Elias does not explain modernity. Rather, he simply describes its self-identity.

I am aware that Elias did not use 'modernity' as a term of reference for his work. Instead, he would have seen himself as attempting to explain the social and historical roots of the consciousness of civilization. However, the point remains that his explanation of the roots does bear a remarkable resemblance to the modern interest in reflexivity. To this extent, he was simply using a specific component of the modern consciousness as the foundation of a historical investigation which could stretch back virtually as far as desired and, albeit by implication rather than express statement, into the future. In other words, and despite his avoidance of the term 'modernity', Elias demonstrates how modernity imagined itself as a continual process of civilization. He was rather less successful in moving outside of modern identities.

Arguably, the work of Emile Durkheim can be seen as a more nuanced moment in the tradition of the interiorization of the wild. Durkheim operated on the terrain of the interiorization of the wild, but he never lost sight of the tensions which were built into that narrative, and of their disturbing implications. The sociological problem that Durkheim posed for himself embodied a Cartesian variation on the theme of the wild. Durkheim tried to explain how the self-sufficient individual can be understood as a part of a society. He wanted to know how the individual who was antithetical to society could become a moral subject. He saw both the problem and the resolution as issues which were interior to the individual.

Throughout his work, Emile Durkheim spoke in precisely the language of opposites which so irritated Norbert Elias. It cannot be doubted that Durkheim certainly did tend to assume that the opposites of his sociological construction actually were ahistorical constants. For Durkheim, it was indeed the case that there are, on the one hand, individuals, who, on the other hand, enter into some distinctive realm called society. (This is an expression of precisely the kind of conceptual compartmentalization that Elias wanted to overcome through the emphasis on figuration.) Durkheim suggested that such a way of coming to terms with the order of things was latent within each social individual. After all, 'It is not without reason ... that man feels himself to be double: he actually is double. There are in him two classes of states of consciousness that differ from each other in origin and nature, and in the ends towards which they aim' (Durkheim 1960: 337). The one set of states of consciousness is derived from the awareness of self, while the other states 'come to us from society; they transfer society into us and connect us with something that surpasses us' (Durkheim 1960: 337). On the basis of this Cartesian model, Durkheim understood the individual in society as homo duplex: 'On the one hand is our individuality ... on the other is everything in us that expresses something other than ourselves' (Durkheim 1960: 328).

The things 'other than ourselves' are the basis of the moral regulation of the individual. They are derived from the moral density of social relationships. It would rather seem that Norbert Elias had read Durkheim on this point, and restated the notion of moral density in terms of the role in the civilizing process of the chain of interdependency. (To this extent, it might be suggested that Elias's work can be read as 'Durkheim on wheels'.) Elias's emphasis on the implications of the frequency and complexity of social relationships for the patterns of behaviour of the individual has a distinctly Durkheimian ring. But whereas Elias saw these relationships in terms of figurational tensions, Durkheim rather tended to speak in terms of the social production of morality. According to Durkheim, the external regulations which make homo duplex social are generated by the 'network' of reciprocal bonds within the division of labour (Durkheim 1984: 332). After all, 'it is not possible for men to live together and have constant dealings without getting a sense of this whole which they create by close association' (Durkheim 1957: 24). The proposition represented a clear expression of the self-images of the modern imagination: 'Man is only moral because he lives in society, since morality consists in solidarity with the group, and varies according to that solidarity. Cause all social life to vanish, and moral life would vanish at the same time' (Durkheim 1984: 331).

The individual can therefore only become a moral subject in so far as he is fully involved within the reciprocal bonds of social solidarity. As Durkheim put it, 'adherence to some thing that goes beyond the individual, and to the interests of the group he belongs to, is the very source of all moral activity' (Durkheim 1957: 24). If the individual falls outside of the boundaries of society, whether through societal negligence or personal wilfulness, then he becomes amoral. The individual who is outside of society cannot be immoral as such because, for Durkheim, outside of society there are no moral standards. The outside is without morality (a claim which recalls Hobbes and, of course, Rousseau). Consequently, Durkheim was quite unable to agree with the natural rights type of theories which were developed by John Locke (with his talk of the right of the individual to life, liberty and the pursuit of private property). Durkheim saw the matter rather the other way around: 'the State was not created to prevent the individual from being disturbed in the exercise of his natural rights ... rather, it is the State that creates and organizes and makes a reality of those rights' (Durkheim 1957: 60).

For Sigmund Freud and, perhaps even Norbert Elias, the wild is some kind of residue within the psychological formation of the individual which has to be deconstructed through the practices and requirements of civilization. Durkheim managed to offer a rather less frighteningly mythological account of the residue, relating it instead solely to the egoistic perception of the world. Indeed, Durkheim sees the problem in terms of the inability of the individual who has not been rendered moral to externalize perceptions of the world and therefore practise reflexivity. For Durkheim, the difficulty is one of ensuring that the man who is in part outside of society can be cut to the measure of the moral life.

This problem was dealt with at length by Durkheim in his posthumously published book, *Professional Ethics and Civic Morals*. The argument of the book is very finely textured indeed and reveals many, if not all, of the stakes in the imagination of civil society. It is also a fine introduction to Durkheim's thought. In it, Durkheim reveals that the complex modern division of labour does not only mean that individuals become increasing dependent on one another. He stresses that the division of labour can also imply the emergence of a diversity of possibly opposing forms of morality. In other words, Durkheim is trying to deal with the question of how any homogeneous system of morality might be possible (and that means, for Durkheim, how any universal community of society might be possible) given the tendency of the division of labour to generate a heterogeneity of moral communities. (Perhaps it can be suggested that, to this extent, some of the questions confronted by Alasdair MacIntyre were anticipated by Emile Durkheim.)

Durkheim was saying, on the one hand, that the division of labour leads to homogeneity through the emergence of social solidarity. But he was also saying that with the appearance of professional groups, the division of labour also means particularity and heterogeneity (and that means the emergence of the possibility of a collapse of reciprocity in the face of a multiplicity of moral and social strangers): 'Thus, centres of a moral life are formed which, although bound up together, are distinct, and the differentiation in function amounts to a kind of moral polymorphism' (Durkheim 1957: 7). But the need to render the individual moral through involvement in society means that these professional groups are extremely important in the creation of society: 'Professional life ... takes on increasing importance, as labour goes on splitting up into divisions' (Durkheim 1957: 103). Clearly, Durkheim is struggling to straddle two stools which are toppling in different directions. The one stool suggests that professional groups are too particular to allow for a single society. The other stool suggests that without professional groups, society is impossible.

Codes of professional ethics overcome the possibility that the individual might never be pulled into a moral community (that is, that the individual might be in the condition of normlessness called anomie). The professional ethics are, in many ways, the representation of civil society because they operate in the space between the family and the state (Durkheim 1957: 5). For Durkheim, professional ethics were in principle able to take the individual outside of the directly experienced milieu of the family and involve him in a greater society. However, it was necessary that each professional group displayed some degree of organizational solidarity. Durkheim was aware that 'professional ethics will be the more developed, and the more advanced in their operation, the greater the stability and the better the organization of the professional groups themselves' (Durkheim 1957: 8). For example, medical doctors are well known for the very high standard of professional morality which is a product of a very high level of professional organization. Sociologists, meanwhile, are in comparison rather lacking in ethical solidarity because they are not so well organized (sociologists tend to be interested in ethics only as the subject matter for textbooks on methodology).

In other words, Durkheim thought that in societies which were characterized by a deep and diverse division of labour, the tendencies towards anomie which confronted the individual (the possibility that the individual might be able to slip through the net of moral norms) could be overcome if the individual was immediately subjected to regulation through occupational or vocational groupings. That is, the family was incapable of providing an adequate moral basis for the socialization of homo duplex, and so that function could be taken over at the point of the individual's point of entry into the division of labour in society. But Durkheim knew that there was a very serious problem at the heart of any such turn to professional ethics.

If the individual is defined through participation in particular codes of professional ethics, then, for Durkheim, the possibility arises that the individual might be too closely defined and thus cease to be the defining subject of his own actions. The possibility of individual reflexivity and freedom might be undermined by precisely the professional groups which help to make sure that homo duplex is made a member of society. Here, Durkheim reveals much of the subtlety of his thought; he argues that the professional ethics which are the basis of immediate morality in complex societies, and which therefore make the individual a free moral subject, might also have the effect of denying any freedom of the individual. Durkheim often called the professional groups 'secondary groups' and he wrote: 'The formation of secondary groups ... is bound to occur, for in a great society there are always particular local or professional interests which tend naturally to bring together those people with whom they are concerned'. But there is a sting in the tail because 'if there is nothing to offset or neutralize their activity, each of them will tend to swallow up its members' (Durkheim 1957: 62).

So, the very agencies which make modern civil society imaginable imply also a dilution of the deconstructive project of modernity. The possibility of freedom can only be confirmed through institutions and arrangements which imply an attack on the freedom of the individual. Durkheim thought that a careful system of institutional checks and balances could square this circle.

In many ways, the argument is quite reminiscent of Rousseau and similarly emphasizes the role of standards of homogeneity in overcoming the particularistic thrust of 'secondary groups'. 'The only means of averting this collective particularism and all it involves for the individual, is to have a special agency with the duty of representing the overall collectivity, its rights and its interests, *vis-à-vis* these individual collectivities' (Durkheim 1957: 62). That special agency is, of course, the state.

Now, Rousseau was prepared to put the state beyond reflexivity (indeed, he made it something like the precondition of reflexivity) if it meant that man as a universal species could avoid the reification of particularity. But Durkheim took great care to include the state in reflexivity. Instead, his precondition of reflexivity was society and he was prepared to give it an almost absolute status: 'Every society is despotic ... still, I would not say that there is anything artificial in this despotism: it is natural because it is necessary, and also because, in certain conditions, societies cannot endure without it' (Durkheim 1957: 61).

The state could defend the practice of reflexivity precisely because it could free the individual from absolute definition on the part of professional ethics or even the family. According to Durkheim, if the state could 'permeate all those secondary groups of family, trade and professional association, Church, regional areas and so on ... which tend to absorb the personality of their members', then it could be nothing other than 'the liberator of the individual' (Durkheim 1957: 65, 63).

As such, the state sets the individual free from definition and therefore involves the individual once again in a moral way of life in which nothing can be done as if by nature: 'Wherever ... particular collective forces exist, there the power of the State must be, to neutralize them: for if they were left alone ... they would draw the individual within their exclusive domination' (Durkheim 1957: 65). However, the state does not stand in lofty isolation, looking down on everything else. Durkheim thought that the state can only be the arrangement of universality thanks to the professional groups. These groups guarantee both the freedom of the state from individuals (that is, the professional groups are a bulwark) and yet also its ability to act (that is, the groups constitute the connection of the state to individuals). The homogeneous state requires, and is impossible without, the heterogeneity of the professional groups. The interstices and connections between the two are the spaces in which individuals can be free and moral (Durkheim 1957: 96).

Durkheim was struggling to do a number of things. Firstly, he was seeking to explain how the egoistic side of homo duplex can be reconciled with the social and moral side. Secondly, and closely following the concerns of Rousseau, he was attempting to explain how universality and homogeneity might be possible in a world which is otherwise particular and heterogeneous. Thirdly, Durkheim tried to provide the sketch of a delicately balanced institutional framework which could enhance reflexivity (and therefore modernity) without resorting to reification. But his work is more interesting than it might have been if it was just a blueprint of modernity which embodied the self-proclaimed ideals of the modern imagination. The point is that Durkheim went to such great lengths to secure the moralization of the wild and the deconstruction of reification precisely because he thought that the forces of modernity made the aims of modernity increasingly difficult.

The commerce and big business which provided the resources of modernity (a freedom from the physical reification of biological need and scarcity) also meant a slackening of the moral bonds without which the symmetric reciprocity of modernity would not be possible. In particular, the pursuit of economic life, exempt from moral regulation, could mean only anarchy. Durkheim argued that economic relationships involve the subordination of the weak by the powerful, 'But since this subjection is only a *de facto* condition sanctioned by no kind of morals, it is accepted only under duress until the longed-for day of revenge' (Durkheim 1957: 11). As such, to the extent that in industrial societies more and more individuals only encounter other individuals in economic relationships, they are also involved in relationships which are outside of morality and which therefore can result only in a weakening of the social aspect of homo duplex.

Durkheim writes that:

> this amoral character of economic life amounts to a public danger. The functions of this order to-day absorb the energies of the greater part of the nation. The lives of a host of individuals are passed in the industrial and commercial sphere. Hence, it follows that, as those in this *milieu* have only a faint impress of

morality, the greater part of their existence is passed divorced from any moral influence.

(Durkheim 1957: 12)

Professional groups and the professional ethics offer the best hope of a move out of the condition of amorality. Hence, the urgency of Durkheim's work and its moral force. Durkheim knew that he was essentially doing nothing more than keeping his finger in the dyke which, hopefully, would burst later rather than sooner.

This kind of interpretation of modernity was, perhaps, an inevitable consequence of the narrative of interiorization of the wild. Any identification of a place which was outside of regulation and reciprocity was also the identification of a place which would eventually take its revenge on the forces of moral restraint. One version of this story was told by Emile Durkheim, but it was perhaps expressed most forcefully by Sigmund Freud.

Most obviously, Freud relentlessly hammered home the theme that, thanks to civilization, men cannot be happy, but that without civilization, men cannot be secure. Freud does not deny that civilization aims to achieve human happiness, but he does deny that the achievement is a realistic possibility. As Freud said, 'It almost seems as if the creation of a great human community would be most successful if no attention had to be paid to the happiness of the individual' (Freud 1985: 334). This is to concentrate on the tragic effects of the relationships which are internal to any given society, but Freud saw the relationships between societies as, perhaps, even more disturbing.

Freud knew quite well that the identification of a society or a civilization also means the identification of groups or individuals who are strangers to the demands of those particular orders of things (this point had, of course, also been recognized by Adam Ferguson). These strangers can be found within and therefore identified as standing in need of either assimilation or expulsion (in the history of Europe, the Jews were typically identified in this way), or they can be found without and thus seen as standing in need of enforced regulation (the 'savages' in need of the civilization of empire and involvement in the communities of God and money).

To identify *this* civilization, and to universalize its reciprocity through moral codes which are not only forgetful of their own history but also ostensibly apply at all times and in all places, is to elevate it in relation to *that* civilization and *those* codes of social relationships. Freud was aware of all of this and, consequently, saw the dark side of any fine moral standards. He deconstructed the canons of reciprocity and revealed them to be dubious constructions. 'When once the Apostle Paul had posited universal love between men as the foundation of his Christian community, extreme intolerance on the part of Christendom towards those who remained outside it became the inevitable consequence' (Freud 1985: 305). But nothing could improve the situation.

The way in which Freud concentrated on the civilization and moralization of the wild within reveals him to be one of the most important interpreters of the imagination of modernity. Moreover, and unlike Norbert Elias, but perhaps not unlike Emile Durkheim, Freud was able to use the self-images of modernity to reveal a deep existential and ontological *malaise*. Freud and Durkheim saw civilization as a metaphysic, in a story which is reminiscent of the legend of the 'Fall' but without the faith in transcendental redemption. Freud saw the only chance of redemption in psychoanalysis, whereas Durkheim saw it in the establishment of society as *sui generis* moral authority. Elias rendered the metaphysic sociological, but by tying it to a developmentalism, he did indeed suggest the hope of something more adequate in the future (i.e., a this-worldly transcendence of the problems of this world, even though that transcendence would itself be merely one stage in a process). For Freud and Durkheim, civilization is the price which has to be paid if man is to be free, and it was quite useless to ask if that price was worth paying. There was no choice. But Freud could never entirely free himself of a concern with the costs.

Chapter 5

The costs

Despite the fear of the mixing of the societal with the wild, which was one of the significant spurs for the seventeenth and eighteenth century imaginations of civil society, and despite the transformation of the pathetic fallacy into something approaching an anthropology for the putatively objective, and certainly objectifying, social science of the nineteenth century, it was nevertheless possible to declare that 'one misunderstands "nature", so long as one looks for something "sick" at the bottom of these healthiest of all tropical monsters and growths, or even for an inborn "hell" in them' (Nietzsche 1973: 118). That sentence from Friedrich Nietzsche's book *Beyond Good and Evil* can, perhaps, be read as an indication of the twists and turns to which the societal construction of the wild could be subject. Essentially, Nietzsche is signalling a complete reversal of the imagination of the state of nature which was systematized by Thomas Hobbes and which thereafter became one of the fundamental narratives of modernity to such an extent that sociologists like Emile Durkheim were prepared, without question, to accept the wild as both an interior and an exterior difficulty.

Nietzsche is trying to foreground this fundamental assumption in modern social and moral theory. He is not at all attempting simply to reverse the conventional evaluation of civilization as good and nature as bad. Jean Jacques Rousseau had already performed that act of table-turning. Nietzsche is not implying that the state of nature is an idyll in which the 'noble savage' lives contentedly. Rather, he helps to force reflexion on the reasons why the likes of Emile Durkheim, Sigmund Freud and Norbert Elias were quite prepared to oppose the 'tropical monsters and growths' to docile domesticity. (I am, of course, aware that these writers were all productive after Nietzsche's work was terminated; Nietzsche is talking about the narrative which is perfectly *illustrated* in Durkheim and the others.) Nietzsche is struggling to deconstruct the assumption which grounded and justified civilization and society.

Nietzsche's purpose was not to inspire a direct turn to nature in the wake of an unmasking of the pretensions of civil society. He was engaged in something more than that. Nietzsche wanted to discover the reasons why 'there exists in moralists a hatred for the jungle and the tropics' (Nietzsche 1973: 119). He continued to ask: why is it that 'the "tropical man" has to be discredited at any cost, whether as the sickness and degeneration of man or as his own hell and self-torment?' (Nietzsche 1973: 119).

The question was directed at the moralists of modernity (a group which would obviously include the sociologists like Durkheim). It was in many ways inspired by the tragedians of ancient Greece, especially Aeschylus and Sophocles. Nietzsche attempted to throw the mythic self-evidences of modernity into a sharp relief through a juxtaposition with the ancients. His point seems to be that it is important to ask why the modern narratives attribute hellishness to men and excuse morality, when for the likes of Aeschylus and Sophocles, hellishness was instead attributed to the moral codes which turned man into a transgressor. (As an example, see Sophocles's version of the Oedipus story; all is well with Oedipus and Jocasta until the moment of the imposition and acknowledgement of moral obligation.)

In somewhat Durkheimian terms, the difference between the ancients and the moderns could be explained with reference to the forms of social solidarity. For the ancients, reciprocity was self-evident, but the boundaries of the community of reciprocity stood in need of definition. (Hence, man as a transgressor of boundaries and as a polluter. The other side of this coin is indicated by the troubles which the gods kept causing for men.) However, in modern narratives, the boundaries of the community were taken as known (and represented in, and confirmed by, the nation-state), whereas continued reciprocity had to be confirmed (hence, man as the wild within). In Durkheimian terms, man must believe that his egoism involves an in-born hell, otherwise symmetric reciprocity would be quite unimaginable. On the surface, the Freudian story is indebted to a similar logic of interpretation and explanation. But Freud is keenly aware of the tragedy and the pathos of civilization.

The point is that whereas Durkheim more or less accepted the claims of civilization and made a case for keeping the wild within the embrace of society, Freud felt compelled to accept civilization. But, for Freud, civilization could only keep the wild at bay at the cost of denying human subjectivity. The 'tropical man' of Nietzsche has to be so aggressively vilified precisely because he is the subjective agent of his own desires. For Freud, the kind of man called forth by Nietzsche is antithetical to society. Consequently, as the demands of civilization on the individual become greater, the fear of the 'sick' and the 'natural' is exacerbated more and more.

Shortly after the outbreak of the First World War, Freud made an observation and drew a corollary out of it. He observed that 'Civilized society, which demands good conduct and does not trouble itself about the instinctual basis of this conduct, has thus won over to obedience a great many people who are not thus following their own natures' (Freud 1985: 71). In other words, the moral conduct, which is the basis and the project of civilization, requires that the individual is alienated from himself. This is the root of the pathos in Freud's diagnosis of civilization and, indeed, the grounds of an explanation why the characteristics of 'tropical man' are so opposed to the demands of society. Freud continued to draw the corollary from the observation: 'Encouraged by this success, society has allowed itself to be misled into tightening the moral standard to the greatest possible degree, and it has thus forced its members into a yet greater estrangement from their instinctual disposition' (Freud 1985: 71). Not, then, just from himself: the individual is alienated also from other individuals. It might be speculated in terms of this interpretation that the societal condemnation of the wild, and of the projects to exclude the natural from the social, represent nothing other than the species- and self-alienation of man in civil society.

Without wishing to enter into a detailed, and probably inconclusive, discussion of the debt that Freud owed to Nietzsche, it cannot be denied that there is a decidedly Nietzschean flavour to Freud's understanding of the costs of civilization. Both are concerned to discover how men can transcend the human condition in civilization, but both assert as the foundation of that discovery the thesis that man can only live if he does without any hope of transcendence from the human condition. (I have derived this formulation from Stern 1978: 68.) For Nietzsche and Freud, civilization is the source of the unhappiness of man and, to put the matter a little more ontologically, it is also the cause of the alienation of man. Man must either become resigned to the demands of civilization or endeavour to go beyond. But, beyond civilization, there is only a vast unknown.

Freud reacted to this existential horror of modernity with an effort to make the human condition marginally less unbearable. Freud advocated an analytic of the enforced reflexivity of the interior wild and habitual places. This response to the confrontation with the boundaries of civilization, and Freud's realization of the impact of civilization on the latent and manifest forms of reciprocity, demonstrated a certain intellectual honesty and, indeed, courage. But perhaps Nietzsche's courage was greater yet. He attempted, paradoxically, to understand the impossibility of transcendence through a demand for transcendence.

In a memorable moment of *Thus Spoke Zarathustra*, Nietzsche commented: 'Man is a rope, fastened between animal and Superman – a rope over an abyss' (Nietzsche 1961: 43). The comment was not made in any Darwinian sense which would imply that man is to be understood as some intermediary between the beasts and perfection. Neither was it directly made in a spiritual sense where man would represent a being which moves from the animal to something approaching the status of the angels. Rather, Nietzsche understood man to be a tightrope in a moral and historical sense. For Nietzsche, the point is precisely that man is a figure which represents a movement away from the tropic of the animal, and which is destined to be overcome. That movement can be identified in the three stages, animal, man and Superman. The reference to the abyss beneath the rope is a warning that most of the men who walk it are unlikely to reach the other end. Either they fall off or they simply freeze in the face of their existential situation.

Nietzsche stimulates an interpretation in which modernity is familiar to such an extent that it has to be gone beyond and rendered obsolete. The story is now totally different to that imagined by John Locke or Thomas Hobbes, for whom modernity promised the obsolescence of the natural artifice. It is a totally different perspective from that of Norbert Elias, the commitment of whom to developmentalism meant that modernity was always something in the making, always something to be done. The image conjured by Nietzsche suggests both the goal of man (although that goal had nothing inevitable about it – it was not a teleology) and yet the impossibility of the achievement of any transcendence by man. For Nietzsche, then, the problem is not alone to transcend civilization. The problem, more significantly, is to transcend man. After all, 'What is the ape to man? A laughing-stock or a painful embarrassment. And just so shall man be to the Superman: a laughing-stock or a painful embarrassment' (Nietzsche 1961: 41–2).

The argument is that man is embarrassed by the tropical and thus pushes it outside of civilization, precisely because the wild represents a challenge to reciprocity. But the wild represents life. As such, Nietzsche declares that modern civilization is actually antithetical to life. For Nietzsche, life, when it is understood properly, is a condition constituted in the will to power. Essentially, he turns the will to power into the driving force of all that is true of man in the world.

In the individual, the will to power represents the will to self-knowledge and self-assertion. For Nietzsche, its project is one of the achievement of the individual life which is lived to the full. The exercise of the will to power is understood to be more or less synonymous with the self-definition of the individual through an overcoming of others. This means two things. Firstly, Nietzsche is implying that the will to power involves the destruction by the individual of everything which leads to self-indulgence and which makes life comfortable and easy. Secondly, it is but a short step from this position to the argument that the will to power consists in nothing other than domination over others and a deliberate lack of concern with the requirements of symmetric reciprocity. The individual who is able to live according to the demands of the will to power stands apart from others. He is the self-defining subject of his own morality and he is the subject of his own history.

The ability to be self-defining necessarily implies the definition of all others. As Nietzsche puts it: 'Everything he knows to be part of himself, he honours, such a morality is self-glorification' (Nietzsche 1973: 195). Consequently, in his relationships with others, this individual does not recognize some symmetry. Quite the contrary. The will to power as the basis of life requires that all relationships with others are known and practised as intrinsically asymmetric. For example, the man of life 'aids the unfortunate but not, or almost not, from pity, but more from an urge begotten by superfluity of power' (Nietzsche 1973: 196). He does not feel pity because he must, but simply because he is able to. In many ways, this philosophical and historical story of Nietzsche was simply taken up and reworked as psychology by Freud when he spoke of a death instinct to destroy the cultural and societal regulations and products which stand in the way of self-definition by the individual (Freud 1985: 308–14).

Just as Freud realized that civilization was impossible without some diversion of the death instinct, so Nietzsche had earlier seen that the will to power is fundamentally and insurmountably anti-thetical to societal relationships. The difference is that whereas Freud was merely seeking to explain civilization in order to come to better terms with it, Nietzsche had tried to go much further. Nietzsche's aim was to try to explain how civilization might be overcome. He wanted to acclaim the case for the unleashing of the will to power and thus the emergence of the Superman promised in the pages of *Thus Spoke Zarathustra*. The emergence would mean the appearance of the moral and historical subject who can destroy all conventional moralities and, indeed, perform an act of the most profound trans-valuation of values.

Given these concerns, Nietzsche understands civilization and society in terms of the restraints which are imposed on the noble; restraints which reduce the noble to a level of mediocrity and which are represented in the noisy denunciations of the wild. The denunciations reflect attempts to keep the will to power under societal control through the vilification of its manifestations. In other words, where conventional moral codes see a problem, Nietzsche sees only so many opportunities. Nietzsche commented: 'When the highest and strongest drives, breaking passionately out, carry the individual far above and beyond the average ... the self-confidence of the community goes to pieces ... consequently it is precisely these drives which are most branded and calumniated' (Nietzsche 1973: 123).

In other words, Nietzsche very strongly claims that civilization and its moral systems do not promote nor protect life. Quite the opposite. Civilization for Nietzsche represents nothing other than an assault on life and the collapse into decadence of the will to definition. The *'fundamental principle of society* ... reveals itself for what it is: as the will to the *denial* of life, as the principle of dissolution and decay' (Nietzsche 1973: 194). Civilization itself could not endure if life was not so diminished. For Nietzsche, morality is the expression of the diminishing: 'everything that raises the individual above the herd and makes his neighbour quail is henceforth called *evil*; the fair, modest, obedient, self-effacing disposition, the *mean and average* in desires, acquires moral names and honours' (Nietzsche 1973: 123). For Nietzsche, such a situation meant the domination of a moral system which trapped the tropical individual and turned him into a slave to the demands of reciprocity: 'within the slaves' way of thinking the good man has in any event to be a *harmless* man: he is good-natured, easy to deceive, perhaps a bit stupid, *un bonhomme*' (Nietzsche 1973: 197).

The domination of the slave morality is revealed in the ethical concern with pity and suffering, and in the political arrangements of democracy. Nietzsche's point is that both of these products of civil society, products which are invariably loudly applauded in the conventional narratives of modernity, should in fact be repudiated precisely because they are predicated on, and in no small way contribute to, an idea of the ontological and anthropological unity of humanity. Nietzsche attacks them 'because they address themselves to "all", because they generalize where generalization is impermissible' (Nietzsche 1973: 119). He argues that imaginations of a grounded and all-inclusive community are only possible at the expense of an awareness of the true asymmetry between the masters and the slaves, the noble and the herd. Nietzsche is not simply arguing for a return to pre-modern arrangements. He is actually deconstructing all the fundamental categories of the narratives of modernity and, in so doing, seeking to rescue the power of life. He is trying to unlock – rather than just abolish – the modern cages which hold the wild.

Nietzsche certainly implied that a false symmetric reciprocity is promoted by universalistic concern with the suffering of others, a concern which identified some homogeneity to the human experience of the world (that is, the universality of pain). To take account of the suffering of others on the basis of the strength of one's own nobility might be one thing, but, for Nietzsche, for us all to take account of the suffering of others purely as a matter of course is quite something else. It is a slave morality which panders to the herd instinct precisely because it denies that each individual should, or even could, sufficiently establish his own definition for dealing with the suffering of others. For example, Nietzsche saw nothing other than a clear expression of the herd instinct in utilitarian ethics. After all, and as Nietzsche quite clearly realized, utilitarianism is basically founded on a very radical reduction of all individuals to the status of morally equal sentient beings who have an interest in avoiding suffering. This identification of a herd morality also meant, for Nietzsche, that the moralists who expressed utilitarian instincts were themselves members of the herd.

The objection was that the symmetric reciprocity assumed by utilitarianism is wholly inappropriate given the demands of life and the will to power. Nietzsche felt able to condemn utilitarians and utilitarianism in more or less the same breath:

> Not one of all these ponderous herd animals with their uneasy conscience (who undertake to advocate the cause of egoism as the cause of the general welfare –) wants to know or scent that the 'general welfare' is not an ideal, or a goal, or a concept that can be grasped at all, but only an emetic – that what is right for one *cannot* by any means therefore be right for another, that the demand for *one* morality for all is detrimental to precisely the higher men, in short that there exists an *order of rank* between man and man, consequently also between morality and morality.
>
> (Nietzsche 1973: 158)

This is a very significant passage. Firstly, it clearly illustrates Nietzsche's thesis that the individual who lives according to the will to power is in many ways a person apart from the mediocre 'herd'. Secondly, the passage shows that Nietzsche refuses to let assumptions of the ontological and anthropological equality of all individuals go unchallenged. He really does believe in asymmetric hierarchies in which some individuals demand and deserve a louder voice than others. Thirdly, Nietzsche is indicating why the fear of the wild goes hand in hand with assertions of things like the general welfare. The point is, of course, that wildness is indivisible from the possession or exercise of qualities which are precisely not general and shared in common. In the narratives of modernity, wildness indicates an illicit sovereignty.

But perhaps more importantly than all those things, the manner in which Nietzsche totally denies the significance of qualities in general indicates also that he was struggling to abandon the modern imagination of society. He is doing nothing other than making a case for the primary importance of the heterogeneous over and above the homogeneous. Nietzsche is struggling to rescue and restore strangeness, whereas the conventional narratives were all going to very great lengths to assimilate, if not annihilate, strangeness. In the face of this kind of challenge to modernity, it is not too surprising that imaginations of bounded moral communities could have absolutely no constructive place (except to the extent that they constituted a fairly clear picture of everything which had to be overcome).

For Nietzsche, there simply should not be any universal bounded community in which every individual is treated as the same in all significant respects. After all, for Nietzsche, individuals are not the same; some are masters and some are slaves, and it is a diminution of life (but a diminution without which society would be impossible) to pretend otherwise. Asymmetric reciprocity becomes the only acceptable form of social relationship. But Nietzsche is not able to ground that asymmetry in the natural artifice because he rejects any criteria of universal and immutable orders of things. Instead, the case for asymmetry can only be made on the grounds of the difference of individuals in terms of the will to power. Against narratives of homogeneity, Nietzsche makes the claim that 'it is *immoral* to say: "What is good for one is good for another"' (Nietzsche 1973: 151). Rather, the will to power requires that some individuals are thoroughly indifferent towards the suffering of others. There is absolutely no bounded community.

The repudiation of democratic political arrangements was founded on much the same argument. Nietzsche argued that democratic arrangements would result in 'a levelling and mediocritizing of man – a useful, industrious, highly serviceable and able herd-animal man' (Nietzsche 1973: 173). That is, democracy, with its assumption of a radical equalization of all members of the political community, was seen by Nietzsche as a form of the creation of a community of strangers, which would mean the subsumption of the noble individuals into the mass. Democracy is nothing other than another of Nietzsche's slave moralities. However, he was prepared to see some kind of benefit in democracy. Since democracy will produce such a mediocre man, it will simply need to produce new masters. The citizens of political communities will be so 'weak-willed and highly employable' (Nietzsche 1973: 173) that new leaders will have to emerge.

The mediocre men will need powerful new leaders 'as they need their daily bread'. While Nietzsche was generally prepared to condemn democracy, he did, then, see some basis upon which to envisage a transcendence of it. On the one hand, 'the democratiz-ation of Europe will lead to the production of a type prepared for *slavery* in the subtlest sense'. But, on the other hand, that same process of democratization was seen by Nietzsche to throw up the chance that 'in individual and exceptional cases the *strong* man will be found to turn out stronger and richer than has perhaps ever happened before' (Nietzsche 1973: 173). Once again, it is possible to see quite clearly the lengths to which Nietzsche was prepared to go as a moralist, and the extent to which he was prepared to push the logic of his analysis, if it meant that some likelihood of the return of the wild could be discovered. For Nietzsche, the problem was one of trying to work out the nature of the individuals who might make the costs of civilization worth paying.

Democracy was, then, repudiated by Nietzsche because it in-volved a false levelling of all individuals. But, in his own terms, he did see benefits coming out of that arrangement which was other-wise so offensive. The same could not be said for socialism. Nietzsche thought that socialist versions of democratic arguments were quite awful on a number of grounds. Firstly, the society aspired to by socialism was simply that of the '*autonomous* herd' which denied the place of the noble and the masters. Secondly, the opposition of socialism to privileged rights and claims means simply that all rights are thus denied: 'for when everyone is equal no one will need any "rights" '. Thirdly, socialist arguments were attacked by Nietzsche because they defended the weak against the strong. But the greatest ill of socialism was that it caused a concern with suffering. For Nietzsche, socialists (note again the conflation of the protagonists of morality with morality itself) are 'at one, one and all, in the cry and impatience of pity, in mortal hatred for suffering in general, in their almost feminine incapacity to remain spectators of suffering, to *let* suffer' (Nietzsche 1973: 126). Nietz-sche understands socialism and socialists as protagonists of a false community of internal homogeneity. They are 'at one, one and all, in their faith in the community as the *saviour*, that is to say in the herd, in "themselves" ...' (Nietzsche 1973: 126).

So, according to Nietzsche, civilization is something which must be overcome by the noble individuals who are able to be guided by the demands of the will to power. These individuals are thus compelled to make themselves strangers to any and all criteria of homogeneity. They are, instead, representations and subjects of heterogeneity and, consequently, stand in perpetual danger of vilification as too monstrous for civilization and its mediocre men. Indeed, when Nietzsche posed his question of why the tropical man is so hated by moral theories and theorists, he answered that such condemnation is carried out in the interests of temperance and mediocrity. Basically, Nietzsche is implying a recognition of something approaching a pathetic fallacy, in which attitudes and sentiments which are conceived as antithetical to society are deliberately projected on to, and indeed made constitutive of, the otherness of nature.

However, although Nietzsche quite keenly recognized the emergence and the operation of the pathetic fallacy and, for that matter, while he identified societal stakes behind the natural artifice, his response remained thoroughly modern. Instead of taking the opportunity to deconstruct of the taken-for-granted foundations of modernity, and instead of pursuing reflexivity to the lengths which, in many ways, he anticipated, Nietzsche responded to one version of the myth of the wild with a turn to its opposite version. Quite simply, Nietzsche ended up working around the proposition that if civilization is decadent, and if civilization condemns certain practices, relationships and individuals as wild, then a true and non-decadent life must look exactly like everything which civilization abhors. As such, if civilization upholds the reciprocity of pity simply on the grounds that a fellow being can suffer, then true life must be based on an indifference towards the suffering of others.

Nietzsche sought a path out of modernity, and implicitly out of civil society, and he thought that he had found it. But, basically, all he found was the mirror-opposite of civil society. Civilization promotes and assumes homogeneity; therefore, Nietzsche promoted heterogeneity. Civil society involves and promotes symmetric reciprocity, therefore, Nietzsche demands asymmetric reciprocity. The noble individual, the Superman, has to stand apart and establish his own strangeness to any conception of symmetric reciprocity and community. After all, for Nietzsche, nobility consists in never 'degrading our duties into duties for everybody; not to want to relinquish or share our own responsibilities; to count our privileges and the exercising of them among our *duties*' (Nietzsche 1973: 210). This is social and moral philosophy in the service of the remythication of the order of things.

But it cannot be denied that Nietzsche inspired an extremely sharp awareness of the costs of civilization. His thought provides a most profound counter-point to the arguments of the seventeenth and eighteenth century philosophers who saw civilization and civil society as the milieu of the freedom of reflexivity. Nietzsche also adds a measure of pathos to the dominant narrative of nineteenth century sociology which boiled down to the argument that civilization might not be totally wonderful, but it is the only hope of avoiding a return to reification. This emphasis on the costs of civilization was basically possible because Nietzsche did not see the state of nature, with its wild practices, as a report of some historical reality which had to be kept firmly 'out there'. Rather, Nietzsche was operating in terms of an assumption of the state of nature as an anthropological condition which could be attained through a critique of the resources of civilization. For Nietzsche, the wild was interior to both civil society and, indeed, the individual.

Perhaps the difference between the theories which identified the state of nature as an 'out there' and those which identified it as something interior can be explained in terms of different apprehensions of modernity. (The following points have been stimulated by a comment in Sayer 1991: 4.) Perhaps it can be proposed that the narratives which identify the wild as 'out there' are reflections of modernity experienced as in the making. As such, John Locke, Thomas Hobbes and even Adam Ferguson were all writing in social situations in which the sharp division of the order of things between the societal and the natural, the defining and the defined, was still to be accomplished. The division was in the making; therefore, the primary problem in the interpretation of the world of strangers was one of establishing the boundaries of the community of civil society and of making sure that it would also be a community of reflexivity rather than of the natural artifice. In these schemes of things, it would be difficult to talk in terms of the costs of civilization simply because civilization itself could not be interpreted as a secure realm.

This story of modernity in the making was given a historical twist in the long-term optimism of Karl Marx (who saw costs in the short run but an eventual utopia), and in the developmentalism of Norbert Elias (who sees the growing complexity of societal relationships as something like a precondition for a more pliable and separate – because more resolutely and accurately defined – nature).

But the tendency of the likes of Nietzsche, and later Freud and even Durkheim, to talk in fairly ahistorical terms meant that they also tended to lapse into talk about the human condition in society. This is most obvious in Freud, but the inclination is not at all absent from the work of Nietzsche. While Nietzsche is very aware of the historical contingency of modern arrangements, he is nevertheless prone to see them as meaning much the same thing for everyone (everyone, that is, except those few noble individuals who can transcend this history). It might be proposed that the assumption of the wild as an interior quality goes hand in hand with an apprehension of modernity as something grown familiar. As such, the arrangements, narratives and imaginations of modernity and civil society cease to be identified as straightforward defences of expressions of reflexivity. Quite the contrary, they are seen as something of a second nature. They are therefore identified as restrictions on freedom and interpreted in terms of their costs.

I should make it plain that I am not arguing that the different attitudes of modernity in the making and modernity grown familiar stand in a line of succession. The attitudes do not follow one after the other with the simple passage of time. Rather, modernity, and specifically civil society, is experienced as either something in the making or as something grown familiar on the basis of the grounding assumptions of the interpretations of modernity and civil society. In other words, each attitude is an intellectual and hermeneutic response by the moralist (by the intellectual) to his own social and historical conditions of existence. If man is seen as anthropologically sufficient unto himself and as a self-contained being who comes to civil society, then modernity is seen as familiar. It is familiar because the assumption of man as possessed of constant wild elements operates as an immutable yardstick for an analysis of the human condition.

Alternatively, if man is seen as something which has to be made human through the work of societal relationships (that is, if man is seen as a being who is made in civil society), then there is no immutable yardstick for an analysis and therefore modernity is experienced as something in the perpetual making. Consequently, it is possible for someone like Elias to come after Freud, or indeed for someone like Nietzsche to come after Hobbes. These approaches to modernity do not exist in direct genealogical relationship to one another. They cannot be placed on a single family tree; rather, they operate in terms of different ontological and epistemological ground-rules. (I talk about these points in a lot more detail in the discussion of the culture of reflexive discourse in Tester 1992.)

Perhaps one of the most profound expressions of a modernity grown familiar which can be offered by sociology is to be found in the work of Max Weber. Indeed, Weber's work is also interesting because it is morally aware of the costs of modernity, and yet it is analytically compelled to accept those costs. In other words, Weber's work is quite without the kind of faith in transcendence which is in the last instance Nietzsche's only way of coming to terms with a world in which transcendence is impossible.

Weber's interpretation of modernity and of the costs of civilization was, unsurprisingly, predicated on the initial ontological assumption that man comes to civil society. The main question for Weber consequently becomes one of understanding what has happened to that self-sufficient being. One way of initially approaching this dimension of Max Weber's work is to explore some of the themes raised in the closing pages of his book *The Protestant Ethic and the Spirit of Capitalism*. The basic narrative of the book is well known; Weber seeks to understand how the Calvinist theological concept of the calling was historically transformed into the justification and legitimation for an individual responsibility for the production of wealth. That is, Weber tries to understand how and why individuals have been prepared to perform roles in the development of the productive forces and relationships of capitalism.

At the end of his discussion of the emergence of the Protestant work ethic, Weber makes a very interesting comment. It reveals that, for him, the relationships which made possible the production of the resources by which modernity would solve the problem of material scarcity (and instead ostensibly convert it into the problem of how to deal with abundance) went hand in hand with a spiritual impoverishment of what it means to be human. The passage is quite lengthy. In it, Weber begins by typifying the nature of modern work and then proceeds to draw implications from it:

> Limitation to specialized work, with a renunciation of the Faustian universality of man which it involves, is a condition of any valuable work in the modern world: hence deeds and renunciation inevitably condition each other today. This fundamentally ascetic trait of middle-class life, if it attempts to be a way of life at all, and not simply the absence of any, was what Goethe

wanted to teach ... For him the realization meant a renunci-
ation, a departure from an age of full and beautiful humanity,
which can no more be repeated in the course of our cultural
development than can the flower of the Athenian culture of
antiquity.

(Weber 1930: 181)

In many ways, Weber is explicitly drawing on a Romantic variation
of the theme of the wild. Through an encounter between Goethe
and the societal relationships of European modernity, Weber sees
nothing other than a most terrible entrapment of the man who
should be the universal subject of his own intentions.

Weber's argument is based on the thesis that outside of the
demands of modern civil society, with its rational procedures and
concerns with the responsible individual, man is truly homogeneous. This homogeneity evidently prevails at a number of levels: the
passage seems to imply that it is ontological, aesthetic, subjective
and historical. However, the domination of reason, and the bourgeois notion of the requirement of individuals to work hard in
their role in daily economic and societal life, means that the
universal homogeneity of man has been divided. Modernity, and
civil society, has turned man into the mundane representative of
a process towards heterogeneity which now traps him, as if it were
an iron cage.

Instead of Faustian man, Weber sees the man of modernity as
a prisoner of the resources and techniques which were meant to
ensure the continual practice of freedom. Weber talks about 'the
technical and economic conditions of machine production which
to-day determine the lives of all individuals who are born into this
mechanism, not only those directly concerned with economic
acquisition, with irresistible force' (Weber 1930: 181). It would
rather seem that Weber thought that the only chance that man
might be able to overcome this entrapment within the 'iron cage'
would appear only when the material resources which underpin
machine production are themselves exhausted: 'Perhaps it will so
determine them until the last ton of fossilized coal is burnt' (Weber
1930: 181).

Even from these very brief points, it is quite clear that Weber is
using a conception of man as a pre-formed, self-sufficient being to
launch an attack on what are consequently defined as the terrible
costs of civilization. Certainly, it would rather seem that Weber did

not want to abandon all the technical products of modernity, but he was profoundly aware of what the entrapment of man within a complex web of economic production meant for man as an aesthetic subject.

For Weber, for whom modernity was rather too familiar, the point was precisely that the promises of modernity in the making, the promises of reflexivity and freedom from the natural artifice, had led to the emergence of barriers against reflexivity. In other words, Weber saw civilization in terms of the emergence of a second nature. This second nature did not take the form of a supernatural God, nor of a patriarchal order. Rather, it was represented in the wide spread of machines which, thanks to the rational division of labour, most people knew nothing about. (In many ways, this is an argument which had been anticipated by Adam Smith, who was also deeply worried about the implications of the division of labour and the relationships of production.) Consequently, these machines came to be experienced as things which existed outside of human interference.

This awareness was registered on a couple of occasions. In *The Protestant Ethic and the Spirit of Capitalism*, he wrote that 'material goods have gained an increasing and finally an inexorable power over the lives of men as at no previous period in history'. This meant that a possible future for the world was one under the sway of a 'mechanized petrification, embellished with a sort of convulsive self-importance' (Weber 1930: 181, 182). Weber also pursued this question in his lecture on 'Science as a Vocation'. In the lecture, Weber argues that modern science is to be understood in terms of a process of the disenchantment of the world. Essentially, the disenchantment involves the deconstruction of the natural artifice since it is synonymous with an awareness on the part of men that the things and events of the world can be understood without reference to any supernatural principles. In other words, disenchantment is much the same as reflexivity (Weber 1948: 139).

Disenchantment is made all the more possible by the rational division of labour between different specialisms so that scientific activity and knowledge is compartmentalized and, consequently, able to follow its own logic of rational-technical development. But it would seem that Weber saw a sting in this particular tail. Firstly, of course, the compartmentalization of knowledge also means the compartmentalization of the knowledgeable such that, for example, I might know a little about sociology, but I know nothing whatsoever as to how my word processor works. Certainly, I could in principle find out about micro-electronics. After all, 'if one but wished one *could* learn it at any time' (Weber 1948: 139). But if Weber's argument is taken to its logical conclusions, it is likely that I will not be able to understand the manuals. I will have become a prisoner of two processes: firstly, of the hold of the Protestant ethic which compels me relentlessly to practise my status as a sociologist (I have not got the time to learn about computers); and, secondly, the collapse of the Faustian universality which would have enabled myself and a computer specialist to communicate. Instead, we are both specialists who are unable to understand each other. Our knowledge, our commitments, our interests as individuals in civilization, have been rendered heterogeneous.

Weber himself gives a rather more mundane example of the process by which the erstwhile resources of freedom and self-definition become blockages to the practice of reflexivity. He points out that 'Unless he is a physicist, one who rides on the streetcar has no idea how the car happened to get into motion. And he does not need to know' (Weber 1948: 139). The point is precisely that the technical predictability of motor vehicles means that we do not actually think about them. They are treated virtually as if they existed by nature. The individual does not actually need to know how a car works: 'He is satisfied that he may "count" on the behaviour of the streetcar, and he orients his conduct according to this expectation; but he knows nothing about what it takes to produce such a car so that it can move' (Weber 1948: 139). In the face of this turn of society into second nature, and given the entrapment of man, life has, for Weber, lost all its higher cultural and creative dimensions.

According to Weber, then, and in a rather Nietzschean vein, civilization, with its rationality and its technology, has made life mundane. Indeed, the similarities between Nietzsche and Weber continue a little further. Nietzsche saw the only way out of the mediocrity of civilization as the Superman who deliberately makes himself a stranger to the demands of symmetric reciprocity. Rather similarly, Weber thought that one of the few historically viable escape routes from the iron cage of modernity involved the appearance of a charismatic individual.

Weber demonstrates very close connections with Nietzsche when he writes: 'The charismatic leader gains and maintains authority solely by proving his strength in life. If he wants to be a prophet, he must perform miracles; if he wants to be a war lord, he must perform heroic deeds' (Weber 1948: 249). In other words, the charismatic individual rests his claims to leadership on the extent to which he is able to transcend the mundane world of the trapped individual and, instead, practise his own acts of definition. For Weber, then, the argument rather seems to be that freedom can only be gained if this civilization is overcome.

That is certainly one way of reading Weber's pessimistic interpretation of the situation of the individual as he is found in modern civil society. But Weber's analysis is also open to a rather more paradoxical reading. Certainly, Weber does not doubt that to be an individual in modern civilization, in modern civil society, is also to be a prisoner of rationality and technology, but Weber suggests that to be an individual also means being a free moral subject. The point is that the Protestant ethic not only makes the individual a subject of the demands of industry. The Protestant ethic also makes the individual morally responsible for his own actions. In other words, working from his rather Romantic ontological and anthropological assumptions, Weber's sociology works through an analysis of the history of rationality and rationalization to an emphasis on the problem of the ethical conduct of life by the individual.

It is possible to understand the analysis provided in *The Protestant Ethic and the Spirit of Capitalism* in terms of a multi-layered concern with process and regulation as issues confronting the individual in civilization. Weber was able to construct a narrative which worked at these different levels more or less at the same time because he struggled to cling to contradictory modern imaginations. On the one hand, Weber was committed to the idea that man is a potentially Faustian figure whose universal wildness is disciplined and entrapped by civilization. But, on the other hand, Weber was also committed to the argument that it is only through societal relationships, and only through the intrinsically social problem of the moral conduct of life, that the individual can be rendered human. (For a discussion of these points which would not, however, necessarily agree with my interpretation of Weber, see Gordon 1987.)

Weber's sociology contains an implicit recognition of what might be called a pathos of subjectivity. The individual in modern civilization is a subject of the demands of rationality and its associated technologies of the division of the world into a defining societal milieu and a defined natural milieu. But precisely because modern techniques require so much of the individual, and indeed precisely because each individual is simply a specialist who relies on other specialists, the individual must also be the self-conscious subject of his own actions. The societal community can only be maintained in so far as each individual reflexively recognizes the depth of his involvement in it, and the magnitude of the stakes of continued participation. That which renders the individual as a subject makes the individual also a subject of his own consciousness. Ironically, then, the freedom of the individual as a moral agent presupposes, and to a very considerable extent actually requires, the devastation of the Faustian potential of universality.

The pathos which runs through the sociology of Weber is exactly the impossibility of knowing if the trade-off between wild man and societal man is worth the effort. All Weber could offer in response was a melancholy call for the men of civilization and, by extension, civil society to think about what it is that they glory. For Weber, 'of this last stage of this cultural development, it might well be truly said: "Specialists without spirit, sensualists without heart; this nullity imagines that it has attained a level of civilization never before achieved" ' (Weber 1930: 182).

However, while the theme of the pathos of subjectivity is indeed contained in Weber's work, its full implications were perhaps best realized by Michel Foucault. (The relationship between Weber and Foucault is discussed in Foucault 1988 and Gordon 1987.) Foucault made a comment which can be read as implying that his work should be read as a series of analyses of how certain forms and areas of social relationships were objectified and turned into problems of rationality. Foucault wrote that he was trying to 'create a history of the different modes by which, in our culture, human beings are made subjects' (Foucault 1982: 208).

Consequently, Foucault identified 'three modes of objectification which transform human beings into subjects'. Firstly, he identified the modes of inquiry, called sciences, which seek to objectify the activities and relationships of humans by saying something definite about them. Secondly, Foucault pointed to the emergence of the 'dividing practices' by which the individual is transformed into a subject who is different from all other individuals (in his studies of insanity and discipline). Thirdly, Foucault sees his work on sexuality as recognizing 'the way a human being turns him- or herself into a subject ... how men have learned to recognize themselves as subjects of "sexuality" ' (Foucault 1982: 208).

The result of Foucault's encounters with the techniques by which humans are transformed into social subjects was in many ways a simple clarification of the themes already implied by Weber. Foucault understood the individual in society, or it could be said, the individual in the process of civilization, in terms of the formation of a set of objectifications and identities. Consequently, the individual was understood by Foucault as constituted in and through power relationships. As Michel Foucault put it:

> power applies itself to immediate everyday life which categorizes the individual, marks him by his own individuality, attaches him to his own identity, imposes a law of truth on him which he must recognize and which others have to recognize in him. It is a form of power which makes individuals subjects. There are two meanings of the word *subject*: subject to someone else by control and dependence, and tied to his own identity by a conscience or self-knowledge. Both meanings suggest a form of power which subjugates and makes subject to.
>
> (Foucault 1982: 212)

Now, there is more than just a hint of the elaborate pun about this passage, but it is perhaps worth spending a little time considering precisely why that suspicion is aroused.

Arguably, when he talks about the individual in society, Foucault is trying to do at least two things. Firstly, he is trying to understand the old problem in political philosophy of why and how it is that standards of legitimacy and obligation are formed and accepted. Secondly, Foucault is trying to explain what 'liberation' might mean. The first concern is in itself not too interesting, but the second concern is rather more intriguing.

Basically, most if not all of Foucault's work on sexuality can be understood in terms of an attempt to unravel the question of why the issue of sexual liberation has been given so much importance and, extending out of that, why all the glorious dawns of sexual liberation have invariably turned out to be experienced as new kinds of entrapment. His answer is that sexual ethics represent a way of disciplining the individual (through the prohibition of certain kinds of sexual activity) while also tying the individual to a very specific identity (i.e., heterosexual, homosexual or whatever). Consequently, to argue that *this* form of sexuality can be liberated through *that* form of sexuality is simply to reinforce the definitions of the individual as a sexual subject. The individual as a self-conscious subject is being asked to subject himself to different forms of sexual subjection. He is not being allowed to define his sexuality for himself.

As such, for the individual to be truly liberated, the meaning of that liberation cannot be spoken. 'We have to promote new forms of subjectivity through the refusal of this kind of individuality which has been imposed on us for several centuries' (Foucault 1982: 216). In other words, Foucault ends up making the case for nothing other than reflexivity and homogeneity.

The connection between Foucault's position and the by now unsurprising concern with reflexivity is reasonably clear. Quite simply, Foucault implies that if he were to specify the meaning of liberation, or indeed if he were to tie that meaning to the old kinds of individuality, it would immediately be placed within the objectified and objectifying narratives of science. Consequently, liberation properly understood cannot be said; it must always retain the ability to reflect on itself without the interference of external authority. Of course, by the very logic of his own analysis, Foucault could not possibly say if this was indeed what he meant by liberation. If it is, then Foucault is, perhaps, to be seen as something like one of the last protagonists of modernity. If it is not, then Foucault is perhaps doing nothing other than trying to pass off an aporia as a revelation.

The case for the connection between Foucault's unspoken imagination of liberation and homogeneity is rather harder to make. But it can be made nevertheless. The point is that Foucault says that it is through the institutions and the arrangements of subjectivity that each individual is tied to an individual identity and thus created as an independent, responsible, person. Now, it would be wrong, and extremely simplistic, to suppose that Foucault is therefore saying that if this individualization did not occur, then all humans would be the same. He is not founding his analysis on the assumption of some grand anthropological or ontological universal constant which stands outside of civil society. But it would rather seem that Foucault carried out another kind of move with a similar effect.

Instead of looking back or outside to some ahistorical condition of human being, Foucault instead looks forward. His argument can be read as suggesting that given that we have all been created as subjects (in the double sense of that word), we cannot know what it means not to be a subject. For us, to be a subject is to be a more or less egoistic, responsible, individual, who experiences the world and others as separate; as strangers and as strange. Therefore, and purely within those terms, liberation for us can be imagined as involving something approaching an entirely homogeneous universal condition of humanity. He is using the products of modernity to call forth their own antithesis. Foucault is using the existential particularity of modernity as the foundation of yet another imagination of the transparent universe of complete homogeneity. Once again, Foucault could not possibly say that he was carrying out such a move, since to do that would be to objectify the chance of liberation and, consequently, disallow it.

So, there are distinct similarities linking the work of Nietzsche and Weber and even Foucault. Indeed, it might even be proposed that all three are connected, and connected with Freud as well, by a concern to explain and understand the costs of civilization. But there is one major difference. Nietzsche, Freud and Weber all appreciated the costs on the basis of an identification of what they took to be the anthropological and ontological condition of the wild. They all shared the assumption that the wild was in some way the mark of self-sufficient and reflexive humanity. Consequently, civilization was a form of symmetric reciprocity which necessarily implied the restraint and repression of that wildness. Foucault worked the other way. He explored the historical conditions of the objectification and the mythication of symmetric reciprocity. He then used that knowledge as the basis of the imagination of an antithetical condition of sufficiency and reflexivity. In other words, whereas Nietzsche and the others imagined a real condition of discontent, Foucault to some extent wanted to stimulate discontent.

And so, once again, all these accounts of what it means for man to live in civilization end up sounding desperately modern. They are all operating, not just on the terrain of reflexivity, but also on the terrain of scarcity. This problem of scarcity is, of course, one of the key themes which runs through the imaginations of civil society. Invariably, scarcity is understood as a lack of one kind or another of material resource. Civil society is put forward as the solution to that material lack. The solution involves nothing other than the consolidation of arrangements and institutions of sym-metric reciprocity. That is, civil society is an architecture for the odd which shows each individual the interdependency and consequently the formal equality of all the members of the community.

However, the imagination of civilization which sees it in terms of its costs to man logically sees civilization as the cause of scarcity. But in this reinterpretation, the meaning of scarcity is redefined quite fundamentally. In this tradition, the problem of the abundance of, and access to, material resources is relatively marginalized in favour of a concentration on the scarcity of the emotional resources of life. As such, the very pressing external physical worries, which were so important for John Locke and Thomas Hobbes (to name just two), were redefined by Nietzsche, Weber, Freud and Foucault as largely interior psychological worries. Indeed, this tendency could go so far that physical resources occasionally disappeared from the picture altogether.

Nietzsche hardly utters a meaningful word about the problem of material resources and scarcity since he is so concerned to rescue the noble from the mediocre. In many ways, this absence could also be due to Nietzsche's not insignificant failures as a social philosopher. He certainly possessed the ability to ask all the right questions, and he relentlessly pushed deconstructive efforts to astonishing lengths. But Nietzsche's answers to his own questions were not too useful or helpful. To be quite honest, all the talk of the Superman hardly represents a meaningful or a terribly practical solution to the problem of civilization.

Furthermore, Michel Foucault seems to suggest that any analysis and narrative of modernity can simply take the matter of material and physical scarcity as already, and presumably permanently, resolved. He admits: 'Outside the Western world, famine exists, on a greater scale than ever; and the biological risks confronting the species are perhaps greater, and certainly more serious, than before the birth of microbiology' (Foucault 1979: 143). In other words, outside of the boundaries of the community of the 'West', there exists a vast milieu in which material scarcity continues to be an overwhelming issue. The existence of the inhabitants of the non-West in conditions of scarcity defines them. But, inside the 'West', the situation is radically different. Here, scarcity has been overcome and, instead of being defined, the 'West' is able to be defining of itself. Foucault says: 'what might be called a society's "threshold of modernity" has been reached when the life of the species is wagered on its own political strategies' (Foucault 1979: 143). Once again, the ostensible critique of modernity reveals an inability to go beyond the foundations of the modern narratives.

Perhaps it is unfair to highlight the failure of Nietzsche and Foucault, and it must be said Freud and to a lesser extent Weber, to confront the very basic conditions of possibility of the critique of modernity, civilization and civil society. After all, for all of them, modernity was to some extent a milieu which was simply at hand; for them, it was something familiar. The tradition which emphasized the costs of civilization was approaching modernity as a problem to be interrogated and, if possible, overcome rather than as a possibility of reflexivity and self-sufficiency which had to be established and vigilantly defended. As such, it was perhaps inevitable that the once longed-for arrangements of symmetric reciprocity should be identified as institutions of mediocrity, and of the domestication of the wild; or that the problem of securing the creature comforts which allow reflexivity in the first place should be frequently forgotten. (Elias's concern with modernity in the making, and the huge debt of Marx to the problematic of the making, meant that they did not lose sight of the question of the production and distribution of material goods.)

For Nietzsche and the others, modernity was not in the perpetual making. Consequently, the questions raised by physical want and material scarcity were of nothing more than historical significance. The problems of living in the modern world were of a rather different status.

Chapter 6

The contradictions

I have argued that civil society is best understood as a socially and historically specific attempt to achieve a number of aims. Firstly, civil society was an invention from the conditions of European modernity which was able in principle to explain the reciprocity of people who experienced themselves as individuals in relationships with strangers. Secondly, it was the milieu in which individuals entered into voluntary associations and thus freely carried out the social construction of a bounded community called society. Thirdly, civil society was the guarantee and the achievement of societal self-sufficiency and of the deconstruction of the natural artifice.

In other words, civil society was an imagination which attempted to identify, represent and legislate some basic unity in the experience of being human, and an essential sameness about what it involves to be an individual who lives a life of external compulsion and obligation. It had to be imagined simply because, outside of the act of the calling forth of the milieu called civil society, it was quite impossible to identify some regularity or essential reciprocity in the relationships between people. The terrain was so vast and cosmopolitan and, in the cities, so strange that it could not possibly be assumed to exist as if by nature. But neither could the contours of the landscape simply be apprehended through an act of cognition or direct empirical observation. The landscape could only be understood in terms of an imaginative constitution of the category of civil society. It is the map of civil society which establishes the regularities and the relationships of civil society. It is a very serious mistake, and it is certainly historically and methodologically naïve, to assume that the category simply and perfectly clearly represents some determinate reality existing 'out there'.

A certain kind of dialectic is, then, intrinsic to the imagination of civil society. The dialectic is at the same time analytical, historical and moral. On the one hand, civil society is identified as that which has been achieved. On the other hand, civil society is imagined as that which stands in need of achievement. That is, the milieu is called forth as something like its own condition of existence and its own destiny. The social construction of civil society is taken as a proof of civil society. Of course, the effort required for the achievement of civil society was never, if ever, taken to be slight. After all, if not much effort had been needed, the prize of a mannered reciprocity would not have been half as alluring. Neither would the costs of civilization have been worth paying, and, quite probably, neither would the redemption offered by the products of civil society have been worth the wait. Civil society was always imagined as a difficult achievement. But, of course, it was precisely the difficulty which made it an attractive destiny in the first place. Similarly, and perhaps as a perfect illustration of this point, Faust would hardly have become some kind of metaphor for the tragic history of freedom and knowledge if his struggles to wrest the secrets of philosophy, medicine and law had involved nothing more than the accessing of a database on a mainframe. (Here, I am thinking of both Marlowe's and Goethe's versions of the Faust legend.)

The charge of civil society consisted of the fact that while it was seen as a costly or a very difficult achievement, it was seen as a distinctly possible achievement nevertheless. There was little or no doubt that the voluntary associations of independent, mannered ('polished') and civilized individuals were actually occurring, and could be made to occur for the indefinite future, if only the representations and requirements of civilization and reciprocity could be made to have an even greater part to play in the engineering of human souls.

However, it was perhaps the case that the imagination of civil society was seen so optimistically, and perhaps the stakes placed on it were so great, precisely because, behind the gloss of civilization and refinement, there lurked what amounted to an existential crisis. The point was not so much that civil society was possible, but rather that it needed to be possible. It was the only viable way that the world could be reconstructed in terms of a meaningful order of things. The existential crisis was not a dimension of the human condition in society; it was not a historical constant which was present for all individuals in all societies at all times. Rather, it was a socially and historically contingent crisis which was generated in seventeenth and eighteenth century Europe, to be projected into the nineteenth century. It was largely due to the collapse of the old orders of things which were based on the time-immemorial structures of asymmetric reciprocity.

The old asymmetry collapsed in the face of urbanization, cosmopolitanism and the consequent redundancy of any and all criteria of firm ascription in the context of a world of achieved strangers and strangeness. (Only some groups were consigned to ascription and there was a limitation on their otherwise intrinsic strangeness. They were so consigned if they lacked, or were denied, the ability to define themselves.) It is the close connection between civil society and the themes of achievement, and a self-sufficient social construction of the societal, which makes it necessary to see civil society as an imagination specific to the circumstances and concerns of European modernity.

The narratives, imaginations and hopes of modernity all implicitly assumed that civil society meant, and indeed itself promoted, symmetric reciprocity. The status and the experience of all individuals was subjected to a kind of ontological and anthropological reduction, so that each individual counted equally with any other, and was invested with the same intrinsic value purely as a human being regardless of societal position. (This was precisely the reduction which so irritated Friedrich Nietzsche.) The reciprocity assumed by the modern orders of things was symmetric to the extent that it was presumed that, irrespective of surface appearances, all individuals counted the same and, indeed, actually were the same. The notion of symmetric reciprocity was, then, taken to be both descriptive and evaluative. It is arguably best represented in the moral narratives which are based on either rights theory (whether those rights are held to be natural or societal) or utilitarian calculations.

Rights theories reduce all relevant subjects to some single trait or characteristic which is taken as itself to be defining of their significance to others. For example, for John Locke, the individual is relevant only to the extent that he is something striving for life, liberty and private property. In comparison with that central core which constitutes moral significance, any other qualities that the individual might or might not possess are taken as entirely contingent and of no value. In many ways, this kind of reduction of the individual reaches an apotheosis in the narratives of human rights which are predicated on the assumption that all individuals are morally significant purely because of their being human. Once this postulate of the relevance of all individuals, regardless of contingent conditions of time and place, is accepted, the debate then becomes one of defining precisely what it is that is constitutive of being human.

To some extent, it is this debate on the rights of the individual as a human who is identical in all morally significant respects to all other humans which runs through the disputes surrounding abortion. The debate revolves around how, when and in what ways a foetus is human and therefore an individual with rights. The inability to settle the abortion debate shows more clearly than anything else that the different sides are not talking to each other. Rather, they are talking past each other because they are basing their arguments on significantly different definitions of what it means and is to be human. (For the one side, the foetus is relevant; for the other side, the foetus becomes relevant. Once again, this is a dispute between ascription and achievement, definition and defining.) As such, the abortion debate is both aggressive and quite unresolvable as a moral question. (For more on this point, see Minson 1985.)

The move of reduction which utilitarian approaches carry out is broadly similar to that carried out in rights theories (although, of course, the narrative and the conclusion are extremely different). In its dominant forms, such as those associated with Jeremy Bentham and John Stuart Mill, utilitarianism reduces the complexity of individual existence to the ability to suffer pain. The argument is, basically, that all sentient creatures have an interest in not suffering pain and that, therefore, any action which causes an increase in the net amount of pain in the relevant community is morally indefensible. An action which causes a net decrease in the amount of pain is, then, morally defensible.

So, in this utilitarian expression of symmetry, there are two important strands. Firstly, all individuals are identical in so far as they have an interest in the avoidance of pain. In the face of that ontological fact, everything else is rendered quite insignificant (such that Bentham at least was able to speculate that animals might be considered as morally equally to humans to the extent that they can suffer, and have an interest not to). Secondly, utilitarianism emphasizes the social relationships of the individual.

Those relationships are understood as reciprocal (the utilitarian problem is what I do to you; it is not concerned with you as such; you have no right not to suffer, just an interest not to be caused to suffer pain by me) and universal. The moral calculation explores the global consequences of my actions on you in so far as those actions have an effect on the net amount of suffering. In other words, the utilitarian calculation presupposes the existence of an already established bounded community which can be treated as universal precisely because it is internally homogeneous. Utilitarian approaches only make sense if they presuppose this kind of a bounded community of significance.

Through the narratives such as those of rights and utilitarianism, the symmetry of individuals within civil society was turned into a moral fact. Moreover, those two narratives can be taken as indications of the processes by which the free and responsible individual presupposed by the basic assumptions of civil society became something of a grounding of modernity. Institutionally, the identification of civil society with the responsible reciprocity of self-defining individuals took the form of democracy. This connection could be made to such an extent that, for many, the relationship of civil society with democratic forces, aspirations and institutions is completely and utterly self-evident.

Prime examples of this kind of mythication can be found in many of the commentaries on the collapse of the Soviet-type system of actually existing socialism in central and eastern Europe (for example, Dahrendorf 1990), or in the logical drift of much of the work on civil society of a writer like John Keane. Keane is in no doubt that civil society represents the ability of democratic pressures to escape any attempt to totally control them. He says that civil society is 'marked by a multitude of opinions' and that 'Precisely because of its pluralism, and its lack of a guiding centre, a tongue-wagging and sign-waving, fully democratic civil society could never reach a condition of homoeostasis' (Keane 1991: 148). (Compare Keane's comments with Carl Schmitt's comments on the uses of principled disagreement in Schmitt 1985: 35.) It is simply asserted that civil society involves democratic pressures; the connection is never really deconstructed nor interrogated.

The simple identification of civil society with free self-definition and achievement was frequently given a rather more ontological twist. The supposed aspiration for democracy became elevated to the status of life as opposed to, and in opposition to, the reifying interests of the state and of technology. (This story was anticipated by Adam Ferguson and Adam Smith. More recently, it was a particular favourite of Václav Havel when he was bravely opposing actually existing socialism, and immediately after he became the President of Czechoslovakia. Variations on the theme can also be found in the work of Milan Kundera and of a number of other novelists from central and eastern Europe. See especially Havel 1987 and Tucker 1990.) Once again, these connections are simply assumed and accepted as beyond question; they are fundamental assumptions without which civil society would be impossible. Consequently, they are pushed beyond the compass of reflexivity.

However, although the project of civil society was, to this extent, both powerful and persuasive, it contained within itself very serious difficulties. Quite simply, the combination of the reduction of all individuals to some homogeneous quality shared by all (be it human-ness or the interest not to suffer or whatever) with the corollary premise of the homogeneity of civil society was logically impossible. This point was realized quite clearly by Carl Schmitt, although he did not use the terminology of 'civil society'. Instead, Schmitt discovered what can be seen as the logical impossibility of civil society through a critique of democracy.

Of course, Carl Schmitt is not a terribly lionized thinker because of his not unfriendly relationship with Nazism, and because of the rather distasteful conservatism of many of his theses (even though he became increasingly popular in the late 1980s and early 1990s). However, intellectually, Schmitt was saying things which resonated with the general thrust of elite theory in the early twentieth century, and it is perhaps precisely his carefully expressed distrust of democracy (and much else besides) which makes him a particularly telling critic of some of the most cherished images of the age. Unlike a number of more popular thinkers, Schmitt possessed a special ability to irritate.

His discussion of democracy is couched in terms which directly compare with the terminology that I have been using to try to understand civil society (although I discovered the similarities after I had developed the concerns expressed in this essay). In his book *The Crisis of Parliamentary Democracy*, Schmitt usefully comments: 'Every actual democracy rests on the principle that not only are equals equal but unequals will not be treated equally. Democracy requires, therefore, first homogeneity and second – if the need arises – elimination or eradication of heterogeneity' (Schmitt

1985: 9). In other words, Schmitt is clearly saying that democracy is a viable political and institutional arrangement only to the extent that it is founded on the basis of some established bounded community. Within that bounded community, all individuals and all relationships can be treated as homogeneous. The individuals and the relationships which fall outside of the boundaries are, on the contrary, identified as heterogeneous. These sites of difference consequently stand in need of assimilation, or even annihilation, if the community of homogeneity is to be reproducible. Schmitt quite rightly remarks: 'Since the nineteenth century it [i.e., the principle of equality] has existed above all in membership in a particular nation, in national homogeneity' (Schmitt 1985: 9). Indeed, it might be suggested that one of the dominant strands of nineteenth century history was precisely the struggle to establish nation-states which contained within their boundaries no traces of an illicit heterogeneity.

Obviously, Schmitt is not explicitly talking about civil society. But it is quite clear that, in many ways, he is identifying in democracy and its representation in the nation-state more or less, the same processes and concerns which can be seen in the imagination of civil society. The parallels are numerous. Firstly, Schmitt is making the point that democracy has to be founded on, and itself contributes to the reproduction of, a bounded community. Perhaps Schmitt's reticence to talk in societal and sociological terms can be simply put down to the self-definition of his work in terms of constitutional theory. Secondly, Schmitt argues that there is a logical narrative requirement, which is represented in political, social and cultural strategies, to establish homogeneity through an identification of the heterogeneous. *Their* difference is the proof and the justification of *our* similarity (and our similarity is itself taken as a sufficient proof of their difference). For example, Schmitt points out that the free entry of immigrants into Australia was restricted through the operation of laws weighted in favour of those who, 'conform to the notion of a "right type of settler" ' (Schmitt 1985: 9). Thirdly, Schmitt is aware that the homogeneous members of the community are inevitably treated equally, but that this necessarily involves the treatment of the heterogeneous as unequal in one way or another (a point which is much the same as the conclusion that Freud reached in his comments on St Paul).

In other words, the principle of equality only makes sense in so far as it is based on a clearly identified milieu of reciprocity and homogeneity, and to the extent that the extension of the ostensibly universal principle of equality is itself bounded. Schmitt was, in many ways, showing that the arrangements of modernity are fundamentally contradictory of the myths of modernity. Consequently, it can be suggested on the basis of Schmitt's work that the imagination of civil society is intrinsically incompatible with any notion of the symmetric reciprocity of individuals who are identical in all significant respects. The idea of a society means that all individuals are not equal; the members are necessarily treated as more equal than the non-members.

Schmitt says that the principle of equality is a practical impossibility: 'An absolute human equality ... would be an equality understood only in terms of itself and without risk; it would be an equality without the necessary correlate of inequality, and as a result conceptually and practically meaningless, an indifferent equality' (Schmitt 1985: 12). The equality supposed by democracy is, then, universal or it is nothing. But if it is universal, it cannot have substance, because equality is meaningful only to the extent that it exists hand in hand with inequality. Moreover, if equality is universal, neither can it be grounded in any definite community. Instead, Schmitt sees only the collapse of the ideal of equality in the face of the requirements of equality. Indeed, he believed that if a universal and, consequently, 'indifferent' expression of equality, 'without the necessary correlate of inequality, actually takes hold of an area of human life, then this area loses its substance and is overshadowed by another sphere in which inequality then comes into play with ruthless power' (Schmitt 1985: 13).

For Schmitt, the point was that any conception of the universal equality of humankind rather flies in the face of the practical circumstances of existence in a complex society. He implies the argument that the central moral tenet of symmetric reciprocity, the idea that participation in a community is equal from one individual to another solely on the basis of their involvement in that community, ignores the fact that 'people do not face each other as abstractions, but as politically interested and politically determined persons, as citizens, governors or governed, politically allied or opponents – in any case, therefore, in political categories' (Schmitt 1985: 11). Schmitt is explicitly denying the validity of the kind of ontological reduction which was a fundamental premise of the modern imagination of civil society. He is thoroughly contemptuous of the argument that it is possible to 'abstract out what is political, leaving only universal human equality; the same applies in the realm of economics, where people are not conceived as such, but as producers, consumers, and so forth, that is, in specifically economic categories' (Schmitt 1985: 11).

Basically, Schmitt was attempting to deconstruct the principle of equality, and implicitly the ideal of symmetric reciprocity, on the basis of the practical requirements of equality and reciprocity. He demonstrated, in an argument which might well be unpleasant but is certainly internally consistent and compelling, that the modern narratives of universality are only sustainable as abstract ideals which must be more or less deliberately ignorant of the circumstances of societal relationships and activity. In other words, Schmitt was in some way turning on its head the modern assumption of a fundamental reality of universality lurking somewhere behind the transient appearances of particularity. In the process, he managed to put quite a lot of question marks against the universal figures of modernity. He showed that the universals could only be reproduced if the practical inequalities, or at least the differences, of society were pushed to one side.

Schmitt's assault on the project of homogeneity has yet another strand. Quite simply, Schmitt suggests that the ideal of equality is incompatible with the ideal that the individual is a personally responsible and self-determining subject. Modern democratic arrangements are based on a conflation of two rather different theses and, according to Schmitt, they cannot uphold the aims of homogeneity and individual responsibility at one and the same time. According to Schmitt, 'The equality of all persons as persons is not democracy but a certain kind of liberalism, not a state form but an individualistic-humanitarian ethic and *Weltanschauung*. Modern mass democracy rests on the confused combination of both' (Schmitt 1985: 13).

Schmitt argues that the contradiction between these two principles is perfectly revealed in Jean Jacques Rousseau's work. On the one hand, Rousseau, according to Schmitt, bases the legitimacy and the right of the state on its ability to represent the entirely homogeneous 'general will'. Rousseau understands the 'general will' as involving nothing other than the complete unanimity of the community. Schmitt says quite accurately that in Rousseau's system, there is no allowance for any sort of heterogeneity. The 'general will' supposes, and indeed is seen as defending, a complete homogeneity. For Schmitt, this is where the problem comes in. Rousseau's version of democracy is a contradiction of his understanding of the responsible individual. The contradiction is clear in the emphasis that Rousseau places on the social contract.

Rousseau's democracy assumes agreement, but Schmitt points out that, 'A contract assumes differences and oppositions'. Schmitt continues: 'Unanimity, just like the general will, is either there or not and it may even be ... naturally present. Where it exists a contract is meaningless. Where it does not exist, a contract does not help' (Schmitt 1985: 14). So, if Rousseau's understanding of democracy as homogeneity makes sense, the social contract is utterly superfluous. But if the social contract is needed, then democracy cannot be homogeneity. The problem is that the liberal conception of the responsible individual, separated from other individuals by the opposing interests and differences that the contract presupposes and ostensibly overcomes, is incompatible with the democratic conception of unanimity. For Schmitt, this tension is one of the most significant reasons for the specific crisis of parliamentary democracy and for the more general problems of the epoch. Where others saw civil society and unanimous contracts, Schmitt saw only 'the inescapable contradiction of liberal individualism and democratic homogeneity' (Schmitt 1985: 17).

The individuals of liberalism are not at all equally and homogeneously reducible to some single ontological or anthropological characteristic. Quite the contrary, Schmitt made the point that individuals are socially determined through societal, political and economic relationships of individualization. However, Schmitt did not thereby cast doubt on all universal figures of humankind; he did not recognize that individuals are also socially determined in terms of gender relationships.

But according to the analysis of Carole Pateman, it is quite impossible to understand fully the modern imaginations of civil society, and of the moment of the social contract, without recognizing the significance of gender relationships of inequality. Indeed, it might even be argued through a bringing together of Schmitt and Pateman that it was precisely the heterogeneity and the inequality of women which made possible the universal equality and homogeneity of civil society in the first place. The problem was that the pushing of women outside of the bounded community of symmetric reciprocity, and the consequent legitimacy of the universal figure of 'man', meant that this foundation of civil society was invariably taken for granted and never actually questioned.

In her book *The Sexual Contract*, Carole Pateman reveals that while the emergence of civil society involved the deconstruction of one meaning of patriarchy, it simply assumed another meaning of patriarchy. Certainly, someone like John Locke launched a quite devastating attack on patriarchy in so far as it was represented in the notion of the divine right of the monarch. It was exactly this kind of patriarchy which was expressed by Sir Robert Filmer, and which Locke took as the occasion of the *Two Treatises of Civil Government*. In this sense, it is perfectly justifiable to call civil society a post-patriarchal order. But in another sense, civil society is profoundly patriarchal. Locke was attacking the notion of patriarchy which was understood as paternal right (that is, the domination of the father over his family, however that family is constituted). For Pateman, this is but one part of the picture:

> Paternal right is only one, and not the original, dimension of patriarchal power. A man's power as a father comes after he has exercised the patriarchal right of a man (a husband) over a woman (wife). The contract theorists had no wish to challenge the original patriarchal right in their onslaught on paternal right ... Modern civil society is not structured by kinship and the power of fathers; in the modern world, women are subordinated to men *as men*, or to men as a fraternity.
>
> (Pateman 1988: 3)

In other words, the universality of the figure of 'man' is predicated on the construction of women as heterogeneous and as unable to practise modern self-definition.

Women were so silenced in the imaginations of civil society through a series of moves. Women were defined by men as closer to nature and therefore as ambivalent in relation to the sharp separation of the order of things into the natural and the societal. As such, women were equated with a natural sphere which was at the same time societal, and their implication in a grey realm which was neither one thing nor the other meant that they had to be excluded from the properly societal milieu. According to Pateman, the contract theories of civil society are all predicated on the postulate that 'Women have no part in the original contract, but they are not left behind in the state of nature – that would defeat the purpose of the sexual contract!' She continues to spell out the intrinsically heterogeneous position of women: 'Women are incorporated into a sphere that both is and is not in civil society. The private sphere is part of civil society but is separated from the "civil" sphere' (Pateman 1988: 11).

If civil society is, for the sake of argument, understood in geological terms, where it is a middle layer with the private sphere underneath and the state above, then it is quite clear from Pateman's analysis that the equation of women with the private milieu meant not only their exclusion from civil society but, perhaps more significantly, the patriarchal construction of their inadequacy for it. As such, the private sphere is seen in the dominant versions of the imagination of civil society as that place to which 'man' goes home in between participation in the defining acts of civilization. The private realm was simply taken for granted as something like the foundation of civil society, a foundation which was, however, entirely insignificant to the problems of the voluntary association of individuals. (The family is hardly mentioned by Emile Durkheim, for example; he simply takes it and its relationships for granted. On this matter, Pateman provides an excellent interpretation of Freud. See Pateman 1988: 103–10.)

The point is, of course, that since the private realm was identified by men (or at least by the men who invented civil society) as beneath the public, it was therefore more natural and less up to the measure of the demands of modern reflexivity. By extension, since the private realm was the natural place of women, they too were defined through the defining act of men as by themselves incapable of modernity. For example, Pateman suggests that Hegel's version of civil society presupposes that 'Women are what they are by nature; men must create themselves and public life, and they are endowed with the masculine capacity to do so. Women must remain in the natural private sphere of the family' (Pateman 1988: 176).

Indeed, without this exclusion of women from the milieu of civil society proper, and instead their natural attachment to the private sphere which is outside of reflexivity, it would be impossible to establish the universal freedoms of individuals (individuals here meaning men operating under a universal sign). Pateman is quite correct to refuse to take for granted the presence of women in universal systems which announce their own homogeneity. Instead, Pateman emphasizes the operation of the interpretive strategy in which 'the meaning of civil liberty and equality, secured and distributed impartially to all "individuals" through the civil law, can be understood only in opposition to natural subjection (of women) in the private sphere' (Pateman 1988: 114). She continues to cast yet more doubt on the ideals of civil society:

> Liberty and equality appear as universal ideals, rather than the natural attributes of the men ... who create the social order within which the ideals are given social expression, only because the civil sphere is conventionally considered on its own. Liberty, equality and fraternity form the revolutionary trilogy because liberty and equality are the attributes of the fraternity who exercise the law of male sex-right.
>
> (Pateman 1988: 114)

In other words, the lofty aims proclaimed so loudly by the individual subjects of reflexivity are founded on nothing other than might and the deliberate (or at least the not entirely accidental) denial of the ability of certain groups to practise, or even to achieve, their own modernity.

Of course, this silencing of voices on the grounds of their evident heterogeneity is indicated in the ability of words like 'man' to operate as universal categories which apply to all individuals everywhere irrespective of their construction as particular kinds of individuals through gendered relationships of inequality. The universalization of 'man' operates at a narrative level to naturalize the exclusivity of a certain interpretation of society. It also operates at an ontological and anthropological level to make men the definitional standard of what it means to be human and, therefore, to make women intelligible only in so far as they are heterogeneous in relation to that standard.

However, the relative ease with which it is possible for women like Carole Pateman to puncture the intellectual universality of 'man' shows very clearly that the modern constructions of homogeneity were fundamentally incoherent. To a large extent, the projects of homogeneity placed a central stress on the ability of individuals to recognize and do something about their responsibilities in reciprocal relationships with other individuals. In other words, homogeneity was only possible if individuals were actually represented in it. However, the heterogeneous position of women as not quite civilized meant that they had to be defined as different and in need of assimilation (since they could not be annihilated).

That is, the attempt to construct homogeneity under the sign of 'man' resulted only in the multiplication of difference around 'man'. Consequently, the ostensibly universal categories of civil society could be shown to be highly particular, and the previously assumed identity of all individuals to 'man' could be deconstructed from the point of view of the voices which had been silenced.

Jurgen Habermas has highlighted a similar kind of undermining of the ostensibly inevitable principles of universality and homogeneity. He has explored the transformations of the category of the public. He argues that the notion of the public sphere was developed in the late eighteenth and early nineteenth centuries by the press which spoke to and for the bourgeoisie. Consequently, the standards and the practices of the bourgeoisie were identified as synonymous with the meanings of the public sphere, and, moreover, the sphere was seen as universally embracing all individuals. The problem was that other social groups took these claims of universality at face value and, as such, the exclusive identification of the bourgeoisie with the homogeneous public sphere collapsed. Habermas argues that the expansion of the press to groups beyond the bourgeoisie meant that 'the public body lost not only its social exclusivity; it lost in addition the coherence created by bourgeois social institutions and a relatively high standard of education'. The result was that the standards of universality were destroyed: 'The public sphere ... becomes a field for the competition of interests, competitions which assume the form of violent conflict' (Habermas 1990: 141).

The founding statements of civil society either deliberately ignored the importance of particularities such as gender relationships or simply pushed them into a position of utter insignificance. But the involvement of that homogeneity with individualism meant that gender relationships became quite central to the experience of civil society. As such, and despite the efforts of the seventeenth, eighteenth, nineteenth and for that matter twentieth century theorists, it is no longer acceptable nor accurate to refer to individuals as 'he' or as 'man'. The very contradictions of civil society mean that any post-modern discussion of civil society must employ a gender-specific vocabulary.

Carole Pateman is, in many ways, making the point that the subsumption of all individuals under the sign of 'man' was a political and intellectual move which established some kind of identity between the governors and the governed. This question of identity was also important to Carl Schmitt. It can even be suggested that it is precisely this matter which lies at the heart of his diagnosis of the difficulties of parliamentary democracy. Schmitt argues that the principle of democracy is based on the argument that there exists a series of identities between the governors and the governed (he suggests that the idea is expressed particularly clearly by Rousseau). However, parliamentism is based on a very sharp lack of identity between the governors and the governed. Indeed, Schmitt proposes that parliamentism represents nothing other than 'the antithesis of a democratic concept of identity' (Schmitt 1985: 36).

According to Schmitt, then, 'all democratic arguments rest logically on a series of identities' (Schmitt 1985: 26). For example, democratic arrangements presuppose the identity, not only of the governors with the governed, but of the sovereign and the subject; the people and the representatives; the state and the electorate; the state and the law (Schmitt 1985: 26). In other words, democracy presupposes a perfect homogeneity of the political community. But, for Schmitt, nothing could be more disastrous for parliamentism. Indeed, he was quite clear in his own mind that the connection between parliamentism and democracy is a historical accident and not at all necessary (Schmitt 1985: 32).

Schmitt's problem was that he wanted to make the case for more parliamentism but also for less democracy. It rather seems that Schmitt saw parliamentary arrangements as the institutional milieu of reflexivity. He believed that 'through discussion and openness' (Schmitt 1985: 3) freedom could be both known and enhanced. Schmitt's description of the basis of parliamentary arrangements in the open discussion of principles and opinions irrespective of interest is quite clearly a statement of reflexivity. He writes that: 'The *ratio* of parliament rests ... in a "dynamic-dialectic", that is, in a process of confrontation of differences and opinions, from which the real political will results'. Schmitt continues to spell out the implication of this thesis, which is, of course, so different to Rousseau's understanding of the basis of political will. 'The essence of parliament is therefore public deliberation of argument and counterargument, public debate and public discussion, and all this without taking democracy into account' (Schmitt 1985: 34–5).

But the accidental coupling of parliamentary arrangements with democracy has made sure that this practice of reflexivity cannot occur. Schmitt argues that, thanks to the democratic assumption of identities between the governors and the governed, politicians now pay more attention to self-interest and short-term gains than to principled discussion. That is, Schmitt seems to imply something approaching a thesis that the ideals of modernity are quite incompatible with the arrangements of modernity. In particular, the principle of homogeneity has led to the establishment of democratic identities, but this means in turn that reflexivity is made impossible. Schmitt was in no doubt that 'The situation of parliamentarism is critical today because the development of modern mass democracy has made argumentative public discussion an empty formality' (Schmitt 1985: 6). More specifically, political parties exist simply to secure the votes of the masses through 'a propaganda apparatus whose maximum effect relies on an appeal to immediate interests and passions. Argument in the real sense that is characteristic for genuine discussion ceases' (Schmitt 1985: 8).

Political parties which involve an identity of the governed with the governors have turned parliamentary arrangements into a simple, interested, pragmatism which is ethically meaningless. Schmitt cautioned: 'If in the actual circumstances of parliamentary business, openness and discussion have become an empty and trivial formality, then parliament, as it developed in the nineteenth century, has also lost its previous foundation and its meaning' (Schmitt 1985: 50). Virtually wherever Schmitt looked, he saw only serious logical contradictions which threatened to either pull themselves apart or, more likely, to cause a complete banalization of humanity.

In a rather different way, and to rather different ends, it was this question of identity, and its implications for the meaning of civil society, which ran through the analysis of civil society put forward by the Italian Communist Antonio Gramsci. Indeed, much of the interest in civil society during the late twentieth century has been directly inspired by Gramsci's rendition of the problem.

Despite his proclaimed Marxism, Gramsci's understanding of civil society stands in a curious relationship to the interpretation which can be found in the work of Karl Marx. It would rather seem that Gramsci was inspired more by Marx's journalistic uses of the notion rather than by its analytically developed and sophisticated expressions. Certainly, Marx used civil society as a way of coming to terms with the social and historical uniqueness of the bourgeois order, but, notwithstanding this practical concern, Marx's civil society is a largely philosophical affair. On the one hand, Marx was trying to appreciate the relative status of the milieu of particular appearances in comparison to the milieu of universal reality. On the other hand, he was using the principle of the fundamental world behind appearances to launch a critique of the existing bourgeois arrangements.

Consequently, the general thrust of Marx's interpretation is an attempt to recover the truths of human being through a reflexive deconstruction of the necessarily reifying impact of bourgeois institutions and arrangements. In many ways, this philosophical enterprise (which owed not a little to the influence of Hegel) reached a highpoint in Georg Lukács's profound essay 'Reification and the Consciousness of the Proletariat'. Lukács followed the philosophical lead and drastically redefined the meaning and the status of the proletariat. It more or less ceased to be a social or a political entity. Instead, Lukács made the proletariat a primarily epistemological figure which could overcome the deeply reified subject-object distinction of bourgeois thought (Lukács 1971).

Gramsci's concerns were less philosophical and far more linked to the problems of political strategy. For Gramsci, the proletariat is, or can become, a social and political movement. He betrays little, if any, worry about its epistemological role. However, just as Marx and Lukács were trying to find a place and a basis of reflexivity in a world which was apprehended as otherwise immutable, so Gramsci tried to use civil society to explain the basis of the evident reification of the bourgeois order, a reification which was expressed in the identity (through the strategies of the construction of hegemony) of the governors with the governed. (For a thorough discussion of the debates on hegemony, see Bocock 1986.) Gramsci also used civil society as the basis of the deconstruction of the second nature of the existing arrangements which was to be achieved by the revolutionary proletariat.

So, for Gramsci, civil society was primarily a political question. Thanks to this shift of emphasis, reification came to mean something different than it had meant before. Whereas Marx (and Georg Lukács) had seen reification in philosophical and possibly even existential terms, and whereas the founding statements of civil society had equated reification with the state of nature (a theme which fed into the problem of the wild in modern sociologi-

cal discourse), Gramsci understood reification as a threat generated by the institutions and the arrangements of the capitalist here
and now. Consequently, Gramsci paid the greatest attention to the
matter of the identity between civil society and the state.

According to Gramsci, civil society can be defined as the realm
in which the state rules, not primarily through coercion, but rather
through 'ever-more conspicuous elements of regulated society'
(Gramsci 1971: 263). That is, civil society is seen by Gramsci as the
milieu in which the state takes the form of a moral force which can
regulate and control the activities of individuals without having to
resort to armed force. Gramsci realized that this interpretation of
civil society (which in many ways simply puts a negative sign
against existing moral order when someone like an Emile
Durkheim put a positive sign against it) is based on a reductive
'premise that all men are really equal and hence equally rational
and moral, i.e. capable of accepting the law spontaneously, freely,
and not through coercion, as imposed by another class, as something external to consciousness' (Gramsci 1971: 245). In other
words, civil society represents something like the superstructure
which simultaneously hides and yet legitimates the base of the
state. Essentially, Gramsci took civil society in an explicitly tactical
direction by making it the cushion which establishes the state as
common sense, inevitable and seemingly natural.

This kind of analysis resulted in Gramsci adopting a terminology which made him rather become a Toby Shandy of
revolutionary theory. Gramsci writes that in the most advanced
states, by which he means those of western Europe and North
America (exactly the states which Max Weber would have identified as the homes of modernity), civil society 'has become a very
complex structure and one which is resistant to the catastrophic
"incursions" of the immediate economic elements (crises, depress-
ions, etc.)' (Gramsci 1971: 235). He continues in a decidedly
Shandean vein:

> The superstructures of civil society are like the trench-systems
> of modern warfare. In war it would sometimes happen that a
> fierce artillery attack seemed to have destroyed the enemy's
> entire defensive system, whereas in fact it had only destroyed
> the outer perimeter; and at the moment of their advance and

> attack the assailants would find themselves confronted by a line
> of defence which was still effective.

(Gramsci 1971: 235)

The argument is that where an identity has been constructed
through civil society between the governors and the governed, 'a
frontal assault' on the institutions of the state is doomed to be a
bloody failure. The only occasion in (then) recent history where a
frontal assault on the state had met with success was, according to
Gramsci, during the Russian Revolution of 1917. It had succeeded
precisely because the state had not been buttressed by a civil society
which had become deeply entrenched in institutions and in the
minds of individuals.

The analysis taught Gramsci the political and tactical lesson that
a direct attack on the state was not the appropriate revolutionary
strategy for western Europe and North America. In these centres
of capitalism (of modernity), civil society had indeed become
highly developed and entrenched (Gramsci 1971: 235–9). Gramsci's analysis leads to the conclusion that it is only through civil
society that the state can be properly approached and undermined. Consequently, a revolutionary strategy appropriate to the
circumstances of the West would involve nothing other than a
deconstruction of existing arrangements, institutions and associations of civil society, and their replacement with new forms which
would, by definition (or perhaps it should be, by supposition), be
less prone to reification. (For a good and open-minded discussion
of Gramsci's conclusion, see Bellamy 1987.)

In other words, and despite his detour into the politics of civil
society, Gramsci ends up making very familiar claims. Certainly,
Gramsci saw civil society as a problem to the extent that it represents a naturalization of unequal relationships which are
themselves possessed of a tendency towards reification. But, significantly, he also believed that civil society represents a potential site
of reflexivity and, by implication, a chance to deconstruct freely
the existing arrangements in the name of making the world a
better place. This conclusion owes everything to the imaginations
and self-images of modernity. Its connection to Marx and Marxism
(or, the old chestnut of Gramsci-studies, its connection to Lenin
and Leninism) is, relatively speaking, of a purely secondary
importance.

To a large extent, the only modern solution to this exceedingly obvious (dare it be said, boring) set of conclusions was simply to deny the importance of civil society. Whether that solution was itself terribly constructive is, of course, a very different matter. This approach was adopted quite thoroughly by Nicos Poulantzas. He wanted to rescue the Marxist tradition from erroneous concepts.

Poulantzas rejected the concept of civil society largely because it 'refers exactly to the "world of needs" and implies the anthropological perspective of "concrete individual" and "generic man", conceived as subjects of the economy, which is the correlate to the historicist problematic' (Poulantzas 1973: 124). Basically, Poulantzas wanted to understand the operation and relationships of capitalist society, and his objection to civil society was, in the first instance, primarily methodological. He argued that with its assumption of the pre-formed individual possessed of anthropological needs and ontological attributes, civil society works as an ideology which disguises the true nature of the state and, of course, the relationships of economic production. Poulantzas rejected the distinction between civil society and the state and saw simply a universal capitalism.

Indeed, Poulantzas believed that if civil society was rejected, the understanding of capitalism could become scientific. For Poulantzas, there was little or no doubt that, 'in the scientific Marxist problematic, this famous real existence of "individuals–subjects" which is ultimately the basis of the problematic of "civil society" and its separation from the state, cannot be accepted' (Poulantzas 1973: 127). The difficulty for Poulantzas was that the methodological denial of civil society caused his brand of allegedly 'scientific Marxism' to be nothing more than a contemplation of society. Ultimately, the thought of Poulantzas looks rather like a simple reversal of the antinomical thought which Georg Lukács saw as typical of bourgeois order. Poulantzas gained the possibility of intellectual control of civil society (and thus, in his own terms at least, qualified himself for leadership of that society). But the gain was at the cost of a loss of control over the details of social existence (see Lukács 1971: 121).

It should be clear that, in many ways, the imagination of civil society is a thoroughly contradictory affair. Perhaps to a large extent, this is because it is actually very difficult to establish what civil society actually means. Certainly, it refers to the voluntary associations of individuals, and certainly it reflects a concern to identify some possibility of the social construction of society, and of the ability of the bounded community called society to be a milieu of a reproducible symmetric reciprocity. But as soon as these narrative conventions of civil society are either extended or developed in a little more detail, the precise meaning of civil society begins to disappear. It might even be said that civil society is rather like the Cheshire cat; all that remains is its smile.

As such, it is quite easy to identify two dominant modern attitudes towards civil society. They are at the same time linked and yet quite distinct. Firstly, civil society is seen as the milieu of societal self-definition and, by extension, of the possibility of societal transformation through a reflexivity which is frequently collapsed into democracy. Perhaps this perspective has its roots in the apprehension of modernity as something in the making.

Secondly, civil society is seen as an intrinsic component of the existing societal arrangements. This appreciation follows either of two paths. Firstly, civil society is therefore criticized as oppressive. This perspective is, of course, clearly expressed in Marx and Gramsci. Secondly, civil society (as civilization) is accepted as a moral regulation of the interior wild places. This strand is expressed most clearly in the sociological and philosophical narratives in which modernity is apprehended as something grown familiar. Whether the moral regulation was seen as a good or a bad thing was a consequence of foundational assumptions about the ontological and anthropological attributes of man (women were incidental to the story).

Moreover, and in their different ways, Carl Schmitt and Carole Pateman (and, of course, Jurgen Habermas) reveal that the central interpretive issue of civil society, the matter of the construction or identification of homogeneity out of the heterogeneous and strange things of the world, is incoherent. Schmitt concentrates on the logical incoherence of the assumption that all individuals are morally equal but that those within the bounded community (of the nation-state) are more equal than those without. Pateman helps to show that the universality of the figure of man was only possible to the extent that the difference of women was either deliberately ignored or turned into the basis of an exclusion of women from the practices of reflexive self-definition because of their alleged proximity to natural reification. Habermas shows that the standards of universality could only collapse if they moved beyond a highly particular constituency.

Now, the deconstructive implications of Schmitt, Pateman and

Habermas are actually very useful, since they highlight contradictions which were either not recognized or wilfully underplayed in the dominant modern narratives of civil society and civilization. Indeed, in many ways, the imaginations of civil society could only continue so long as there could be no possibility of reflexion directed at civil society. That is, within modernity, there could be no deconstruction of the imagination of civil society since civil society was tantamount to being the sociological distillation of modernity. Any narratives which did suggest any such deconstruction were either marginalized on the basis of their supposed heterogeneity in relation to mainstream tradition (perhaps this explains some of the uneasiness surrounding Schmitt), or identified as self-interested and therefore inadequately objective (a common justification for the rejection of feminist discourse). Either that, or the hints at deconstruction were simply not followed as far as they might well have been.

But as soon as it becomes obvious that civil society is not all that it is meant to be and that, in fact, the imagination is thoroughly contradictory, then civil society itself comes to seem rather less than inevitable. It ceases to be interesting or even useful to treat it as an existential or societal reality. Instead, civil society becomes something to be examined. Once that examination begins, the imagination can no longer be treated as if it is a report of reality (although the history of civil society was one of the forgetting of the important 'as if'). Rather, it has to be treated as a myth constructed in the conditions and circumstances of European modernity. It is a story we live (or lived) by. It might not be the same thing as living itself.

This point was realized quite clearly by Michel Foucault. He saw that as soon as civil society is seen as an item of intellectual interest, then it begins to seem rather less than obvious. Quite the contrary, what begins to come across quite distinctly is the extent to which the imagination is very starkly based on a series of binary oppositions in which one side is labelled 'good' and the other side is labelled 'bad'. In an interview which was carried out towards the end of his life, Foucault offered some thoughts on the Polish Solidarity movement. One of the conventional ways of understanding Solidarity was to see it in terms of a movement of civil society against the state. Foucault suggested that the explanation of Solidarity in these terms seriously over-simplifies complex relationships in Poland. Foucault suggests that 'when one assimilates the powerful social movement that has just traversed that country to a revolt of civil society against the state, one misunderstands the complexity and multiplicity of the confrontations'. After all, 'It is not only against the state-party that the Solidarity movement has had to fight' (Foucault 1988: 167).

This is, of course, an empirical objection to civil society. But Foucault was also prepared to reject civil society on analytical grounds. He did so in a fashion which, firstly, ties civil society to a specific social and historical moment and, secondly, emphasizes the simplistic dualities of the imagination. Foucault says that the idea of civil society as a milieu separate from, and even opposed to, the state emerged in the late eighteenth and early nineteenth centuries. The idea might have been useful at that time as a way of restricting the activities of the state and of ensuring the 'victory' of economic liberalism. But as for the present: 'I'm not at all sure that it [i.e., the notion of civil society] is still operational' (Foucault 1988: 167). This was to emphasize the emergence of civil society out of a very specific set of circumstances, but Foucault was also worried by the formal logic of the idea. He said: 'there is something else that bothers me about this notion: it's ... never exempt from a sort of Manichaeism that afflicts the notion of "state" with a pejorative connotation while idealizing "society" as a good, living, warm whole' (Foucault 1988: 167–8).

The point is, of course, that without the state–society opposition, it would have been quite impossible to have established civil society as the homogeneous and defining terrain of achieved human being. Foucault's empirical and formal rejections of the continued usefulness of civil society certainly hit the mark. But the imagination of civil society as good and reciprocal and intrinsically democratic goes much deeper into the status of the modern than Foucault seems to think. The imagination was not simply about a series of formal divides and Manichaen evaluations. It was also about what it means to be a modern individual living in the modern world.

Civil society was a means by which the existential and interpretive flux and intrinsic strangeness of modernity could be explained and controlled. Quite simply, it could explain, as safe and pleasant, normal and indeed natural, a symmetric reciprocity between people who knew nothing whatsoever about each other, and who probably cared about each other rather less. Civil society tied these disconnected strangers into communities of mutual responsibility which were expressed in mutual connections of trust, consideration and, for that matter, embarrassment. It did not really matter if the reciprocity was as empty as the hat-doffing described by Jean-Paul Sartre in *Nausea* just so long as individuals continued to prove themselves to be tied to each other as morally identical citizens of the community. Indeed, in the work of Norbert Elias, the very emptiness and formality of civilization is taken as an indication of the tightening of reciprocity.

Moreover, the marks of a civil condition were taken to be products of the ability of society to polish and refine the raw stuff handed over to it by nature. Consequently, and with its assumption of the pre-formed individual, civil society came to mean much the same as the ability of man to achieve his own society and to define for himself his own existence. The ever-widening distance between this bounded community and the 'out there' of nature was seen as nothing other than a guarantee that the reflexive defining ability of man could be reproduced. Reproduced, that is, just so long as the beast within could be kept firmly under lock and key, just so long as the deliberately silenced groups did not answer back.

However, it is very significant that it is now possible to ask questions of, and about, civil society. In many ways, an awareness of the mythication of civil society and a recognition of the logical contradictions, if not incoherence, of the imagination, means that it is not possible to treat civil society in good faith as if it actually is what it claims to be: a direct and objective report of reality. Perhaps it has become inappropriate to talk any longer about the possibility of civil society.

Indeed, I have, in some ways, signalled nothing other than the impossibility of civil society. Now, that might represent something of a liberation from the frequently oppressive, or at least unpleasant, interpretations of homogeneous community and identity which were so important in the conditions of modernity. However, it is not too clever, nor indeed very useful, to simply destroy the time-honoured narratives of civil society and replace them with nothing (a nothing which, following Foucault, could be justified, however, because it evidently reflects the unsayability of freedom). The challenge of accounting for the reciprocity and order of strangers remains.

Chapter 7

The aesthetics

Despite the logical incoherence that Carl Schmitt and Carole Pateman emphasized in their different ways, it nevertheless remains the case that the narrative of civil society was actually quite clear. Perhaps this is almost completely attributable to how the imagination was predicated on a more or less simple, and a more or less consistent, opposition between the wild, on the one hand, and the milieu of civil society itself, on the other hand. In many ways, it is quite easy to see the same problems and solutions of the construction of a meaningful order of things running from Locke and Hobbes, through the philosophers of the Scottish Enlightenment, and into the ostensibly objective foundations of the modern sociological discourses.

Moreover, it can be suggested quite reasonably that the theme of the opposition between the wild and the societal was so popular and, for that matter, held to be so compelling precisely because it reconciled so many of the problems and possibilities associated with the deconstruction of the natural artifice. Indeed, the theme played no insignificant part in the consolidation of the mythical second nature of society. It might even be said that civil society can be read as both the condition of possibility and the product of continuing modernity.

Yet, and as I hope to have shown with the help of the likes of Schmitt and Pateman, civil society was not all that it was said to be. In particular, civil society not only collapsed in the face of the incoherence of the social relationships and institutions associated with its homogeneity and universality, it also collapsed because of the implications and consequences of its antinomies. That is, it is possible to see in the imagination of civil society a number of propositions and themes which are in themselves quite reasonable, and yet deeply inconsistent when put together. Two such anti-nomical couplets come to mind immediately:

1.1 Civil society is that which is known. It is largely synonymous with reflexivity, the free associations of individuals, and social self-definition.
1.2 Civil society is that which is unknown. As soon as something definite is said about civil society, the meanings of voluntary association, self-definition and so forth are fixed. Consequent-ly, as soon as civil society is known, it is reified.
2.1 Civil society is a milieu of security and certainty (or, at least, of a decrease of uncertainty) thanks to the promotion and ident-ification of a bounded community of symmetric reciprocity.
2.2 Civil society is a milieu of fear, anxiety and disgust thanks to the domestication of a wild which wills to escape societal boundaries.

The fact that within the modern imagination of civil society the antinomies were simply not recognized, or, if they were, pushed to one side without too much difficulty, can be seen as an indication of what can happen to the logical construction of an order of things when it comes against the images and interests of mythication.

I have been concerned to emphasize the absolutely central connection between civil society and moral order. Indeed, it is quite impossible to appreciate the complexity and subtlety of civil society if a great deal of attention is not paid to how it was taken to involve the imposition or inculcation of moral regulation in the relationships between the individual subjects of society (otherwise known as the citizens of civil society). Certainly, that kind of perspective can help to reveal a number of the implicit assump-tions which were simply taken for granted by modern sociology. But a consideration of the antinomies reveals that civil society was about something more than morality. Civil society was not simply imagined to be a force of the moral good.

Through the antinomies, it is possible to see fairly clearly that civil society was imagined as a force of the good in quite another sense. It was also a force of the aesthetically good. Put another way, the symmetry of civil society did not solely refer to the relationships between individuals. It also referred to the aesthetic quality of those relationships. This aesthetic dimension went beyond the relatively simple procedures of classification of the pathetic fallacy in which the emotions or qualities which societal life denied were projected on to things defined as natural. In the imagination of civil society, there was an implicit collapse of the morally good into the aesthetically beautiful.

One very useful meaning of the beautiful was outlined by Immanuel Kant in his *Critique of the Faculty of Judgment*. Basically, Kant suggests that beauty is not a quality that a thing possesses in itself, but rather beauty is a quality which is invested in the thing in its perception. That is, we make something beautiful through disinterested reflection on it. The disinterested reflection is the basis of aesthetic judgement and, therefore, of taste. As Kant put it: 'Taste is the faculty of judging an object or a way of representing it by an entirely disinterested satisfaction or dissatisfaction. The object of such satisfaction is called *beautiful*' (Kant 1988: 357). It is beautiful since a sense of pleasure arises from the extent to which the object fits the capacities of the subject to perceive it. To quote Kant once again, the aesthetic judgement of an object 'has to do with no concept of the character and internal or external possibility of the object through this or that cause'. Rather, Kant continues, the judgement 'has to do with', 'the relation of the representative powers to one another so far as they are determined by a representation' (Kant 1988: 365). So, beauty is a subjective judgement which is stimulated by the cognitive ability to represent an object. Beauty is not directly caused by the object. But the emphasis on subjective judgement does not mean that one person's standard of beauty is possibly another person's standard of the ugly.

For Kant, any judgement of the beautiful is both universally and subjectively valid. Here, Kant's comments on the universality of aesthetic judgement directly parallel his position on the universality of moral judgement. It is one of the main precepts of the categorical imperative that the individual should only will for all others what he would will for himself. Similarly, when the individual passes a subjective aesthetic judgement of an object, he is making a judgement of the object which must be accepted by all other judging subjects. Kant's concern with the subjective act of perception did not mean that his aesthetic theories collapsed into an uncontrollable subjectivism as it might have done had he been a straightforward empiricist.

Kant directly relates aesthetic judgement to the ability of the individual to, firstly, subjectively and self-sufficiently define the meaning of things and, secondly, reciprocally establish that self-definition as acceptable for all others. Thirdly, Kant tries to see through the operation of procedures like that represented in the pathetic fallacy. He manages to make the point that objects only possess some qualities and not others because of the judgements which are made of them, and the meanings which are constructed around them. Kant's approach implies the point that any statement of ostensibly innate qualities is best understood as a statement which attempts to construct a universal order of things and thus avoid the possibility of absolute heterogeneity. Kant says:

> It would be laughable if a man who fancied his own taste thought to justify himself by saying, 'This object (the house we see, the coat that person wears, the concert we hear, the poem submitted to our judgment) is beautiful *for me*'. For he must not call it beautiful if it pleases only him ... he judges not merely for himself, but for everyone, and speaks of beauty as if it were a property of things. Hence he says, 'The *thing* is beautiful', and he does not just count on the agreement of others with this his judgment of satisfaction because he has found this agreement several times before; rather he *demands* it of them.
>
> (Kant 1988: 358)

Interestingly, Kant simply presupposes a knowledge on the part of the individual of all previous agreements over the beauty of an object. Perhaps more importantly, he assumes that the judging individual exists in a community in which agreement is possible.

On the basis of his analysis, Kant felt able to express the nature of the beautiful in four propositions. He said that, firstly, the beautiful is that which pleases immediately, as a reflective intuition. Secondly, Kant said that the beautiful 'pleases apart from any interest'. Thirdly, it represents the freedom of the imagination to judge. Fourthly, 'The subjective principle in judging the beautiful is represented as universal (i.e., as valid for every man), though not knowable through any universal concept' (Kant 1988: 386).

Now, Kant was in no doubt that these aesthetic questions were also of deep moral significance. After all, 'Now I say the beautiful is the symbol of the morally good, and that it is only in this respect ... that it gives pleasure with a claim for the agreement of everyone else' (Kant 1988: 385–6). It is worth taking up Kant's technical use of the word 'symbol' as meaning an indirect presentation and an analogy. Through Kant's comment, the suggestion can be made that the universal and yet subjective definition of the beautiful can be read also as a symbol of the universal and yet subjective definition of moral restraint and constraint. Or, put another way, and admittedly moving way beyond Kant's own position, the aesthetics of the beautiful can be read as a symbol of the imagination of civil society.

Indeed, it is quite clear that Kant's theses on aesthetic judgement are quite impossible without some presupposition of a bounded society. Firstly, the disinterested treatment of things, which is so important in aesthetic judgement, is impossible without some kind of distanciation between the defining subject and the defined object. In other words, there has to be some kind of imagined boundary between the subject and the object. Otherwise, if there was no distanciation, the defining subject would not be able to treat anything disinterestedly since it would impinge too much on him. Secondly, the argument that, in subjectively defining beauty, the individual is also defining beauty for all others presupposes some kind of community with effective channels of communication in which subjective judgements, individual acts of definition, can be known and can be made known to others. Thirdly, Kant makes a fairly ambivalent comment about the individual knowing about previous agreements over definition of the beautiful; this presupposes some kind of communal memory which would be impossible if the production and reproduction of the community was not expressed and confirmed in some kind of institutional arrangements or societal practices and rituals (see Connerton 1989).

In many ways, then, Kant's comments on the beautiful can indeed be interpreted as a symbol of the imagination of civil society. Like Thomas Hobbes, Kant seems to be fundamentally worried about how it is possible to construct a universal order of things out of a series of basically subjective judgements. The problem for both of them can be read in terms of the difficulty of explaining how civil society can be homogeneously self-defining when the act of definition is itself heterogeneous and individual. Hobbes got around this problem by placing all his hopes in the Leviathan, which was a universal epistemological legislator every bit as much as it was a universal political legislator. In many ways, Kant was rather more devious. He universalized and rendered homogeneous the heterogeneity of particular judgements through an anthropological ontology which would mean that all individuals would perceive things in terms of the same categories of knowledge. But it would rather seem possible to propose that

Kant, without quite admitting it, linked that ontological position to the imagination of a bounded community of societal self-definition.

In these terms, it can be suggested that civil society was imagined as that which allowed things to be known as objects 'out there'. Civil society was the category in terms of which the aesthetic meaning of the thing could be judged. In other words, civil society was itself the standard and the condition of possibility of the beautiful. Civil society actually was the beautiful. Indeed, this connection is not entirely absent from Agnes Heller's term 'symmetric reciprocity', which I have been using throughout this essay. Like many, if not all, sociological categories, the phrase involves the representation of an order of things which can be construed to be beautiful in the Kantian sense. Modern sociology renders relationships beautiful in this way precisely because it deals with them from an allegedly disinterested position. Moreover, the purpose of sociology was conventionally to construct the categories through which the relationships could be represented with clarity in their entirety.

Civil society was the milieu which guaranteed that a meaningful order could be constructed out of the things of the world, an order which was in principle perfectly clear to perception because it perfectly matched the subjective ability to pass defining judgements. Those places which escaped firm definition were, instead, equated with the milieu of strangers. It can be proposed that in so far as there is a direct connection between civil society and the beautiful, so there is a direct connection between the milieu of strangers and the sublime. In other words, the aesthetic delight of civil society was in no small part enhanced by the aesthetic fear and terror occasioned by strangers.

I have stressed throughout this discussion that the presence of strangers gives rise to an interpretive difficulty which cannot possibly be overcome through the natural artifice. The point is, of course, that the natural artifice derives legitimacy and credibility from its evident immutability and existence since time-immemorial. The presence of strangers makes assumptions of immutability quite redundant because the coming and staying of strangers is an intrinsically historical event. Civil society was an imagination which could make sense of the presence of strangers and, more importantly, elevate it into something approaching a precondition for morality, solidarity and reciprocity in society. In terms of its internal operation, civil society made the milieu of the strangers small by making it regular; it transformed quantity into a quality. But the strangers outside of the boundaries of civil society (the strangers who had to be made to stay outside in order to make the meanings of inclusion known precisely through their exclusion) were thereby continually overwhelming. When they were not ordered as orderly members of society, the strangers were instead terrifyingly sublime. (For a general discussion of the aesthetics of the sublime, see Monk 1960. For a discussion on the sublime in contemporary social theory, a discussion which grinds some very specific axes indeed, see Appignanesi 1989.)

According to Kant, there is a very real formal difference between the beautiful and the sublime. He writes that the beautiful 'is connected with the form of the object, which consists in having [definite] boundaries' (Kant 1988: 376). In these terms, civil society is the precondition and the knowledge of the beautiful because one of its most basic concerns is the identification of things with definite boundaries. But the sublime is extremely different: 'The sublime, on the other hand, is to be found in a formless object, so far as in it or by occasion of it *boundlessness* is represented while yet its totality is also present to thought' (Kant 1988: 376). This presence in thought which Kant talks about refers to his assumption of the operation of Ideas in Reason; they are so called precisely because they are ideas which cannot possibly be derived from experience. We cannot experience the complete milieu of strangers, but we can discuss it; consequently, there must be some idea of that milieu which operates on the basis of cognitive reason. So, while the totality and the bounds of the milieu of strangers can be represented as an Idea in Reason, the point is that the objective milieu of strangers is boundless. It goes beyond all faculties which might make it open to perception. Put more simply, the milieu of strangers is formless; we cannot perceive it. It is sublime.

Kant suggests that it is possible to divide the sublime into two analytic dimensions. Firstly, he identifies the mathematical sublime, which is a product of the enormity of an object. As Kant put it, the mathematical sublime 'is a magnitude which is like itself alone ... *The sublime is that in comparison with which everything else is small*' (Kant 1988: 377). Secondly, Kant talks about the dynamical sublime, which is represented in might. In particular, Kant linked this dynamical sublime to nature (Kant 1988: 378–9).

There are clear similarities between Kant's interpretation of the sublime and the problem of strangers, which was tackled, and to some considerable extent successfully overcome, by the imagination of civil society. There would rather seem to be a set of common interpretive problems and solutions which can also be found in the work of Thomas Hobbes in particular, but also quite noticeably in the sociological discourses which upheld the status of civilization as moral regulation. There is a more or less hidden equation of the 'out there' beyond the societal boundaries with qualities which are not very different from those which Kant (subsequently to Hobbes but rather before the development of an explicit sociology) associated with the sublime. More obviously, Sigmund Freud and Emile Durkheim, in different ways, and with differing degrees of enthusiasm, were both prepared to concede that the costs of civilization were worth paying if it meant that some form, some order, could be imposed on the otherwise massive and mighty flux of the strangers. For them, and perhaps indeed for all the strands of the modern sociological discourse, civilization was nothing other than the form which brought some meaning to the content of social relationships.

In other words, sociology was working in terms of the aesthetic assumption that the milieu of strangers is sublime and, therefore, an otherness to the beauty of civil society and civilization. But sociology also clung to the idea that despite the formlessness of the milieu of strangers, it was still possible to say something definite about it (notably, that it was a wild state of nature). The totality of that other milieu could indeed be represented in thought. As such, the milieu of strangers could be universally known as sublime. Instead of epistemological and ontological disorder, the very formlessness of the wild 'out there' offered the possibility of a restatement of the homogeneity and universality of society (the 'in here').

The boundlessness of the milieu of strangers (that is, its sublimity) did not give rise to the overwhelming presence of a multiplication of particularity outside of the bounded community of civil society. The ability to say what the world out there was like, even if that world was said to be highly particular and heterogeneous, meant that it was also possible to imagine a universal meaning and nature of that extra-societal milieu. The particular itself became aesthetically universal; as such, it became a problem which threatened to destroy societal universality, not simply through seepage but rather through its status as a parallel world.

The very ability to conceive of the totality of the milieu of strangers led to the juxtaposition of one homogeneous universal with another, with the societal being labelled morally and aesthetically good.

A similar conclusion might also be found in Kant. He too denied that the boundlessness of the sublime meant that it confronted each individual as an overwhelming object, to which each responded in his own particular way. Kant admitted that the sublime goes beyond our sensual ability to perceive it, but he argued that the very fact that we can still talk about the sublime means that we are still able to establish some universal meaning of it. What sociology achieved as a social and historical discourse, Kant said could be achieved by the individual subject who was also a universal subject. Where sensual capacities failed to create order and meaning, Ideas in Reason quickly stepped in.

There is a distinct hint that Kant was attempting to dig himself out of an undesirable hole of his own making when he said of the sublime:

> in the immensity of nature and in the insufficiency of our faculties to adapt a standard proportionate to the aesthetical estimation of the magnitude of its realm, we find our own limitation. In our rational faculty, however, we find at the same time a different, nonsensuous standard which has that infinity itself as the unit in comparison with which everything in nature is small; thus in our mind we find a superiority to nature even in its immensity.

> (Kant 1988: 379)

The result of the sensual inability to grasp the sublime is, then, a reconstruction of the universal ability of the individual subject to know. The very fact that the individual subject can experience something as sublime and boundless proves that the individual can impose a totality on the order of things. The individual subject is nothing other than a universal legislator.

As such, the thing itself is not sublime; rather, it is the subjective perception of the thing which is the basis of its boundlessness. Kant turns the threats to societal self-sufficiency and self-definition into the most excellent proofs of self-sufficiency and self-definition. The very ability to know through an Idea in Reason that the sublime is boundless means not the particularity of humanity, but instead its universality. 'Thus humanity in our own person remains unhumiliated, though as mortal creatures we have to submit to the dominion of nature' (Kant 1988: 379). While humans wither and die, humanity goes on.

But behind the confident facade of Kant's argument, there was undoubtedly a degree of doubt. Kant stared the modern horrors of chaos and epistemological uncertainty firmly in the face. He went to the very edges of modernity, and perhaps quite understandably he very quickly ran back to the middle. It is this tension between wanting to know and wanting to be certain that makes Kant's work so rich and wonderful. Indeed, there are hints in the *Critique of the Faculty of Judgment* that Kant was quite aware that the confidence he placed in the universalizing capabilities of Ideas in Reason might only be an attempt to work a way around the basic particularity of the experienced world. Kant seems to have been aware that all the effort to establish the universality of reason and humanity was essentially an aesthetic and moral act of definition which denied the acceptability and viability of certain other defining acts of judgement. In other words, Kant seems to have known that his universalizing philosophical project could only succeed if it assumed a more fundamental order of things somewhere behind the appearances of things, and if it disallowed some judgements as illicit.

For example, Kant was prepared to admit that the ostensibly universal judgements of beauty might not be all they seemed. He wrote: 'The judgment of taste itself does not *postulate* the agreement of everyone ... it only *imputes* this agreement to everyone, as a case of the rule in respect of which it expects not confirmation by concepts but assent from others' (Kant 1988: 361). In other words, Kant is here approaching a sociological conclusion that the universality of judgements is only possible in so far as competing voices, competing definitions, are ignored or disqualified on the grounds that they are not expected. As such, the expectation of 'confirmation by concepts' could be understood as nothing other than a legitimating and seemingly incontrovertible gloss on a basically tawdry social struggle over meaning.

Indeed, Kant was even prepared to acknowledge the possibility that it is impossible to universalize subjective definitions of beauty. Kant wrote that the individual subject might assume the universality of judgements simply because he assumes that what holds good for himself also holds good for everyone: 'this is all on which he promises himself the agreement of everyone – a claim which would be justified under these conditions if only he did not often make mistakes, and lay down erroneous judgments of taste' (Kant 1988: 361).

Kant was, then, driven by his desire to know the conclusion that it is impossible to be certain. He ended up looking at either an epistemological abyss in which all standards of universality would collapse into the particularity of subjective judgements, or at a field of social relationships in which universality would simply be a product of the forced silencing of particularity. There is more than a hint of desperation to Kant's attempt to work a way around this especially tricky dilemma. Kant could ultimately establish the place of universality, and of the certainty that judgements would be symmetric and homogeneous, only by asserting the significance of a realm of reason which was beyond societal interference. He was aware that criteria of universality could be overwhelmed by the particularity of subjective acts of definition, and so he basically slipped a ghost into the machine which promised to create some essential order out of the muddle of appearances. This is, of course, a characteristically modern tactic.

Kant looked for an escape route from the logic of his analysis of the sublime and the beautiful. But Edmund Burke, who had reflected on the sublime before Kant, did not turn away from the epistemological and ontological difficulties which were posed by boundlessness. As such, Burke provides a way of understanding how and why the ostensible universality of civil society ultimately collapsed in the face of particularity. While Kant's version of the sublime can reveal the aesthetic possibility of civil society, Burke's far more radical version can reveal the aesthetic impossibility of civil society. There is a basic and very important difference between Kant and Burke on the sublime. Whereas Kant denied that things are sublime in themselves, independent of the subjective act of judgement (and used this point as the foundation of a chance of the construction of a meaningful order of things), Burke was indeed of the opinion that it is the thing itself which is sublime.

Burke argued that the sublime is a quality of an object which causes a collapse of all rational abilities to come to terms with it. (Instead, the argument seems to involve an implication that the thing can only be known through the emotional vestiges of the wild.) The sublime also prejudices all stable identities by anticipating them, and by undermining any conception of their fixity. Burke wrote of the sublime that 'the mind is so entirely filled with its object, that it cannot entertain any other, nor by consequence reason on that object which employs it'. Burke continued: 'Hence arises the great power of the sublime, that far from being produced by them, it anticipates our reasonings, and hurries us on by an irresistible force' (Burke 1990: 53).

So, for Burke, it is the enormity of the thing itself which is the origin of the sublime. Sublimity is attributable to our inability to apprehend an object and, thus, the terror it stimulates. The terror works at a number of levels. Most obviously, it is an ontological terror because while man is meant to be the self-sufficient maker of his own being in the world, he becomes aware of nothing so much as the self-sufficiency of a multitude of other things. Secondly, the terror is epistemological. Burke did not take the path that Kant later followed, a path which restored the epistemological sovereignty of man in the universe; instead, Burke simply knew the ability of things to escape the rigid order which allegedly and putatively contained them in their entirety. Thirdly, the terror is existential because the sublime confronts man, not with his self-sufficiency and his ability to define, but rather with a definition of what it is to be human. In these terms, to be human is to be frightened.

However, it is important to note that when he talks about the terror associated with the sublime, Burke is using the word 'terror' in a quite specific way. The sublime does not require that the individual is actually in a condition of absolute fear, but, rather, that the individual has the idea of being in such a state. As such, the sublime is an aesthetic matter because it is a question of the emotional responses stimulated by an object. If objects cause simple and absolute terror, 'they are simply painful', but 'they are delightful when we have an idea of pain and danger, without being actually in such circumstances ... Whatever excites this delight, I call *sublime*' (Burke 1990: 47). In other words, it is possible to see one more expression of the problem of boundary drawing.

Arguably, this set of aesthetic worries can be applied with relative ease to the social, historical and cultural problem of the construction of a meaningful order of things out of the milieu of strangers. From the point of view of looking out from civil society, the milieu of strangers is apprehended as content without form. And, precisely because it is formless, it is able to overflow the societal ability to understand it. Indeed, a Burkean argument would suggest that, from the societal perspective, there is actually no possibility of meaningfully understanding the milieu of strangers because there cannot possibly be any map to make it meaningful. As such, the strangers inspire only the idea of terror.

But the terror does not lead to societal neurosis nor, indeed, to a freezing in the face of fear. Quite the contrary. Through Burke, it might be suggested that the milieu of strangers causes delight. After all, it is precisely this other of civil society which makes civilization and moral regulation so compelling in the first place. Basically, it can be proposed that the delight in the face of terror can be read as a representation of a condition in which the object of terror is distant. Consequently, the subjects of civil society do not know terror itself, but instead the rather delightful idea of terror: 'When danger or pain press too nearly, they are incapable of giving any delight, and are simply terrible; but at certain distances, and with certain modifications, they may be, and they are delightful, as we every day experience' (Burke 1990: 36–7). The milieu of strangers might inspire terror, but it is not thereby terrible. It is not terrible because, thanks to the boundary-drawing exercises of civil society, it is distinct from us, and, moreover, through the idea of terror stimulated by the other, we know who and what we are.

Continuing this interpretation of civil society in terms of an interpretation of themes from Burke, it can be proposed that the effect of the distance is such that it leads to a tightening of the bonds of symmetric reciprocity. Since, for Burke, terror is only known at a distance, it causes a certain delight which itself involves the generation of a feeling of sympathy with the distress and suffering of others. In other words, Burke saw the reciprocity of societal relationships as primarily aesthetic, but moral as well. He was indicating the double goodness of the pity which so infuriated Friedrich Nietzsche.

Burke was in no doubt that 'we have a degree of delight, and that no small one, in the real misfortunes and pains of others' (Burke 1990: 42). He suggested that when we read of the fall of great empires of monarchs, for example, we are terrified and yet delighted at the same time. We pity and yet avidly wish to know more of the disaster. This combination of responses is due to a distance which inspires sympathy: 'for terror is a passion which always produces delight when it does not press too close, and pity is a passion accompanied with pleasure, because it arises from love and social affection' (Burke 1990: 42). Burke argues quite strongly that the delight in a tragedy is proportionately linked to the amount of sympathy felt for the victims of the tragedy. As such, and to give an obvious example, the widespread popular delight which used to be caused by public hangings can be interpreted as a source of great sympathy with the murderer who had not been adequately pulled within the boundaries of civilization. Where sympathy is most needed, there also is the most delight.

In other words, the sublimity of the 'out there' strengthens and justifies symmetric reciprocity by linking it with a sympathy which seems to be instinctive. Burke wrote:

> there is no spectacle we so eagerly pursue, as that of some uncommon and grievous calamity; so that whether the misfortune is before our eyes, or whether they are turned back to it in history, it always touches with delight. This is not an unmixed delight, but blended with no small uneasiness. The delight we have in such things, hinders us from shunning scenes of misery; and the pain we feel, prompts us to relieve ourselves in relieving those who suffer; and all this antecedent to any reasoning, by an instinct that works us to its own purposes, without our concurrence.
>
> (Burke 1990: 43)

There is yet more to societal reciprocity than this sympathy. Burke argues that 'one of the strongest links of society' is imitation (Burke 1990: 45). But imitation is due to affection rather than jealousy. He argues that whereas through sympathy the individual is concerned with what others feel, through affection the individual becomes concerned with what others do. Indeed, 'It is by imitation far more than by precept that we learn every thing; and what we learn thus we acquire not only more effectually, but more pleasantly' (Burke 1990: 45). Consequently, imitation is the most pleasurable and the most profound form of reciprocity: 'it is a species of mutual compliance which all men yield to each other, without constraint to themselves, and which is extremely flattering to all' (Burke 1990: 45).

In many ways, Burke sees imitation as a means by which humans can practise the modern ability to be self-defining and, moreover, the ability to construct a self-sufficient society. The links of imitation were enhanced yet further by ambition. The point, for Burke, was that while imitation can be the basis of society, it cannot be the basis of a process of civilization. This is where jealousy does become important. After all, if every individual simply copies every other individual, 'there never could be any improvement amongst them' (Burke 1990: 46). As such, all individuals attempt to outdo others in some activity which is held to be valuable. In particular, this ambition often takes the form of attempts to encounter the sublime. The 'swelling and triumph' which ambition nourishes 'is never more perceived, nor operates with more force, than when without danger we are conversant with terrible objects, the mind always claiming to itself some part of the dignity and importance of the things which it contemplates' (Burke 1990: 46).

Burke and Kant provided aesthetic theories which bear direct and sustained comparison with the narrative procedures and evaluations of the imagination of civil society. Not least, the analysis of the sublime, like the imagination of civil society, shares a concern to understand the basis on which some things are evaluated as good, and some evaluated as bad. They share the conclusion that the good is that which can be accommodated within an order of things; and the bad is that which either overflows classification or becomes ambivalent in relation to those ways of making sense of the world which either cannot or do not resort to the natural artifice. Secondly, the imagination of civil society and the narrative of the sublime are both concerned to tackle the problems of homogeneity and heterogeneity. The problems of the sublime and civil society are similarly concerned to identify procedures by which the universal (that is, the homogeneity of either symmetric reciprocity or aesthetic experience) can subsume the particular (that is, the heterogeneity of strangers and of reaction to the formless sublime).

It is precisely at this point, and thanks to the investigation of the sublime, that it is possible to appreciate why the imagination of civil society was ultimately incoherent. Basically, the problem was very simple. Civil society was the standard and the milieu of universality, but it could only assimilate or annihilate the terror of the strangers, it could only build on the sublime as a basis for sympathy, to the extent that it spoke the meaning and the truth of its universality. The universality of civil society had to be expressed (or, at the very least, some means had to be developed and adopted by which competing definitions of the meaning could be pulled together). But precisely in the moment of the statement, the universality of civil society collapsed into particularity.

The logical implication of civil society, as for the sublime, is not the intended subsumption of particularity by universality. Rather, the implication is the subsumption of universality by particularity and, thereafter, the continuous subsumption of one particular by another. To put the matter into somewhat more concrete terms: the imagination of a single internally homogeneous society was impossible because any definition of homogeneity came from a specific societal space. Consequently, it was a particular definition. That is, of course, more or less exactly the kind of point that Carole Pateman would wish to stress.

Civil society was ultimately quite undone by its own contradictions and Manichaen simplifications. On the one hand, the emphasis on universality and homogeneity led to the imaginative, and for that matter, frequently the practical expansion of bounded communities. Increasingly, the strangeness of the outsiders was defined as irrelevant, trivial in relation to the universality underneath, or insignificant in the face of their destruction. Through any one of these measures, or a mixture of them, the standard of universality and the demand for homogeneity was imposed over ever-greater areas and encompassed ever more social relationships. That is, universality led to the massification of the community and, indeed occasionally, to its expansion even beyond the boundaries of the nation-state. This process was, of course, to a considerable extent, facilitated and generated by communication technologies. It reached something of a highpoint with the McLuhanesque talk of the global village.

However, and on the other hand, the logic of civil society was pushing in a very different direction indeed. While the commitment to universality implied the expansion of the community and increasing massification, the need to define the meaning of universality increasingly meant the subsumption of the universal by the particular. The boundaries of the community were prone to contraction as each definition of the meaning of universality was made from the point of view of a particular societal group (or a particular nation-state). As such, groups or communities which had previously taken their inclusion within the boundaries for granted deliberately excluded themselves (or were deliberately excluded by others) as soon as the meaning of universality was spoken and revealed to be highly exclusive. Instead, the societal groups which had been thus marginalized emphasized their own particular meanings of universality, or they were simply annihilated.

The playing out of the antinomies of civil society involved nothing other than a simultaneous playing out and exhaustion of the myths of modernity. From being a condition of possibility and a guarantee of societal self-definition, civil society led to the emergence of two more or less irreconcilable modes of definition. One form of definition gelled around participation in massified social networks which operated over and above individuals. The second form of definition gelled around participation in relatively small-scale communities which allowed no place whatsoever for those defined as outsiders. Morally, the situation implied the involvement of the individual in ever-larger networks of symmetric reciprocity, and yet also the implication of the individual in relatively restricted communities for which those outside are simply foes. Aesthetically, the situation implied a simultaneous deepening of the gulf between the sublime and the beautiful milieu of symmetric reciprocity, and also an ever-increasing nearness to the sublime milieu of the strangers. Tolerance and ignorance, and absolute terror and sheer delight, seem to go hand in hand after the realization of the incoherence of civil society.

Michel Maffesoli has tried very hard to capture this paradoxical situation. He has gone so far as to suggest that civil society is a 'worn out' idea from nineteenth century political philosophy. Perhaps the rhetoric rather gets the upper hand over the analysis, but Maffesoli suggests that the idea of civil society only continues to be seen as useful because, without it, 'Much of the intelligentsia seems unable to understand the qualitative changes taking place within society'. In other words, civil society provides easy answers. Maffesoli goes on to suggest that the use of civil society, 'has the double advantage of avoiding analysis and of covering up the split running through the social body' (Maffesoli 1990: 89). Maffesoli sees contemporary social relationships in a radically different way. He is certainly aware of the simultaneity of pressures towards enlargement and contraction. He writes: 'within massification, processes of condensation are constantly occurring through which more or less ephemeral tribal groupings are organized'. Maffesoli explains that these 'tribal groupings ... cohere on the basis of their own minor values, and ... attract and collide with each other in an endless dance, forming themselves into a constellation whose vague boundaries are perfectly fluid. This is the characteristic of postmodern society' (Maffesoli 1991: 12).

Maffesoli is suggesting that there is certainly a process of massification but that, beside that trend, something very different is taking place. Firstly, the clear boundaries which were established through the projects of modernity have become extremely contingent. Secondly, Maffesoli is proposing that post-modern societies (I wonder about the applicability of the word society, given that a society is precisely the kind of fixed bounded community which Maffesoli stresses is now fluid) are characterized by a multiplicity of particularity and by an absence of any and all standards of the universal. That is, post-modern societies are thoroughly heterogeneous and not at all homogeneous. Thirdly, Maffesoli stresses that the assumption of fixed identities has collapsed in the face of the emergence of thoroughly contingent and temporary 'tribal groupings'. In many ways, Maffesoli seems to paint a picture of ceaseless and remorseless self-definition, but of an utter absence of reifications and immutable definitions against which it is possible to be defining.

When Maffesoli talks about tribes and neo-tribalism, he is not at all trying to indicate that the post-modern condition is essentially atavistic. Rather, he is trying to grasp a rather different kind of transformation: 'In fact, contrary to the stability induced by classic tribalism, neo-tribalism is characterized by fluidity, by punctuated gathering and scattering' (Maffesoli 1988: 148). Maffesoli equates neo-tribalism with a 'world of incessant movement'. That is, and to put words into his mouth, Maffesoli equates neo-tribalism with the sublime flux of the milieu of a ceaseless strangeness.

In modern societies, the identity of individuality is constructed in and through the function which the individual performs. But such a close connection between the identity of the function and the identity of the individual means two things for Maffesoli. Firstly, the individual is de-individualized as identity collapses into function (a possibility which had worried Emile Durkheim). Secondly, the function becomes the location of individuality and, consequently, a role (Maffesoli 1988). It is this combination of de-individualization and of role that the concept of neo-tribalism attempts to grasp. It implies a quite fundamental redefinition of the terms of social inquiry. In particular, Maffesoli sometimes stops talking about society and the social and instead occasionally talks about sociality.

The redefinition is indicative of basic changes. According to Maffesoli, 'The characteristics of the social are that the individual can have a *function* in the society, and also function within a party, an association, or a stable group'. However, and by contrast: 'The characteristics of the sociality are that the person (persona), plays *roles* within his professional activities, nurturing the various tribes in which he participates' (Maffesoli 1988: 148). Consequently, the meanings of individuality and reciprocity are reduced to the transient appearances of 'the diverse games of the *theatrum mundi*'. Maffesoli continues to draw out the implication of this situation which can be read as one more indication of the collapse of societal universality and homogeneity into the particularity and heterogeneity of sociality. He writes that the emphasis on doing rather than being involves 'the importance of appearance ... [T]he esthetic is a means of testing, of feeling in common. It is also a means of recognition'. He continues: 'The theatrical founds and comforts the community. The cult of the body and games of show are meaningful only because they are part of a vast scene in which everyone is at once both actor and spectator' (Maffesoli 1988: 148).

The consequence is an ethics of aesthetics. Of course, in its orthodox sense, ethics is concerned with the definite standards of moral conduct and judgement which apply to all relevant subjects, or with the system of morals which is universal to a group or community. In other words, ethics, conventionally understood, is concerned with those rules and foundations which make sustained communal life possible. But, according to Maffesoli, this status of ethics is no longer tenable. Instead, he proposes that universal ethics has collapsed in the face of particular neo-tribalist moralities. The basis of ethical judgement has been relocated from epistemological or ontological foundations to the entirely transient question of how the individual constructs personal moral ties (Maffesoli 1991).

It would be very easy for such an argument to lead to disquiet, and to a more or less implicit assertion that since universal ethics are no longer tenable, symmetric reciprocity and moral regulation are no longer tenable either. Maffesoli manages to avoid such nihilism, but perhaps only thanks to a sleight of hand. The thrust of his thesis is one of the impossibility of a sustained imagination of a bounded community of self-definition called civil society. But he can only make the case for the continuation of symmetric reciprocity thanks to a slipping in of an assumed society. In a distinctly Durkheimian formulation, Maffesoli argues that neo-tribalist affiliation, which is of course purely aesthetic, 'is a question of a socialization which might be specific but which nevertheless presents the characteristics of all socialization: integration into the collectivity and the transcendence of the individual' (Maffesoli 1991: 19). The memory of Emile Durkheim is made yet greater when Maffesoli continues to say of neo-tribalism that 'the accent is placed more on collective sensation than on a common rational project. But the result is no different: participation in the general body of society' (Maffesoli 1991: 19).

It would rather seem to be the case that, in the final analysis, Maffesoli's attempt to think through some of the implications of the redundancy of civil society only flatters to deceive. Certainly, Maffesoli makes a series of useful points when he reflects on the ethics of aesthetics and the emergence of neo-tribalism, but the conclusion he reaches is actually not terribly original. Ultimately, and like the main thrust of modern sociological narratives, Maffesoli merely restates as an erstwhile report of reality the necessity of reciprocity between individuals.

But the identification of neo-tribalism, and indeed of the argument which Maffesoli makes at one stage of his analysis (only, it would seem, to abandon it at the end), that the concept of society should be replaced with the concept of sociality, contains leads which are worth pursuing. The leads might make it possible to develop some more or less coherent picture of how it might be possible to interpret social relationships after civil society.

Of course, it would be very easy to suggest that since sociality is about the contingencies of display and the fluidity of change, it is highly tolerant and permissive towards the different. It could be concluded that sociality means nothing other than an overcoming of the difficulty of the stranger. But sociality can be interpreted in a very different manner. These trends, to some extent, reinforce and restate the implications of the trends towards the massification and condensation of community. After all, since sociality is highly fluid, it cannot ground any firm identities and neither can it establish any firm basis of the community from which it would be possible definitively to know and order the multiplicity of things. Consequently, in these terms, the problem of the sublime becomes of quite fundamental and overwhelming significance. In the context of Burke's analysis, there would be no safe haven from which the sublime could stimulate the idea of terror; instead, the sublime would occasion terror itself. And there would be no escape route from fear other than a more or less frantic attempt to turn away from any intellectual or physical confrontation with the immensity of a world which escapes clear knowing. The escape route involves fundamentalism of one kind or another. The ethics of aesthetics have a rather nastier and unpleasant face than Maffesoli, with his ultimately fairly conventional sociological worries, seems to acknowledge.

To the extent that neo-tribalism can be taken to be an indication of the hold of an ethics of aesthetics, and since the meanings of community and identity are reduced to the appearances of community and identity, it is possible to identify three main themes to the social situation which is left after the playing out of the incoherence of civil society. Firstly, social relationships are not predicated on any imagination of fixed identities or essences. Consequently, the meanings of social relationships are themselves highly fluid and remarkably contingent. Secondly, since neo-tribalist identifications are absolutely meaningless outside of their appearance, their grip over individuals must be very powerful indeed. Consequently, they can admit of no internal inconsistency, doubt or qualification. They are hermeneutically fundamentalist in relation to other instances of neo-tribalism and practically highly aggressive. If they were not, they would be quite meaningless and of no value. Thirdly, and despite Maffesoli's turn to society, the logical impact of neo-tribalism is the emergence of an impossibility of societal universality. Not only would any criteria of the universal and the homogeneous be incapable of reproduction given the flux and transience of identification but, perhaps more importantly, a plurality of neo-tribalism implies the absence of any single bounded community which can be taken as the terrain of the universal. To this extent, the continuation of universalizing projects (just because they are incoherent doe not mean that they cease) can only lead to the identification and establishment of bureaucratic structures which attempt to fix meanings in a futile and never-ending cycle of the anticipation of identity. In other words, massification ultimately and ironically involves an acceleration of particularity and heterogeneity.

When Maffesoli's analysis is used to reach these kinds of conclusions, it can be seen that, to some extent, he has rediscovered, albeit through an explicitly sociological method, a problem which has been known to moral and social philosophers for some time. Basically, the problem is that if universal imaginations of community are untenable (for one reason or another), then it becomes very difficult, and indeed extremely important, to attempt to

understand how and why individuals might continue to be tied to
some rules of responsible reciprocity in their relationships with
each other. Put another way, if individuals do not live in homogeneous societies which make universal demands through
universal regulations, then it becomes very difficult to explain why
and how they should and could live together.

Precisely this kind of problem has been confronted in a very
sustained way by Alasdair MacIntyre. The little book *Secularization
and Moral Change* can be read as a succinct introduction to many
of the main themes in MacIntyre's work (MacIntyre 1967). MacIntyre's basic point is that universal moral regulations are not only
descriptively untenable, but that they are also, perhaps ironically,
morally indefensible. He argues that modern societies are characterized by the existence of a number of different communities
which shape the imaginations and destinies of individuals (the
most obvious examples of such communities are social classes).
Each of these communities has its own moral code – for example,
in the nineteenth century some fractions of the English working
class upheld strong principles of temperance and responsibility,
while the middle classes equally strongly upheld precepts of professional propriety – which results in a moral pluralism. As such,
when they tried to lead moral lives, these groups potentially did
different things, and their statements of the meaning of morality
were not necessarily talking about the same problems, even less
giving the same answers. This pluralism means that 'the notion of
authoritative moral utterance [is] inapplicable; at worst ... the lack
of a shared moral vocabulary makes the use of explicit moral
assertion positively pernicious' (MacIntyre 1967: 57).

MacIntyre is arguing that it is quite unjustifiable to make moral
claims which are universal in a society which is fractured between
a multiplicity of different communities which are frequently in
conflict with one another. As MacIntyre says: 'What is pernicious
is the illusion that is created [by authoritative, universal, moral
statements] of a society united not as in fact it is by harsh utilitarian
necessities, but by common standards and ideas' (MacIntyre 1967:
57).

The core of MacIntyre's concern is the argument that for there
to be universal moral authority, there must first be a recognized
bounded community. After all, 'the notion of authority can only
find application in a community and in areas of life in which there
is an agreed way of doing things, according to accepted rules'

(MacIntyre 1967: 53). In those terms, it might be proposed that the practice of symmetric reciprocity is logically prior to the moral regulation of symmetric reciprocity (just as the critiques of contract theory pointed out that agreement must have been prior to the contract which allegedly established it). MacIntyre illustrates his argument with the game of chess, and he makes the point that there can exist recognized authorities on chess 'only because the game of chess exists as a set of established and agreed practices, both in respect of following the rules and in respect of legislating about them' (MacIntyre 1967: 53). Similarly, moral codes can only be universally binding if the constituency of universality has been established already. Of course, it needs to be added that the universality of morality subsequently reproduces the boundaries of the community.

However, according to MacIntyre, modern societies are bedevilled with a problem that the moral legislators of chess are unlikely to have to confront. While morality presupposes a moral community, the division of labour and yet solidarity of modern societies means that the universal community is a union of the different and, therefore, a union of different moralities (MacIntyre 1967: 52). According to MacIntyre, that awkward situation is especially due to the inter-relationships of social classes. He emphasizes a dilemma which is already well known; the dilemma of the impossibility of speaking the meaning of universality from a particular location. Quite possibly following the lead of Emile Durkheim, MacIntyre is aware of the social and economic pressures towards solidarity, but the 'needs that were met by co-operation between classes and the accompanying moral schemes led to a situation in which every attempt to universalize, to give cosmic significance to, the values of a particular group was bound to founder' (MacIntyre 1967: 25).

But any attempts to construct universal moral regulations were also bound to failure because of the impact of liberal beliefs. (This is virtually the self-same difficulty that Carl Schmitt saw as one of the central problems in the relationship between parliamentary arrangements and mass democracy. The problem is, of course, expressed in rather different terms by MacIntyre.) According to MacIntyre, the problem with liberalism is that it asserts the moral responsibility and self-sufficiency of the individual. Such an assertion is contradictory because it suggests, on the one hand, that moral values are highly personal and private, but, on the other hand, that such values are objective and impersonal because they can be chosen by the individual (MacIntyre 1967: 45).

Consequently, it is impossible to pass moral judgements on others or, indeed, to have any great trust in the permanence of one's own moral rules. According to MacIntyre, we deny 'that there are objective standards underlying and authenticating that list of the virtues of which the agent's group is the bearer'. But quite simultaneously, we adhere to 'the incompatible notion that what values a man has depends upon his free choice and that nobody has the right to act as moral legislator for anyone else' (MacIntyre 1967: 45). The result is that the virtues of modern society are of an entirely secondary order (they are about means; the question of ends never arises), if not completely empty. In particular, MacIntyre argues that the term 'duty' originally referred to the function which an individual performed in society, but the impact 'of industrialism and of a liberal and individualist ethos' has been an erosion of the specific universal meaning of duty with, instead, its reduction to simple problems of particular circumstances (MacIntyre 1967: 72).

Whatever the attitude adopted towards his conclusions, it cannot be denied that MacIntyre's attempt to understand some of the moral implications of the collapse of universality are extremely valuable. Quite simply, the logical incoherence of any imagination of a universal bounded community of self-defining individuals (that is, the logical incoherence of civil society) suggests also the logical incoherence of any universal moral regulations. The attempt to overcome particularity by subsuming it within some universal category ultimately meant not only the meaninglessness of the universal but also the multiplication of particularity.

The imagination of civil society was meant to be good in both the moral and the aesthetic senses of that term. But, outside of coercion, it led to a complete inability to know the meanings or requirements of the good. Even less, did it allow the possibility of a general acknowledgement of what the good actually consisted in. Civil society was an imagination which was ostensibly able to render the things of the world small, beautiful, manageable, static and clear. Instead, it rendered them opaque, sublime and perpetually transient.

Civil society, that specific resource of modernity, which was ostensibly so positive, achieved its own negation.

Chapter 8

Conclusion

The logical incoherence of civil society, and the inability of the imagination to provide any legitimate and reproducible standards of the homogeneous and the universal (that is, the inability of civil society to achieve its ostensible purpose), should not cause too much surprise. Perhaps the incoherence was inevitable. But while civil society was not a terribly water-tight idea, perhaps the incoherence was not directly the fault of the imagination itself. Perhaps the problem can be identified as one especially telling instance of a deeper contradiction in the very meanings and practices of the modernity which civil society expressed, and indeed the modernity which was the condition of possibility of civil society. Basically, that contradiction consisted in the two aims which emerged in the wake of the deconstruction of the natural artifice; the two aims which were so much the heart and soul of civil society.

On the one hand, there was the interest and the enterprise of reflexivity so that the social and the societal could be defining of itself, and so that individuals could operate in terms of the demands of a symmetric reciprocity. On the other hand, there was the interest and the enterprise of societal order. The enterprise of order was so vitally important because after the deconstruction of the natural artifice (thanks to the arrival of the urban and cosmopolitan strangers), the world was a possibly meaningless and chaotic place if social constructions of the order of things were not imposed upon it. Both reflexivity and order were absolutely fundamental in the arrangements and the practices of modernity. In many ways, it might even be said that reflexivity and order were the central principles of modernity. They were certainly the central concerns and priorities of civil society.

However, and it might even be said, rather unfortunately,

reflexivity and order were deeply contradictory of each other. The two principles were quite irreconcilable. After all, the thrust of reflexivity is to deconstruct more or less everything which might be construed as a reification or as a definition of the meanings of society. But the thrust of order is precisely to solidify some meanings and practices so that they become the taken-for-granted preconditions of human freedom in the world. Despite the kinds of hermeneutic somersaults and blind alleys which were associated with modernity and with civil society, the simple fact of the matter was that reflexivity undermined the possibility of order, and order denied the possibility of reflexivity. In other words, the incoherence of civil society was largely an example and an illustration of the incoherence of European modernity.

Of course, this kind of contradiction was spotted very keenly by Karl Marx and Frederick Engels although, as fine upstanding moderns, they laid the blame firmly in the lap of some of the existing arrangements of modernity rather than in the lap of the myth of modernity itself. They explained the problem quite clearly in the discussion of the curious history of the bourgeoisie which can be found at the beginning of *The Communist Manifesto*. Marx and Engels spoke about bourgeois order as something which had been accomplished already and, to some extent, already made into a second nature. They were prepared to talk in fairly definite terms about 'Our epoch, the epoch of the bourgeoisie' (Marx and Engels 1942: 205). But along with this virtual naturalization of bourgeois order, Marx and Engels identified a very different tendency indeed. The bourgeoisie was constantly, consciously and necessarily destroying every possibility of the reproduction of order. Marx and Engels saw the bourgeoisie as a societal and historical achievement which was achieving nothing other than its own deconstruction. After all, 'The bourgeoisie cannot exist without constantly revolutionising the instruments of production, and thereby the relations of production, and with them the whole relations of society' (Marx and Engels 1942: 208).

To this extent, the bourgeoisie can be identified as being tantamount to the universal subject of reflexivity, and also as the subject of the modern ability of the social and the societal to be defining of itself. Marx and Engels were indicating the universality of the bourgeoisie when they invested it with the profound ability to change deliberately the world in all the many ways highlighted in the first chapter of *The Communist Manifesto* (Marx and Engels 1942: 204–18).

But the appearance of universality, and the production (and for a while the reproduction), of a homogeneous societal order was achieved at a fairly high cost. Behind the facade of universality and of order, there was a process of reflexivity which was running out of control. The process took the form of a perpetual subsumption of the particular and the homogeneous by another category, or other categories, of the particular and the heterogeneous. Famously, the out-of-control reflexivity (which Marx and Engels reduced to the question of the forces of production unleashed by the bourgeoisie, but which I wish to see more in terms of a wider modernity) meant that 'All fixed, fast frozen relations, with their train of ancient and venerable prejudices and opinions, are swept away, all new-formed ones become antiquated before they can ossify'. Marx and Engels continued: 'All that is solid melts into air, all that is holy is profaned, and man is at last compelled to face with sober senses his real conditions of life and his relations with his kind' (Marx and Engels 1942: 208–9). (This passage was the occasion of Marshall Berman's splendid discussion of modernity Berman 1982). So, the world becomes clearer, but it becomes quicker as well. It is highly reflexive but fundamentally chaotic.

Now, while Marx and Engels memorably revealed this contradiction at the very centre of the enterprises of the bourgeoisie, their way of talking shows quite how deeply contradictions of this kind, contradictions between order and reflexivity, ran in the imaginations of modernity. Marx and Engels seem to betray a certain admiration for the historical ability of the bourgeoisie to free itself from the restrictive definitions of the feudal order and to sweep away the 'ancient prejudices and opinions'. Marx and Engels were actually applauding the modernity of the bourgeoisie. Yet they were gleefully aghast at the inability of the bourgeoisie to halt the efforts of sweeping away. They saw the bourgeoisie as something approaching a 'sorcerer's apprentice'. And, of course, in the story of the sorcerer's apprentice, there is a very thin line between laughter and panic.

Marx and Engels were working in the light of the consequences of the deconstruction of the natural artifice. They were writing from deep within the camp of modernity, and they showed that the modern worries with order and reflexivity were actually quite irreconcilable. Marx and Engels overcame this contradiction by more or less turning it into a teleology and an inversion of the existing societal arrangements. They placed their hopes in a future in which reflexivity would cease because nothing would exist which would need to be rendered clear, and a future in which order would cease to be a problem or a project because it would be self-evidently universal and self-sufficient.

But with this argument, Marx and Engels simply worked around the contradiction between order and reflexivity at the expense of turning modernity into its own utopian myth; a utopia which was, however, active in the present and, therefore, actually an acceleration of reflexivity. The utopia meant nothing other than the increasingly rapid obsolescence of any and all orders of things. The status of the future as the achievement of an accelerated reflexivity was intended to overcome the contradictions of modernity which were crystallized in the contradictions of the bourgeoisie. Instead, it simply exacerbated them. (For the idea of an active utopia, see Bauman 1976.)

The difficulty of the irreconcilability of order and reflexivity meant, perhaps inevitably, that the social relationships and the societal arrangements of modernity were invariably characterized by a highly peculiar and potent blend of existential confidence and existential horror; freedom and bureaucracy. More significantly, it was quite impossible to resolve the dilemmas of universality and particularity; homogeneity and heterogeneity; self-definition and just definition. This is basically the series of problems that civil society attempted to overcome. For the most part, however, that attempt to overcome either failed disastrously or simply involved a restatement of the initial problem, although coupled with a faith that it would be resolved in time.

Of course, all the modern narratives and projects struggled very hard to overcome these divides. They attempted to hold together the pressures towards order and reflexivity. But the attempts were doomed to failure because they could always be accused of really being the exact opposite of everything that they claimed to be (as soon as they expressed the meanings of universality and thus revealed their particularity). Consequently, reflexivity became formalized and was made the specific activity of specific professional groups; these groups were able to define themselves as possessed of the ability, the obligation, even the right, to define all others. Order became a virtually meaningless husk which lived on through a bored habit elevated to the status of 'tradition' (although the irony of modernity reliant on tradition was frequently missed). The other face of modern order was its transformation into rigid institutional frameworks which interpreted the speed and certainty of the movement of paper as a sign of the continuing vitality and enthusiasm of everything outside the office.

If order did not undermine reflexivity, and if reflexivity did not undermine order, it was only because they could be, and often were, transformed into the greatest fear of each other and therefore operated as a mutual justification. And, ever since the time of Thomas Hobbes, it has been known that reification through a denial of reflexivity or a rigid institutionalization of order might be acceptable if the horror of the alternative is too overwhelming. As such, the post-modern condition involves a different and simultaneous combination of pressures towards particularity, reification and accelerated reflexivity. In other words, the concern with rigid and definite boundaries has been replaced with a need to come to terms with, and to learn how to make sense of, a world of boundlessness and fundamentalism. The modern imaginations of civil society are based on a series of problems and possibilities which means that they will be largely inadequate for the tasks of interpreting and creating maps of post-modernity. Civil society will only continue to be accepted as a satisfactory imagination to the extent that it can continue to provide easy and comforting answers to easy and irrelevant questions.

The imagination of civil society was the precondition and the product of modernity. And so, just like the challenges associated with modernity, it too could not avoid a most bleak destiny after the initial burst of enthusiasm.

Bibliography

Aeschylus 1956 *The Oresteian Trilogy*, trans. Philip Vellacott, Harmondsworth: Penguin.

Anderson, Benedict 1983 *Imagined Communities. Reflections on the Origin and Spread of Nationalism*, London: Verso.

Appignanesi, Lisa (ed.) 1989 *Postmodernism. ICA Documents*, London: Free Association Books.

Bauman, Zygmunt 1976 *Socialism. The Active Utopia*, London: George Allen & Unwin.

—— 1985 'On the Origin of Civilization: A Historical Note', *Theory, Culture & Society*, 2(3): 7–14.

—— 1987 *Legislators and Interpreters. On Modernity, Post-modernity and Intellectuals*, Cambridge: Polity.

—— 1990 *Modernity and the Holocaust*, Cambridge: Polity.

Bellamy, Richard 1987 *Modern Italian Social Theory. Ideology and Politics from Pareto to the Present*, Cambridge: Polity.

Berman, Marshall 1982 *All that is Solid Melts into Air. The Experience of Modernity*, New York: Simon & Schuster.

Bleicher, Josef 1990 'Struggling with *Kultur*', *Theory, Culture & Society*, 7(1): 97–106.

Bocock, Robert 1986 *Hegemony*, London: Tavistock.

Burke, Edmund 1990 *A Philosophical Enquiry into the Origin of our Ideas of the Sublime and Beautiful*, Adam Phillips (ed.), Oxford: Oxford University Press.

Castoriadis, Cornelius 1987 *The Imaginary Institution of Society*, trans. Kathleen Blarney, Cambridge: Polity.

Clark, Kenneth 1956 *Landscape into Art*, Harmondsworth: Penguin.

Coleridge, Samuel Taylor 1985 *The Oxford Authors. Samuel Taylor Coleridge*, H. J. Jackson (ed.), Oxford: Oxford University Press.

Connerton, Paul 1989 *How Societies Remember*, Cambridge: Cambridge University Press.

Dahrendorf, Ralf 1990 *Reflections on the Revolution in Europe*, London: Chatto & Windus.

Durkheim, Emile 1957 *Professional Ethics and Civic Morals*, trans. Cornelia Brookfield, London: Routledge & Kegan Paul.

—— 1960 'The Dualism of Human Nature and its Social Conditions', trans. Charles Blend, in Kurt H. Wolff (ed.), *Emile Durkheim, 1858–1917*, Columbus: The Ohio State University Press.

—— 1984 *The Division of Labour in Society*, trans. W. D. Halls, London: Macmillan.

Elias, Norbert 1956 'Problems of Involvement and Detachment', *The British Journal of Sociology*, 7(3): 226–52.

—— 1978a *The History of Manners*, trans. Edmund Jephcott, Oxford: Basil Blackwell.

—— 1978b *What is Sociology?* trans. Stephen Mennell and Grace Morrissey, London: Hutchinson.

—— 1982 *State Formation and Civilization*, trans. Edmund Jephcott, Oxford: Basil Blackwell.

—— 1987 'On Human Beings and Their Emotions: A Process-Sociological Essay', *Theory Culture & Society*, 4(2–3): 339–61.

Ferguson, Adam 1975 *Principles of Moral and Political Science*, New York: George Olms. (Originally published 1792.)

—— 1980 *An Essay on the History of Civil Society*, New Brunswick: Transaction Books.

Foucault, Michel 1970 *The Order of Things. An Archaeology of the Human Sciences*, London: Tavistock.

—— 1979 *The History of Sexuality. Volume One: An Introduction*, trans. Robert Hurley, London: Allen Lane

—— 1982 'The Subject and Power', in Hubert L. Dreyfus and Paul Rabinow, *Michel Foucault: Beyond Structuralism and Hermeneutics*, Brighton: Harvester.

—— 1986 'Kant on Enlightenment and Revolution', *Economy and Society*, 15(1): 88–96.

—— 1988 *Politics Philosophy Culture. Interviews and Other Writings 1977–1984*, Lawrence D. Kritzman (ed.), trans. Alan Sheridan and others, New York: Routledge.

Freud, Sigmund 1985 *Civilization, Society and Religion*, The Penguin Freud Library, Volume 12, Albert Dickson (ed.), Harmondsworth: Penguin.

Gordon, Colin 1987 'The Soul of the Citizen: Max Weber and Michel Foucault on Rationality and Government', in Scott Lash and Sam Whimster (eds), *Max Weber, Rationality and Modernity*, London: Allen & Unwin.

Goudsblom, Johann 1987 'The Sociology of Norbert Elias: Its Resonance and Significance', *Theory Culture & Society*, 4(2–3): 323–37.

Gramsci, Antonio 1971 *Selections from the Prison Notebooks*, ed. and trans. Quintin Hoare and Geoffrey Nowell Smith, London: Lawrence & Wishart.

Habermas, Jurgen 1990 'The Public Sphere: An Encyclopedia Article', trans. Sara Lennox and Frank Lennox, in Stephen E. Bronner and Douglas M. Kellner (eds), *Critical Theory and Society. A Reader*, New York: Routledge.

Havel, Václav 1987 *Living in Truth*, Jan Vladislav (ed.), London: Faber & Faber.

Hegel, G. W. F. 1952 *Philosophy of Right*, trans. T. M. Knox, Oxford: Clarendon.

Heller, Agnes 1990 *Can Modernity Survive?*, Cambridge: Polity.

Hobbes, Thomas 1991 *Leviathan*, Richard Tuck (ed.), Cambridge: Cambridge University Press.

Hume, David 1947 'Of the Original Contract', in *Social Contract. Essays by Locke, Hume and Rousseau*, introduction by Sir Ernest Barker, London: Oxford University Press.

Kant, Immanuel 1988 *Kant. Selections*, Lewis White Beck (ed.), New York: Macmillan.

Keane, John 1991 *The Media and Democracy*, Cambridge: Polity.

Locke, John 1924 *Two Treatises of Civil Government*, London: Dent.

Lukács, Georg 1971 *History and Class Consciousness. Studies in Marxist Dialectics*, trans. Rodney Livingstone, London: Merlin.

MacIntyre, Alasdair 1967 *Secularization and Moral Change*, London: Oxford University Press.

Maffesoli, Michel 1988 'Jeux De Masques: Postmodern Tribalism', trans. Charles R. Foulkes, *Design Issues*, 4(1 & 2): 141–51.

—— 1990 'Post-modern Sociality', trans. Russell Moore, *Telos*, 85: 89–92.

—— 1991 'The Ethic of Aesthetics', *Theory, Culture & Society*, 8(1): 7–20.

Marx, Karl 1946 'Theses on Feuerbach', in Frederick Engels, *Ludwig Feuerbach and the End of Classical German Philosophy*, Moscow: Progress Publishers.

—— 1959 *Economic and Philosophic Manuscripts of 1844*, Moscow: Progress Publishers.

—— 1971 *Early Texts*, ed. and trans. David McLellan, Oxford: Basil Blackwell.

Marx, Karl and Engels, Frederick 1942 'The Communist Manifesto', in *Karl Marx. Selected Works in Two Volumes*, Volume 1, London: Lawrence & Wishart.

—— 1970 *The German Ideology*, C. J. Arthur (ed.), London: Lawrence & Wishart.

Minson, Jeffrey 1985 *Genealogies of Morals. Nietzsche, Foucault, Donzelot and the Eccentricity of Ethics*, London: Macmillan.

Moller Okin, Susan 1991 'Gender, the Public and the Private', in David Held (ed.), *Political Theory Today*, Cambridge: Polity.

Monk, Samuel H. 1960 *The Sublime*, Ann Arbor: The University of Michigan Press.

Nietzsche, Friedrich 1961 *Thus Spoke Zarathustra*, trans. R. J. Hollingdale, Harmondsworth: Penguin.

—— 1973 *Beyond Good and Evil*, trans. R. J. Hollingdale, Harmondsworth: Penguin.

Pagden, Anthony 1988 'The "Defence of Civilization" in Eighteenth-century Social Theory', *History of the Human Sciences*, 1(1): 33–45.

Pateman, Carole 1988 *The Sexual Contract*, Cambridge: Polity.

Phillipson, Nicholas 1981 'The Scottish Enlightenment', in Roy Porter and Mikulás Teich (eds), *The Enlightenment in National Context*, Cambridge: Cambridge University Press.

Plato 1963 *The Trial and Death of Socrates*, trans. John Warrington, London: Dent.

Poulantzas, Nicos 1973 *Political Power and Social Classes*, trans. Timothy O'Hagan, London: New Left Books.

Rousseau, Jean Jacques 1968 *The Social Contract*, trans. Maurice Cranston, Harmondsworth: Penguin.

—— 1984 *A Discourse on Inequality*, trans. Maurice Cranston, Harmondsworth: Penguin.

Rundell, John F. 1987 *Origins of Modernity. The Origins of Modern Social Theory from Kant to Hegel to Marx*, Cambridge: Polity.

Sartre, Jean-Paul 1965 *Nausea*, trans. Robert Baldick, Harmondsworth: Penguin.

Sayer, Derek 1991 *Capitalism and Modernity. An Excursus on Marx and Weber*, London: Routledge.

Schmitt, Carl 1985 *The Crisis of Parliamentary Democracy*, trans. Ellen Kennedy, Cambridge, MAS: The MIT Press.

Simmel, Georg 1950 *The Sociology of Georg Simmel*, ed. and trans. Kurt H. Wolff, New York: The Free Press.

Smith, Adam 1976 *The Theory of Moral Sentiments*, D. D. Raphael and A. L. Macfie (eds), Oxford: Clarendon Press.

—— 1977 *Lectures on Jurisprudence*, R. L. Meek, D. D. Raphael and P. G. Stein (eds), Oxford: Clarendon Press.

Steiner, George 1989 *Real Presences*, London: Faber & Faber.

Stern, J. P. 1978 *Nietzsche*, London: Fontana.

Sterne, Laurence 1983 *The Life and Opinions of Tristram Shandy, Gentleman*, Ian Campbell Ross (ed.), Oxford: Oxford University Press.

Swingewood, Alan 1970 'Origins of Sociology: The Case of the Scottish Enlightenment', *British Journal of Sociology*, 21: 164–80.

Talmon, J. L. 1952 *The Origins of Totalitarian Democracy*, London: Martin Secker & Warburg.

Tester, Keith 1991 *Animals and Society. The Humanity of Animal Rights*, London: Routledge.

—— 1992 *The Two Sovereigns. Social Contradictions of European Modernity*, London: Routledge.

Tucker, Aviezer 1990 'Václav Havel's Heideggerianism', *Telos*, 85: 63–78.

Weber, Max 1930 *The Protestant Ethic and the Spirit of Capitalism*, trans. Talcott Parsons, London: George Allen & Unwin.

—— 1948 *From Max Weber: Essays in Sociology*, ed. and trans. H. H. Gerth and C. Wright Mills, London: Routledge & Kegan Paul.

White, Hayden 1978 *Tropics of Discourse. Essays in Cultural Criticism*, Baltimore and London: The Johns Hopkins University Press.

Wolff, Janet 1990 *Feminine Sentences*, Cambridge: Polity.

Name index

Aeschylus 83, 101
Anderson, Benedict 13, 14
Appignanesi, Lisa 154
Auden, W(ystan) H(ugh) 8, 17
Austen, Jane 77

Bacon, Francis 9
Barthes, Roland 13
Baudelaire, Charles 1, 34
Bauman, Zygmunt 9, 53, 71, 90, 175
Bellamy, Richard 142
Bentham, Jeremy 127
Berman, Marshall 174
Bleicher, Josef 9
Bocock, Robert 140
Burke, Edmund 158–62, 167

Castoriadis, Cornelius 13–14
Clark, Kenneth 61
Coleridge, Samuel Taylor 26–7
Connerton, Paul 152

Dahrendorf, Ralf 128
Durkheim, Emile 49, 74–5, 91–102, 112, 135, 141, 155, 165–7, 170

Elias, Norbert 9–10, 84–93, 99–100, 103, 11–12, 123, 147
Engels, Frederick 15, 173–4

Ferguson, Adam 7, 46–9, 50, 52, 98, 111, 129
Filmer, Robert 37–8, 51, 134

Foucault, Michel 11, 73, 118–23, 145–7
Freud, Sigmund 74–5, 78–85, 87, 89–90, 93, 98–103, 105, 111–12, 121–3, 130, 155

Goethe, Johann Wolfgang von 114, 125
Gordon, Colin 117, 118
Goudsblom, Johann 84, 90
Gouldner, Alvin 6
Goya y Lucientes, Francesco José de 56
Gramsci, Antonio 139–42, 144

Habermas, Jurgen 137, 144
Havel, Václav 129
Hegel, G.W.F. 14, 21-2, 24, 135, 140
Heller, Agnes 12, 28–32, 53, 153
Hobbes, Thomas 54–65, 67, 71–2, 74, 76, 80, 83, 85, 90, 93, 100, 103, 111–12, 122, 148, 152, 155, 176
Hume, David 36, 38, 45–6, 48, 50, 52

Kant, Immanuel 1, 33, 150–8, 159, 162
Keane, John 128
Kundera, Milan 129

Lenin (Vladimir Ilyich Ulyanov) 142
Locke, John 7, 10, 24–5, 35–45,

47, 50, 52–4, 61, 72, 76, 85, 93,
   103, 111, 122, 126, 134, 148
Lukács, Georg 1, 140, 143

MacIntyre, Alasdair 94, 169–71
McLuhan, Marshall 163
Maffesoli, Michel 164–8
Marlowe, Christopher 125
Marx, Karl 4–5, 14–24, 26, 35,
   50, 54–5, 63, 65, 74–5, 86, 111,
   123, 139–40, 142, 144, 173–4
Mill, John Stuart 127
Milton, John 9–10
Minson, Jeffrey 127
Moller Okin, Susan 21
Monk, Samuel H. 154

Nietzsche, Friedrich 100–12, 116,
   121–3, 126, 160

Orwell, George 7

Pagden, Anthony 77–8
Pateman, Carole 24, 133–7, 144,
   148, 163
Phillipson, Nicholas 46
Plato 69
Poulantzas, Nicos 143

Robertson, William 28
Rousseau, Jean Jacques 7, 24, 33,
   54, 60, 63–72, 74, 76, 81, 85–6,
   90, 93, 96–7, 100, 132–3, 138
Rundell, John F. 22
Ruskin, John 61

Sartre, Jean-Paul 34, 50, 147
Sayer, Derek 23, 111
Schmitt, Carl 128–33, 137–9,
   144–5, 148, 170
Simmel, Georg 13–14, 32–5, 50,
   76
Smith, Adam 49–50, 52, 115, 129
Socrates 69
Sophocles 101
Steiner, George 2
Stern, J.P. 103
Sterne, Laurence 30–1
Swingewood, Alan 28, 46

Talmon, Jacob 63
Tucker, Aviezer 129

Weber, Max 42, 49, 74–5,
   113–19, 121–3, 141
White, Hayden 62, 74, 75, 78
Wolff, Janet 13

Subject index

abortion 127
achievement 11, 19, 30–3, 38–9, 66, 104, 126–8
aggression 81–4
alienation 102–3
anomie 94–5
artificiality 67–8, 70
ascription 11, 16, 29–33, 37–8, 126–7
assertion 38–9
association, voluntary 5, 8–9, 40, 53, 124–5, 135, 143, 149
authority 35–6, 44, 51, 169: absolute 60; external 4–5, 7, 11, 58–9, 80, 83–4, 120; legislative 42; sacred 29

beauty 149–59
behaviour 77, 85–8, 89, 92, 125
Beyond Good and Evil (Nietzschel) 100
boundaries: boundlessness 156, 158, 176; civil society 51, 77, 111, 154; civilization 161; community 10, 12, 68–9, 82, 128, 130, 144, 147, 163, 168, 170; community of reciprocity 47, 101, 133, 149; community of strangers 42; drawing 48, 159–60; modernity and 165; moral community 108; natural artifice 31; self-definition 153; society 25, 34, 56, 61, 62–3, 70, 74, 89, 93, 103, 124, 143, 152, 155; 'West' 122

bourgeoisie 15–20, 22, 44, 114, 137, 139–40, 143, 173–5

capitalism 15, 18–19, 113, 141–3
civilization, concept of 9–10
coercion 46, 58–9, 65, 72, 124, 141, 171
commonwealth 42, 59–61, 63
consciousness 60, 84, 92, 141
construction of society 6–11, 20–1, 25–6, 35, 125, 143
contract, social 45–7, 53, 57–9, 63, 67–8, 70, 72–4, 87, 133–4, 170
Crisis of Parliamentary Democracy, The (Schmitt) 129
Critique of the Faculty of Judgement (Kant) 150–157

democracy 106, 108–9, 128–33, 137–9, 144, 146
developmentalism 90, 99, 103, 111
discontent 103, 115, 121, 149
Discourse on Equality, A (Rousseau) 63–6
dividing practices 118
duality 17, 21, 146

egoism 55, 57, 65, 82, 84, 93, 97, 101, 107, 121
enlightenment 7, 28, 46, 50, 148
equality 54–5, 57, 68, 107–8, 122, 126, 129–32, 136, 141–2, 144
estrangement 19–20, 102

ethics 36–7, 82, 106, 166: of
  aesthetics 167–8; professional
  94–6, 98; Protestant 113,
  116–17; sexual 119
Eumenides (Aeschylus) 83
existentialism 17, 103, 125, 140,
  146, 159, 175

family 79, 94–6, 135
feudalism 14, 49, 174
figuration, concept of 86–7, 89–92
freedom 5, 20, 35, 49–50, 57,
  70–2, 112, 114, 117, 125, 138,
  147, 173: domination 69; God
  37: humanity 18, 25, 46, 67,
  99; individual 31, 34, 49, 95–6,
  118, 135–6: liberty 53–4, 93,
  119–21, 126, 136; natural
  artifice 115; resources 116;
  society 11, 43–4, 51, 52;
  stranger 32

gender 23–5, 79–80, 133, 136–7
general will 60, 68–71, 132–3
genital pleasure 79–81
guilt 84–5, 87

herd morality 106–9
heterogeneity (particularity) 16,
  42, 51, 66, 76, 94, 96–7, 174–5:
  authority 42; capitalism 19;
  external 48; Foucault on 121;
  Freud on 84; Hegel on 22;
  Hobbes on 59; homogeneity
  11, 96–7, 107, 144–5, 162–3,
  165–6; individuality 47; Kant
  on 151–2, 157–8; Marx on 21,
  23, 140; massification 168;
  morality 94; natural artifice 20;
  Nietzsche on 110; religion 18;
  Rousseau on 63, 66–70;
  Schmitt on 129–30, 132; state
  17; state of nature 51, 76;
  stranger 109; Weber on 114,
  116; women 134–7
hierarchy 32, 34, 107
history, civil society in 14–15, 20
History of Manners, The (Elias) 89
homogeneity (universality) 16,

41, 51, 72, 74, 76, 98, 147, 148,
  155–6, 171: authority 42,
  democracy 139–9; figuration
  87; Foucault on 120–1, 146;
  Freud on 84; Hegel on 22;
  heterogeneity 11, 96–7, 107,
  144, 162–3, 165–6; Hobbes on
  59–63; internal 48; Kant on
  150–2, 157–8; Locke on 44;
  Marx on 21, 23, 140; morality
  93–4; neo-tribalism 168–9;
  Nietzsche on 108–10;
  reification 43; religion 18;
  Rousseau on 66–71; Schmitt
  on 129–33; species-being
  19–20; state 17; suffering 106,
  128; Weber on 114, 118;
  women 24, 135–7
humanity 18–20, 23, 25, 42, 51,
  62–5, 67, 70–1, 88, 117, 127,
  139, 156–7

identity 137–42, 147, 158, 165,
  167–8
imagination, concept of 13–14,
  21, 24–6, 32
imitation 161
individual 102, 104, 107, 109,
  117, 127, 133, 165, 172:
  freedom 31, 34, 49, 95–6, 118,
  135–6; heterogeneity 16, 42;
  homogeneity 129–30; -ity 7,
  15, 17, 92–3, 120, 137, 166; in
  social relationships 29–30,
  40–1, 48, 122, 124, 156, 162;
  in society 5, 8, 10, 20–2, 43–4,
  119, 147; as stranger 33, 121;
  symmetry 66
industrialization 52, 97
interdependency 77, 79, 81,
  87–8, 89–93, 122

judgement, aesthetic 150–2,
  157–8

knowledge 88–90, 115, 125, 151-2

labour: division of 22, 48, 50, 52,
  92–5, 115, 170; estranged 19

law 57, 60, 64–5, 72, 136, 138;
    breaker 68–9
Leviathan (Hobbes) 54, 59, 61
liberalism 132–3, 146, 170–1
*Life and Opinions of Tristram
    Shandy, Gentleman, The* (Sterne)
    30, 32–4, 36
love 82–3, 99

man, concept of 72–3, 114, 136–7
massification 163–4, 167–8
mediocrity 105, 107–8, 110, 116,
    122–3
modernity 25–6, 40, 45, 53–4, 61,
    64, 71–2, 75, 79, 90–1, 115–16,
    120–1, 123, 126, 128, 131–2,
    141, 157, 165, 172–6: ethics 36,
    39; in Europe and North
    America 141–2; freedom 95;
    gender 133, 135; man in 73–4,
    103; morality 101; natural
    artifice 28–9, 43, 78;
    reciprocity 31–2, 124;
    reflexivity 11–12, 97, 110, 136;
    scarcity 122; society in 51, 57,
    67, 76, 106, 144–5, 147, 164,
    171; sociology 113, 148; wild
    98–9, 100, 107–8, 111–12, 114
monarchy 14, 29, 32, 36, 51, 134:
    absolute 37–9, 60
morality 54, 71, 74, 93–9, 101–2,
    104–9, 127, 153, 156:
    regulation 76–7, 83, 92, 97,
    141, 144, 149, 155, 160, 166,
    169–71

natural artifice 12–13, 15, 17, 20,
    22, 24, 28–33, 35, 39, 60–1,
    70–1, 73, 103, 108, 110–11,
    115, 153: deconstruction 40,
    42–4, 51, 52–4, 57, 59, 64, 75,
    77, 89, 91, 115, 124, 148, 172,
    174
nature 11, 19, 25, 30, 36, 62–4,
    77, 100–1, 110, 147, 154:
    human 82, 85–6, 88, 89–91;
    second 49, 115–16, 140, 148,
    173; *see also* state of nature
Nausea (Sartre) 34, 50, 147

neo-tribalism 164–8

order 172–6
Order of Things, The (Foucault) 73
origins of civil society 44, 46–7,
    62, 67, 79, 91

parliamentism 138–9
particularity *see* heterogeneity
pathetic fallacy 61, 71, 73, 100,
    110, 149, 151
Patriarcha (Filmer) 37, 39
patriarchy 24, 29, 36–7, 73, 115,
    134–5
politics 7, 16–18, 131–2, 138–40,
    142
principles 37–9
*Principles of Moral and Political
    Science* (Ferguson) 46
private sphere 4–5, 8, 14–22, 48,
    135–6
Professional Ethics and Civic Morals
    (Durkheim) 93
professions 93–6
property 15–16, 40–1, 43–4,
    53–4, 67, 93, 126
*Protestant Ethic and the Spirit of
    Capitalism, The* (Weber) 113,
    115, 117

reality 13–14, 23, 62, 64, 90, 144,
    147
reciprocity 47, 56, 58, 61–2, 65–6,
    76, 79, 82–3, 93–4, 98–9, 103,
    124–5, 128, 130, 147, 167, 169:
    asymmetric 29–33, 35, 37–40,
    42, 50, 64, 67, 108, 110, 126;
    symmetric 31–2, 34–6, 40–4,
    48–50, 52, 57, 64, 67–8, 70, 74,
    85, 88, 97, 101, 104, 106–7,
    110, 116, 121–3, 126, 131–3,
    143, 146, 149, 153, 160–1, 164,
    166, 172
reflexivity 6, 13, 44, 52, 54, 73,
    75, 111–12, 123, 129, 135, 144,
    147, 149, 172–6: Durkheim on
    93, 95; Elias on 91; Foucault
    on 120–1; Freud on 103, 118;
    Gramsci on 140, 142; Hobbes

on 59–60; Hume on 45; Kant
on 17; Locke on 35–8, 41–3,
53, 71; Marx on 15–16, 18, 20,
22; in modernity 11–12, 97,
136, Rousseau on 63–4, 70, 96;
Schmitt on 138; Simmel on 14;
Smith on 50; Weber on 115–16
reification 11, 18, 24, 28–9, 31,
35, 45, 48, 51–2, 73, 173, 176;
Durkheim on 96–7; Elias on
87; Gramsci on 142; Hobbes
on 54–5, 57, 59–60, 64, 74;
Locke on 40, 43, 45; Maffesoli
on 165; Marx on 21, 23, 140;
Nietzsche on 111; Pateman on
144; Rousseau on 69–71, 74, 96
relationships, social 12, 33, 73,
112, 148–9, 153, 155, 163, 169,
175: Burke on 160; as civil
society 8–11, 14, 76; Durkheim
on 135; Elias on 86–7, 111;
Freud on 81–3; Gramsci on
142; Heller on 28–31; Hobbes
on 56–8, 61; Hume on 46;
individual in 40–1, 48, 122,
124, 156, 162; Kant on 158;
Locke on 36, 38, 53; Maffesoli
on 164, 167–8; Marx on 15–16,
19–21, 23; Nietzsche on 105,
108; Pateman on 136;
reciprocity 34–5; Rousseau on
64, 66–7; Schmitt on 130, 132;
Smith on 49–50; utilitarianism
127–8; Weber on 117
relativism 60
religion 17–18
rights 109, 134: divine 29, 36–8,
40, 51, 134; natural 53–4,
57–8, 93; theories 126–8
rite 34–5, 152
role 165–6, 171

scarcity 55, 57, 66–8, 79, 82, 97,
113, 121–2
sciences 118, 120
Secularization and Moral Change
(MacIntyre) 169
self-awareness 10, 92

self-consciousness 10, 24, 50, 71,
118, 120
self-definition 104–5, 116–17,
120, 126, 128, 134, 144, 147,
149–50, 152–3, 156, 159, 161,
164–6, 171, 175
selfishness 15–18, 20, 22
Sexual Contract, The (Pateman) 134
sexuality 7, 79–81, 118–20
similarity 130
Social Contract, The (Rousseau) 63,
66–7, 70
socialism 109, 128–9
sociology 6–8, 12, 14, 26, 46, 50,
71, 74–5, 84, 89–91, 95, 101,
111, 113, 117–18, 140, 148–9,
153, 155–6, 167–8
Solidarity, Polish 145–6
solidarity, social 22, 92–5, 101,
153, 170
species-being 18–20, 22–3
state of nature 51, 52–3, 73–4,
76–7, 134, 140: Elias on 86, 88;
Freud on 80–1; Hobbes on
54–63, 65, 71, 80, 100; Locke
on 40–5; Nietzsche on 100,
111; Rousseau on 64–6, 69–71,
81
state (public sphere) 8–9, 11,
14–17, 20–3, 43, 93, 96, 129,
132, 135, 137–8, 141–3, 146
status: achievement 30; ascription
32; civil society 22; civilization
89–90, 155; ethics 166;
humanity 72; individual 107,
126; man 64, 73; monarch 29;
proletariat 140; society 96;
stranger 73; women 80
strangeness 59, 65, 107–8, 110,
121
strangers 44, 51, 67, 146, 167;
boundaries 56; contract 58;
freedom 32–4; genital pleasure
as 79; heterogeneity 109,
162–3; identification 47–8, 98,
111; as law-breakers 68–9;
milieu of 153–6, 159–60,
164–5; reciprocity 35–6, 40–1,
50, 70, 94, 116, 147; social

relationships 13, 15, 82, 124;
status 73; urbanization and 62,
74, 76, 126
subjectivism 60, 118, 120
sublimity 153–6, 158–9, 161–2,
164, 167
suffering 106–10, 127–9, 160
superego 83–4, 87
symbolism 151–2
symmetry 66–8, 104, 106–7,
127–8, 149, 158, 162
sympathy 160–2

technology 7, 10, 77, 114–17, 129
terror 159–60, 162, 164, 167
Thus Spoke Zarathustra (Nietzsche)
103, 105
transcendence 102, 104, 109,
112–13, 117, 167
tropical man 101–2, 104, 106, 110

Two Treatises of Civil Government
(Locke) 35, 38, 40, 42, 53–4,
134

universality *see* homogeneity
urbanization 7, 12, 33–4, 62, 76,
126
utilitarianism 106–7, 126–8

war 55–6, 58, 61, 80, 141
Wealth of Nations (Smith) 50
wild 7, 9–10, 62, 71–4, 77, 80, 84,
90, 93, 97, 99, 100, 102, 104–7,
109–10, 114, 117, 121, 123,
140, 148–9, 155, 158;
interiorization 76–7, 83, 91, 98,
103, 111–12, 144
will to power 104–5, 107–9
women 23–5, 63, 79–80, 133–6,
144

For Product Safety Concerns and Information please contact our EU
representative GPSR@taylorandfrancis.com
Taylor & Francis Verlag GmbH, Kaufingerstraße 24, 80331 München, Germany

www.ingramcontent.com/pod-product-compliance
Lightning Source LLC
Chambersburg PA
CBHW050446280326
41932CB00013BA/2259